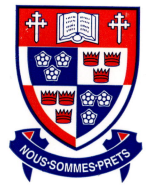

The International Politics of the Persian Gulf

The International Politics of the Persian Gulf examines the causes and consequences of conflict in one of the most important regions of the world. Bridging the gap between critical theories of international relations and the empirical study of the Gulf area, this book expands on the many ideologies, cultural inventions and ideational constructs that have affected relations in the past three decades.

Issues explored include:

- The rise and fall of Arab and Persian nationalism
- The international repercussions of the Islamic revolution in Iran
- The events surrounding the three Gulf Wars
- The 'mindset' of terrorist networks such as al-Qaeda
- Why US neo-conservatism is threatening regional order.

Confronting mainstream discussions of the region written in the 'realist' tradition, Arshin Adib-Moghaddam presents what he terms 'a cultural genealogy of anarchy', analysing the permeation, throughout the Gulf area, of values and beliefs constitutive of the problematic nature of regional relations.

Provocatively written, persuasively researched and conclusively argued, *The International Politics of the Persian Gulf* presents the first comprehensive analysis of international relations in the Gulf from an explicitly multidisciplinary perspective.

Arshin Adib-Moghaddam received a Diploma in Political Science from the University of Hamburg and an MPhil and PhD from the University of Cambridge. In October 2005, he was elected to the Jarvis Doctorow Junior Research Fellowship at St Edmund Hall and the Department of Politics and International Relations at the University of Oxford.

Routledge Studies in Middle Eastern Politics

The International Politics of the Persian Gulf

A cultural genealogy

Arshin Adib-Moghaddam

LONDON AND NEW YORK

First published 2006
by Routledge
2 Park Square, Milton Park, Abingdon, Oxon OX14 4RN

Simultaneously published in the USA and Canada
by Routledge
270 Madison Ave, New York, NY 10016

Routledge is an imprint of the Taylor & Francis Group, an informa business

© 2006 Arshin Adib-Moghaddam

Typeset in Garamond by
Newgen Imaging Systems (P) Ltd, Chennai, India
Printed and bound in Great Britain by
Biddles Ltd, King's Lynn

British Library Cataloguing in Publication Data
A catalogue record for this book is available from
the British Library

Library of Congress Cataloging in Publication Data
A catalog record for this book has been requested

ISBN10: 0–415–38559–8
ISBN13: 978–0–415–38559–6

To my parents Mahmoud and
Mehranguiz Adib-Moghaddam

The change in the balance of power in the instinctual dynamic in favour of destructive energy may again be a turning point in history. The universe of violence in which we live today is no longer the universe of violence which is identical with the history of mankind. The universe of Auschwitz and Buchenwald, of Hiroshima and Vietnam, of torture and over-kill as conventional techniques in international relations is no longer the historical universe of violence.

(Herbert Marcuse, *Towards a Critical Theory of Society*)

Contents

Acknowledgements

I should mention with gratitude the institutional support of Hughes Hall in the University of Cambridge which granted me two research fellowships, the Cambridge European Trust whose generous fellowship enabled me to pursue my studies with relative financial autarky, the Centre of International Studies at Cambridge University whose administrative and academic staff was always available for consultation and the friends and colleagues at St Edmund Hall and the Department of Politics and International Relations in the University of Oxford, my current port of call. Likewise, I am grateful to the International Institute for Strategic Studies (IISS) and the Royal Institute of International Affairs in London, the Gulf Research Centre (GRC) in Dubai, the London embassy of the Islamic Republic of Iran and the School of International Relations in Tehran for inviting me to conferences/speeches and granting me access to their resources. I am grateful to Abbas Maleki who introduced me to academic life and the institutional infrastructure of Iran. I would like to mention with gratitude the helpful encouragements of Raymond Hinnebusch and Peter Avery. Their critical engagement with this study during my *viva voce* at Peter Avery's wonderful fellow suite at King's College, Cambridge, made the cumbersome ordeal of transforming my PhD dissertation into a book manuscript a rather more manageable process. I am particularly indebted to Yezid Sayigh, whose support and friendship is valued beyond its academic merits. Joe Whiting and Nadia Seemungal of Routledge deserve special appreciation for their gnomic editorial style and congenial communication culture. Last but by no means least, I must gratefully acknowledge the endurance, motivation and patience of my supervisor at Cambridge, Charles Jones. He cannot be blamed for all of what follows, but his dedication to the supervisory role was invaluable to the realisation of this project.

Arshin Adib-Moghaddam
Oxford
October 2005

Introduction

In the past few years there has emerged a new and salutary interest in the critical study of culture, an interest that has also ameliorated the study of international politics. Yet despite a recent growth of critical theoretical work in both disciplines, scholars of International Relations and Middle Eastern studies remain generally uncomfortable reverting to cultural concepts to understand the causes of international conflict, particularly with regard to the area under focus here. As a consequence, the idea that identity, norms, institutions and other cultural artefacts shape international politics in the Persian Gulf has remained marginalised.

This book attempts to synthesise the critical study of culture with empirical analysis of conflict in the Persian Gulf. It takes anarchy to be constituted in a cultural context where different constructions of identities engage, compete and sometimes clash with each other. It will become clear that both history and our method privilege interaction between the three main protagonists – Iran, Iraq, Saudi Arabia – but our analysis is not meant to exclude the other littoral states, Bahrain, Oman, the United Arab Emirates, Qatar and Kuwait. Some might argue that the subject is too large or too small: that 'region' is in itself a problematic abstraction or that the international politics of the Persian Gulf cannot be satisfactorily analysed in isolation from the 'Middle East'. I understand that there are contending definitions of what constitutes 'region', and to make a case for analytical autonomy of the Persian Gulf does not mean that there is no interconnectedness between this part of the world and Palestine/Israel, North Africa, Central Asia or other areas. It will become clear that during some periods and political developments I will go beyond the analytic delineation, for instance when the Second Persian Gulf War or competing ideological narratives in the Islamic worlds are discussed. I argue, however, that it would be misleading to subsume constitutive events such as the Islamic revolution in Iran, the Iran–Iraq war and even the Iraq–Kuwait crisis under a 'Middle Eastern' meta-narrative, just because analysis of the Persian Gulf is not departmentalised and institutionalised or because political rhetoric and media representation suggest abstraction from the particular in favour of the general. It is my proposal that for the purpose of this study it is sufficient and necessary to discuss the international politics of the Persian Gulf without *explicitly* positioning the analytical focus within a wider 'Middle Eastern' discourse. A line has to be drawn somewhere and this is where I choose to draw it, partly because of the limits of my own knowledge.

Since the sub-title of this book, 'a cultural genealogy', requires some explanation, Chapter 1 elaborates on my understanding of critical genealogical analysis. The issues here are taken from critical theories and social 'constructivist' ideas and are discussed in relation to the discipline of International Relations (IR). Hence, some terminology might be unfamiliar to area scholars. However, an effort has been made to simplify theoretical language as far as possible. I cannot really say that what follows is 'simple language', but the measure of clarity has become for me an important demand of this study. The second and subsequent chapters form a dialectical analysis of constitutive events in the Persian Gulf. Selecting deductively from empirical studies on the area and drawing inductively on sociological, anthropological, psychological and cultural theories, an effort has been made to trace the ideational sources of conflict in the area. It is risky, I am conscious, to oscillate between theoretical abstraction and empirical description, but it seems to me true that the relationship between them is a real one, and the insights that one realm can lend to the other may be worth taking the risk for.

By choosing critical theory as epistemological orientation, causal rigour and parsimony is sometimes traded for a deeper and broader ontology, appreciating that I am tracing a 'genealogy' of international politics in the Persian Gulf that defies theoretical closure. I know that this study is perhaps ill-equipped to compete with the empirical analysis of area scholars on the one side, and 'positivist' IR theories such as political realism and neo-liberalism on the other, that is both in terms of their parsimonious style and stringent methodology. The strengths of these approaches lie in their axiomatic structure and causal rigour, which permits a level of analytical clarity that other approaches struggle to match. Concomitantly, I assert that those approaches are flawed because they are based on a questionable ontology. The challenge of critical disquisition therefore must be to reread, re-examine and resist reification – to pursue what Nietzsche called the 'skill to ruminate, which cows possess but modern man lacks'.[1] To that end, this study is in opposition to what Andrew Linklater aptly called the 'resistance to radical, idealist or critical modes of enquiry'.[2] Contesting the taken-for-granted facts about the causes of conflict in the Persian Gulf, it is argued, demands radical interpretation and not the reification of apparently authoritative truisms.

Due to its epistemological approach and empirical object of analysis, this study is intrinsically multidisciplinary in its ambition. It agrees with scholars of international relations and area analysts, that due to the limited number of empirical work beyond North America and Western Europe in IR,[3] and the theoretical underdevelopment of Middle Eastern Studies, the two disciplines could benefit from more cross-fertilisation.[4] By necessity then, this study had to balance between the scholarship of two disciplines. To meet the emphatic demands to both International Relations and Middle Eastern Studies, I tried to look beyond scholarship produced in the 'Western' hemisphere, following a generous citation policy to credit these sources – even so readers will still find much ground that has not been covered. I have not limited myself to 'standard' literature, choosing instead to consult the spectrum of sources pertinent to the subject of this study. At the same time, the confines of a monograph do not allow for proper coverage of the vast scholarship produced by IR scholars and those engaged in Area Studies alike. Thus, the bibliography remains selective and not necessarily a measure of what has been seriously engaged in this study. To credit the increasing importance of the Internet for social research, I have included a number of web pages both in the bibliography and the endnotes.

A final note: writing about a geographical area which covers two different languages, I have had to make decisions about words. There is no standard way of transliterating Arabic and Farsi names. In each case, I have employed the most familiar spelling used in the English-speaking world and stuck to it. When the spelling of a book author was different from mine, I reproduced the published spelling. In general, I have tried to guarantee consistency and simplicity.

1 Studying conflict in the Persian Gulf

An epistemological introduction

1.1 Critique, anarchy and genealogy

Far from rejecting or disqualifying a particular theoretical school of thought or methodology in advance, this study tries to radically reinterpret and complement the available literature, with a particular emphasis on those apparently tangential aspects which because of the dominance of 'materialist' or 'realist' theories of world politics remain marginalised.[5] Intrinsic to the overbearing majority of studies about the Persian Gulf (and world politics in general) is the conviction that states are exclusively driven by material rather than cultural and/or social factors and are hence caught in a perennial competition over scarce resources.[6] At present, the study of international relations has gone in two opposed, some would say epistemologically divergent, directions: one, into an empirically rich, parsimonious and positivist paradigm that boasts of policy-relevance, methodological elegance, simplicity and emphatic relevance for the 'real world' of international politics, and two, into a deciphering, unrelentingly critical, yet sometimes also unnecessarily intransigent anti-realism, that identifies itself as 'constructivist' and/or 'post-modern' scholarship – an active, heterogeneous minority whose ideas have been shaped by European traditions of critical or anti-foundational thought, especially by the critique of the Frankfurt School (primarily Habermas, Adorno, Horkheimer and far less Marcuse, Neumann, Fromm, Pollock and Löwenthal), Nietzsche, Foucault, Derrida, Bakhtin, Barthes, Baudrillard and other canonical figures.

Critical practice is, of course, amenable to a great variety of interpretations, transcending disciplinary boundaries and paradigmatic homogeneity.[7] In our discipline of reference – International Relations – it ameliorates 'constructivism',[8] the 'English school',[9] the 'world-polity approach',[10] post-modernism and post-structuralism,[11] and feminist theories.[12] Despite disparate objects of analysis and different nuances of method and methodology, critical IR theories agree on the onto-logical premise that international realities are invented or socially manufactured rather than inert facts of nature. Although I risk oversimplification, it is probably correct to say that this is the smallest common denominator of contemporary critical IR theories.

It is a central ambition of this study to bridge the gap between those critical theories of international relations and the empirical study of conflict in the Persian

Gulf. More specifically, I am driven by the renewed interest in the impact of norms, identities, ideologies and other cultural artefacts on international life in West Asia.[13] An increasing number of IR scholars have already experimented with the study of the 'Middle East'. Scholars writing with neo-realist[14] inclinations such as Barry Buzan, Shibley Telhami and Stephen Walt focus upon perpetual anarchy, security dilemmas, the regional balance of power (or in the case of Walt, balance of threat), polarity and other material variables;[15] scholars borrowing from Marxist and dependency theories see interaction in the region as reflective of the hierarchical structure of the international capitalist system, stressing the causal importance of the international division of labour, core-periphery dependencies, the political economy of oil and ideology;[16] and approaches that may be viewed to stand in 'liberal' tradition focus upon shifting patterns of domestic politics, public opinion, interest groups and the role of institutions.[17]

Yet despite the recent (and rather late) 'discovery' of West Asia by IR scholars, very little attention has been paid to exploring the relationship between ideational dynamics and anarchy in the area. In the period under focus, stretching from 1971 to the present day, international relations between Persian Gulf states were beset by revolution, civil conflict, inter-state wars and transnational upheaval. Is regional interaction consequently reducible to one continuous, unalterable plot of structural enmity? Is anarchy in the Gulf simply *there* determined by ahistorical and primordial continua? Readers of this book will quickly discover that it does not agree with the fatalistic characterisation of the area as a 'perennial' conflict formation.[18] Deconstructing the cultural dynamics which have caused inter-state conflict is crucial to my argument here, my basic point being that anarchy in the Persian Gulf has a 'cultural genealogy', a *Herkunft* which demands what Foucault so aptly termed 'archaeological' exploration.

It is not at all obvious, that the Gulf has to remain trapped in a historically ciphered cycle of violence that has hampered the institutionalisation of communitarian norms and has scared the lives of its peoples with fulminate force. Nor is it clear, that the geo-strategic significance of the area renders violence inevitable, although the 'Western' thirst for the region's vast oil and gas resources played its part in confronting it with the abominations of empire. Anarchy, that is, the lack of a central authoritative and decisive entity beyond the nation-state does, by itself, not explain the high occurrence of violence in the Persian Gulf. Neither does it preclude the emergence of amicable relations between the littoral states a priori. War, Margaret Mead audaciously asserted amidst the devastation caused by the Second World War, is neither a biological necessity nor a sociological inevitability, but an invented social institution which will be rendered obsolete once a better invention takes its place.[19] If war is a human invention, anarchy must be treated as a human product, or more precisely, an ongoing human production as well. As a manufactured, reified, theoretical mnemonic, it is not biologically given, not a fact of nature. Anarchy is not merely limited to what states make of it;[20] anarchy exists *only* as a human fabrication and – by extension – as a produce of nation-states.

Let me say a little here about the normative implications of the idea that that there is one, all-encompassing system around the world and that this system has one logic, self-help anarchy. The culture of thought promoting this pessimistic, almost dismal world-view, accepts and promotes habituating society to accept the 'kill or be killed rationale' as an inevitable fact of international life. We will discover later that this has been the political function of anarchism in Saddam Hussein's Iraq and in other places. In the Iraqi case, the Ba'thist grand foreign-policy strategies were formulated according to the ideology that the 'West', Jews and Iranians have always constituted an existential threat to the Iraqi nation-state. '[T]he indispensable condition of war' Gordon Allport wrote in the 1960s 'is that people must *expect* war and must prepare for war before, under war-minded leadership, they make war.... It is in this sense that "wars begin in the minds of men." ' [21] In other words, in international theory and practice, anarchy is a very powerful concept to legitimate violence, even aggression. For the Ba'thist garrison state, for instance, propagating the self-help nature of the international system was an ideological instrument to habituate its populace to the inevitability of war. Iraqis were told that the 'backstabbing Persians', the 'racist Jews' and the 'imperialistic West' had a prolonged history of hostility against the people of Iraq and the wider Arab worlds. Do theories of self-help anarchy not always legitimate anarchic, aggressive behaviour? Do they not beget, even demand, the invention of the national enemy who has to be fought and hated? I think there is a case to be made that theories of self-help anarchy have implicit and explicit political functions. To put it bluntly, if theory, education, political or cultural indoctrination habituates society to accept war as inevitable, selling warfare as a national or religious duty is greatly facilitated. Anarchy in this political-doctrinaire sense is an ongoing elite pro-duction, a 'reified theoretical fact', that is not detached from human intentionality. 'When any theory so represents itself', Robert Cox rightly cautions, 'it is the more important to examine it as ideology, and to lay bare its concealed perspective'. [22] To that end, showing that war and anarchy in the Persian Gulf are *not* facts of nature but ongoing human productions has become an important epistemological and norma-tive ambition of this book.

If anarchy is not monolithically 'Hobbesian' or self-help as (neo)realists argue, it has to follow that the term refers to a stratified, socially constructed order. This view is at the heart of critical theories of international relations. Anarchy conceived in this sense has a genealogy, a historical differentiation that is coded according to the cultural dynamics prevalent in the international society under focus. Whilst genealogy 'does not resemble the evolution of a species and does not map the destiny of a people', it does take issue with the inventions, asymmetries, perversions and diffusions of human interaction. [23] In our case, the purpose of genealogical analysis must be to critically unravel the cultural manufacturing processes of anarchy and conflict in the Persian Gulf. This method is radically different to realist approaches. Whilst political realism has a priori defined (and in its neo-realist version ahistorical) answers to the way decision-makers behave – balance of power calculations, minimising security dilemmas, power maximisation etc. – a genealogical research design inquires where these *post facto* policy outcomes come from in the first place.

But the critical genealogist does not look back to discover unilinear historical causalities. To the contrary. Genealogical thought challenges the representation of indefinite teleologies, essential systems or law-like propositions, characteristic for positivist reasoning: 'The genealogist needs history to dispel the chimeras of the origin' said Foucault contemptuously of historical determinism 'somewhat in the manner of the pious philosopher who needs a doctor to exorcise the shadow of his soul'.[24] Understood in this sense, a genealogy disputes the existence of objective, historically predetermined realities in international relations. This view is relativistic in at least two senses: first it is 'ontologically relative' in relation to entities and process, denying that the studied phenomena are inevitable, objective manifestations of reality. And second, it is 'relative about rationality', questioning whether scientific theories employed to suggest law-like causalities on the basis of empirical analysis are universally applicable and all-encompassing.[25] In other words, whereas the positivist majority organised around the realist paradigm claim to know how the international world functions, the genealogist attempts to unveil the canopy of facts masquerading as fixed realities. Whereas political realism 'tends to emphasise the irresistible strength of existing forces and the inevitable character of existing tendencies, and to insist that the highest wisdom lies in accepting, and adapting oneself to, these forces and these tendencies',[26] genealogical thought highlights the relative autonomy of subjective action and agency as the dominant stimuli for political emancipation. Whereas political realism is a philosophy of adaptation, genealogical practice translates into a philosophy of change.[27]

1.2 Culture, method and dialectical analysis

I have outlined my understanding of two central terms of this study, anarchy and genealogy. I must explain and briefly discuss my understanding of culture now, so that it can be seen what the phrase *cultural genealogy of anarchy* means for my method and epistemology.

As I use the word, 'culture' does not pretend to unravel an experimental science in search of law-like causalities, a dangerous illusion of orientalist reasoning. Yet unlike some post-modern writers, I do believe in the determining imprint of norms, identities, institutions and other cultural artefacts on the world-views of collective entities; nation-states or other formations with an immanent ideational consistency and a highly articulated set of shared knowledge between their constituent agents. Therefore, I study culture as a dialectical phenomenon. A dialectical approach towards culture focuses as much as possible on the manufacturing, reification, theorisation and institutionalisation of culture. How is culture produced, reproduced, legitimated, ideologised, contested and transformed? How is the meaning of culture fixed or stabilised historically via theory and political practice? How does culture affect strategic preferences and foreign-policy decisions?

As it is pursued here, the duty of cultural analysis is not to demonstrate that the past has a deterministic impact on the present, that behaviour is a priori defined. In our case, following Clifford Geertz, 'culture is not a power, something to which social events, behaviours, institutions, or process can be causally attributed; it is a context, something within which they can be intelligibly – that is, thickly – described'.[28] It is important to remember that cultural inventions, however monolithic and deterministic they may appear, are essentially human fabrications. Their objective status does not divorce them from human action. The relationship between the individual, the producer and the cultural world, the product, is and remains a dialectical one. Both are in constant interaction with each other. I have argued elsewhere that these aspects receive their proper recognition once cultural systems are understood in terms of an ongoing dialectical process composed of four moments: (a) *externalisation*, that is, following Marx and Hegel, the ongoing outpouring of human activity in society as an act of anthropological necessity; (b) *objectification*, the appearance of externalised cultural artefacts such as norms, institutions, values, traditions, as inter-subjectively shared objects of reality; (c) the *internalisation* of that objectivated world by agents and (d) the constitutive effects of dialectical *introjection* on identities, interests and preferences.[29]

Understanding culture as an ongoing social production complements our ideas about a genealogy of anarchy in the Persian Gulf. If a genealogical analysis of anarchy demands revealing inventions, metaphors and myths, investigating the construction, reification and ideological functioning of culture is helpful to understand how invented facts are processed and mediated. Consequently, a cultural genealogy of anarchy analyses the permeation throughout the Persian Gulf area of values and beliefs constitutive of the conflictual nature of inter-state relations between the littoral states. If Arab/Iranian misperceptions persist, what are the structures of thought reproducing this phenomenon? If opposition to the United States is pervasive, what are the agents and ideologies promoting this view? The Persian Gulf area continues to be *the* central theatre where various cultures (political, popular, media etc.) interact and fight each other. A cultural genealogy of anarchy interprets these engagements, exploring the use and abuse of ideational constructs and their role in legitimating aggression. Ultimately, the approach has also a normative connotation. It negates that violence is somehow intrinsic to the regional system – or worse obfuscation – that 'sword-swinging Mullahs' cannot be appeased, that they need to be bombed into rationality, that reactionary military force is the panacea for regional violence.

In the second place, a cultural genealogy of anarchy focuses as much as possible on the impact of exclusionary identity politics on foreign policies. It appreciates, following Ernest Gellner, Eric Hobsbawm, Benedict Anderson and Charles Tilly, 'the element of artefact, invention and social engineering which enters into the making of nations' and looks into the relationship between the ongoing manufacturing of the state and the production of 'enemy-images'.[30] It helps us to understand how and why, regional states reverted to exclusionary state identities that were intrinsically anathema to communitarian relations. More specifically, it investigates the impact of Iraq's Ba'thist brand of Arab nationalism on relations with other Arab states and Iran; the function of Iranian nationalism during the Pahlavi dynasty and the country's changed self-perception during the revolutionary process of the late 1970s. These issues, it will be argued, are immediate causes of anarchy in the Persian Gulf and demand critical exploration and, perhaps, contestation.

Yet even though it is the first study to explicitly investigate the cultural fabric of international politics in the Persian Gulf from the perspective of critical IR theories, this book is not a general account of regional cultures *per se*. It will be clear to the reader that I am primarily focusing on *political* cultural dynamics. Although an effort has been made to include the realms of literature and media, this study is about the social construction of politically shared knowledge. This cultural fabric is so complexly woven and 'thick', that all I could do is to describe elements of it during certain, conflictual periods, and merely to expose a larger whole, complex, intransigent, deterministic, dotted with gnomic personalities, perspicacious discourses and fatalistic events. An important task of future research would be to deconstruct the other dimensions of culture, with a special focus on those existent and strong commonalities that could bring the regional Gulf society closer together. This search for community begets tolerating difference and appreciating congruence, rather than reifying apparently unbridgeable dichotomies. Indeed, there is a case to be made that reifying the myth of a 'perennial Middle Eastern conflict formation', has – almost imperceptibly – condemned the region to recurring periods of self-fulfilling disasters. I am very conscious that these are issues left embarrassingly incomplete in this study; had we moved further down our path, we might have complemented analysis of conflict with appreciation of communitarian exigencies.

1.3   Plan of the book

Ultimately, the preceding epistemological ideas offer three principal methodological questions for studying conflict in the Persian Gulf: (1) What are the dominant political norms, institutions, values, identities and other cultural artefacts at a given period of time? (2) How are they invented, changed, reified and transcended by dominant political actors, most notably the state? (3) How do cultural artefacts condition the appearance of power and interest and how do they manifest themselves in strategic preferences?

All three questions relate to the ideational fabric of international politics in the Persian Gulf and – more specifically – the cultural constitution of regional anarchy. The penetrative power of ideas is of course such, that the ideational structure of the Persian Gulf cannot be artificially detached from the rest of international society. Therefore we will address effects emanating from beyond the region if they are significant for behavioural patterns as well. But the following chapters attempt to present as far as possible 'the' regional perspective, not out of analytical expediency, but scholarly necessity. There are enough studies that dramatise the impact of the 'centre' on the 'periphery', a powerful legacy of two 'grand' theories: Marxism with its focus on the asymmetries of core-periphery relations, and the so called 'state-systemic project' with its propensity for superpower rivalries.[31] But I think that theory and methodology should not predetermine the superiority of one 'level of analysis' over the other. In other words, I believe that the impact global impulses have on regional dynamics is difficult to discern in advance. Ultimately, it is a matter of the empirical analysis to explore the relationship between global and regional norms and institutions, and to determine if they are complementary with – or contradictory to – each other.[32]

The three long chapters and one shorter concluding unit into which this book is divided are designed to facilitate as much as possible exposition of the cultural genealogy of anarchy in the Persian Gulf. Chapter 2 juxtaposes regional relations before and after the revolution in Iran. More specifically it develops three principal arguments: the relative pre-revolutionary security sustained by the complementary roles of Saudi Arabia and Iran which was 'systemically' legitimated by the United States under the twin-pillar norm did not lead to a communitarian order because exclusionary Iraqi and Iranian identity politics reconfirmed pre-existent misperceptions between the Persian and Arab populations inhabiting the area. Second, identity was even more contested after the revolution in Iran because regional states felt that their very legitimacy was threatened. By virtue of its Islamic-revolutionary message, the Iranian movement pushed forward norms and institutions that were in explicit opposition to established forms of governance and inter-state behaviour in the region and beyond. This revolutionary transformation, it will be finally argued, generated a reshuffling of role attributions, triggering a regional 'legitimacy contest' which culminated in the devastating war between Iran and Iraq in September 1980.

Chapter 3 shifts the focus to the Kuwait crisis. It suggests that the international support granted to Saddam Hussein during the war against Iran emboldened Iraq to pursue a second invasion, this time against its smaller neighbour to the south. Concomitantly, it will be argued that despite revolution in Iran and two inter-state wars regional relations did not regress into a state of self-help or 'chaotic anarchy'. The Persian Gulf continued to constitute what English-school theorists have termed an 'anarchical society', a network of states neither in a state of complete chaos, nor community.[33] Moreover, after the period of violence between 1980 and 1991, sovereignty was increasingly accepted as a 'right'.[34] The institution of sovereignty was reinforced due to three developments: the decline of pan-Arabism as an effective foreign-policy programme; the return to state-centrism of the post-revolutionary Iranian state and the presence of the United States as a status quo power. Hence, after a decade of revolution, two inter-state wars and numerous domestic crises, the structure of the regional society remained essentially the same, with striking similarities to relations before the revolution in Iran.

Chapter 4 explores the cultural 'genealogy' of anarchy in the Persian Gulf further. It is argued, that regional relations after the Second Gulf War revealed both processes of reification of the anarchic culture and contestation of its inhibiting properties. Conflictual norms were strengthened due to two developments: the hegemony of neo-conservative strategic doctrines (most notably unilateralism and pre-emption) after the attacks of 11 September 2001 leading to the invasion of Iraq in March 2003. And second, the emergence of a neo-fundamentalist current in political Islam, which was hostile to any negotiations with the 'West' and threatened the stability of conservative regimes in power (especially Saudi Arabia). At the same time, a parallel process contested the conflictual propositions of regional anarchy. At least since the election of Mohammad Khatami in 1997 and the reformulation of Iranian foreign policies towards détente and dialogue, GCC states and Iran embarked upon an open-ended process of mutual trust building. This novel constellation strengthened co-operative incentives in the conduct of regional affairs.

In a brief concluding Chapter 5, the central empirical, theoretical and methodological themes of this study will be evaluated, raising questions about future research and the potential for communitarian policies in the Persian Gulf. To that end, I will return to the three methodological questions raised at the beginning of this section.

2 The Persian Gulf between independence and revolution

Ideational shifts and regional repercussions

2.1 Introduction

In terms of political violence, human losses and material destruction, the period between the Iranian–Islamic revolution in 1979 and the end of the Iran–Iraq war in 1988 was the most devastating in the modern history of the Persian Gulf. Revolution in Iran and the ensuing war between that country and Iraq exacerbated existing insecurities amongst all the littoral states. This process transmuted regional relations into an atypical period of hostility. Never before had there been bloodshed on such a scale and not since the First World War and Vietnam had there been a comparable systematic use of chemical weapons on the warfront. The numbers give an impression about the scale of destruction during the longest conventional warfare in the twenty first century.[35] On the Iranian side, according to Hadi Qalamnevis, Director General of the Statistics and Information Department at the Islamic Revolution Martyrs Foundation, 204,795 people lost their lives in the Iran–Iraq war, including 188,015 military and 16,780 civilians.[36] Earlier estimates by Mohsen Rafiqdust, the former head of the Iranian Revolutionary Guard Force, had stated that 400,000 were wounded during the war.[37] According to a Senior Iranian Foreign Ministry official, about 60,000 Iranians were killed by chemical weapons attacks, with over 300,000 suffering from related syndromes.[38] Overall, it is estimated that 370,000 people were killed on both sides with an additional number of approximately 700,000 people maimed and injured.[39] In terms of material losses, Iranian government estimates indicate that the war caused US$ 440 billion in direct losses to the Iranian economy, with another US$ 490 billion categorised as indirect losses.[40] According to other sources, it is estimated that the costs amount to aggregated direct and indirect costs of US$ 627 billion to Iran and US$ 561 billion to Iraq,[41] with the total costs exceeding the overall oil revenues of the two states in the twentieth century.[42]

This chapter addresses the sources of conflict in the Persian Gulf during this period. Between 1979 and 1988, littoral states were faced with revolution, inter-state war and recurrent domestic upheaval. A great deal of recent theoretical speculation has proposed that these events can be attributed to shifts in the regional balance of power, security dilemmas caused by the Iranian revolution or the impact of superpower rivalry on the politics of the region. This perspective strongly suggests, even to neo-realists who have incorporated 'constructivist' ideas into their analysis (most prominently Barry Buzan and Ole Waever), that the wider 'Middle East' is a near-perfect example for a 'perennial conflict formation'.[43]

The following paragraphs offer an alternative view. They propose that the politics of identity were equally consequential for the way regional states behaved and that the conflictual period after the revolution in Iran was atypical. To that end, it will be explored how the Islamic revolution abruptly transformed the parameters of regional interaction. The short explanation for the paradigmatic shift would be that the Iranian movement had unilaterally determined the politics of regional relations that followed its inception. Eventually, this is why Michel Foucault described it as a revolt against the 'planetary system', inspired by a 'religion of combat and sacrifice', a counter-hegemonic mass movement that could bring about the 'transfiguration' of the world.[44] But the story does not end here. The shift away from the relative co-operative period of the 1970s has been confined to alterations to the terms of conduct, not a revision of the regional system into self-help anarchy. Regional institutions, perceptions and identities did not suddenly yield to the revolutionary fervour emanating from Iran. Not even Saddam Hussein's two wars changed that constellation. International relations continued to be related to – and artificially rooted in – *preceding* interaction. To elaborate on this point and to differentiate the dynamics after the revolution from those before it let me proceed with an interpretative overview of regional relations before the Islamic revolution in Iran.

2.2 The unfinished 'twin-pillar' order and the simmering clash of identity politics

The symmetries of regional interaction before the Islamic revolution in Iran were encapsulated in the 'twin-pillar' norm – the nucleus of the Nixon doctrine formulated in 1969. According to that norm, Pahlavi Iran and Saudi Arabia were expected to act as US surrogates. Both states were empowered to guarantee regional stability as the prerequisite for the free flow of oil from the Persian Gulf.[45] In order to ensure the efficiency of this 'policemen' role, the United States responded to the requests for sophisticated military hardware and training assistance, especially from the Pahlavi monarchy in Iran. The twin-pillar norm as part of US strategy after the defeat in Vietnam and under the condition of bipolarity was largely complementary with the self-perception of Iran and to a lesser extent Saudi Arabia, legitimating and reinforcing their roles as status quo powers in the region.

The Pahlavi state in Iran was considered the linchpin of the twin-pillar doctrine. Regardless of party affiliation, eight consecutive US administrations agreed that 'geo-politics' and Cold War bipolarity required a militarily strong, anti-Communist and pro-Western Iran. These role attributions were readily accepted by Mohammad Reza Shah Pahlavi. The geo-strategic significance attached to the role of Iran was considered especially significant after the Shah was brought back to power by a MI6/CIA sponsored military coup in 1953 which ousted the democratically elected Prime Minister Mohammad Mossadegh. Moreover, with the vocal presence of the Tudeh communist party in Iran and precedents of Tsarist and Soviet intrusion to Iranian sovereignty, most clearly exemplified in the refusal to withdraw Soviet military forces from the Northern Iranian region of Gilan after the Second World War (1946), securing that country from both external aggression and internal subversion was considered imperative. As part of the 'northern tier' bulwark against communism, the role of Iran as the pivotal 'Western' ally in the Persian Gulf was institutionalised by formal treaties (Baghdad Pact or CENTO), deterring the Soviet Union from direct military confrontation. Iran was hence *systemically* legitimated as the regional pillar of 'Western' strategy. That attribution pushed the country into the role of policing regional stability, if necessary by force as in Oman where Iranian troops (at the invitation of Sultan Qabus) defused a Marxist separatist uprising in the Dhofar province of the country in 1973.[46]

Regional manifestations of 'status quo politics' are even more intrusive. Driven by close consultations between Saudi Arabia and Iran, OPEC developed into an effective international cartel, able to influence the direction of the world economy and eager to capitalise on its economic position for political gains.[47] The price rises of 1973 in reaction to the Arab-Israeli 'October war' could not have been accomplished without Iranian backing of the Saudi/Egyptian lead.[48] The Shah did not merely want to cash in during the boycott in order to boost Iranian revenues, he felt obliged to follow the political initiative of Saudi Arabia and Egypt because of a resurgent indigenous Islamic political culture in Iran and the external pull to identify with the cause of the Palestinian people. Already, in the 1960s, the Shah faced assertive and organised opposition primarily targeted against domestic policies such as the modernisation programme enshrined in the 'White Revolution' or his decision to grant legal immunity to US American military personnel. That domestic dissent was part of a larger movement against what was perceived to be the increasing dependence of the regime on 'Western' powers and collusion with Israel. In that context, demonstrating solidarity with Iran's Arab neighbours on the issue of Palestine was meant to please the opposition and raise the 'Islamic credentials' of the regime. The price rise was thus as much a utilitarian-economic decision as it was forced upon the Shah as an act of Islamic solidarity within the context of the Palestinian struggle for independence and the Arab-Israeli wars.

The norm of Islamic solidarity prescribed co-operation between 'Muslim' states on the one hand side and resistance against imperialism and Zionism on the other. Constructivist IR theorists define such 'regulative norms' as specifications of the proper enactment of an already defined identity.[49] This theoretical mnemonic offers two interpretations: the regulative effect of the Islamic solidarity norm ordered the Saudi and Iranian perception of their external environment, and the norm defined the proper behaviour *in that particular situation*, pushing Saudi Arabia and Iran towards a moment of pan-Islamic consciousness. The Shah was under pressure from Arab countries and at home from an increasingly vocal Islamic opposition to respond to the call for solidarity with the Palestinian movement. King Faisal on the other side emphasised the imagery of the pan-Islamic *umma* as a means to appeal to the Arab masses, countering the influence of Ba'thist and Nassirite versions of Arab nationalism.[50] That the norm of Islamic co-operation had entered the plot of inter-state interaction is supported by the fact that Iran and Saudi Arabia (together with

Morocco and Pakistan) were also the primary forces behind the establishment of the Organisation of the Islamic Conference (OIC).[51] The first meeting of the organisation in Rabat in September 1969 was convened one month after the Arson attack on the Al-Aqsa Mosque in Jerusalem.[52] Both the decisions to raise crude oil prices as a protest against Zionism and institutionalising state-centred Islamic co-operation in the OIC were hence taken within the context of a resurgent Islamic narrative, accentuated by King Faisal bin Abdul Aziz as the inherent *raison d'état* of the Saudi state[53] and forced upon the Shah by Arab expectations and the assertive Islamic identity of the Iranian populace.

Despite all the fears of potential destabilisation by communist subversion after the withdrawal of British forces in 1971, the consensus between Saudi Arabia and Iran secured a decade of relatively stable relations in the Persian Gulf area. Between 1968 and 1978 regional states accentuated the role of diplomacy and outlawed the use of massive military force. Legitimisation and complementary norms were central to the consolidation of the regional society. Without a meaningful military presence in the Persian Gulf after the withdrawal of British troops in 1971, the 'West' legitimated the regional equilibrium, relying on Saudi Arabia and Iran as regional proxies. The twin-pillar norm was complementary to the regional roles of both countries, lending them the 'psychological ease' to pursue their alliance in OPEC and the institutionalisation of co-operation without much fear of US antagonism, hence securing global-systemic compliance with Saudi/Iranian notions for the stability of regional order. Richard Haass, Special Assistant to the Deputy Under Secretary of Defense/Policy Review at the US Department of Defense during the period of the Iranian revolution and at the time of writing, Director of the Bush administration's Policy Planning Staff expressed the unexpected persistence of relatively amicable relations in a paper published in 1981:

> [I]t is the large degree of commonality of interests and purpose between Iran and Saudi Arabia throughout much of the past decade that impresses the observer. Despite differences over the price and availability of oil, the two were instrumental to OPEC's ability to both survive and thrive during a period of fundamental change in the international political economy of oil. Massive importation of arms and mutual military development did not bring about deep hostility or conflict between the two countries, while the absence of formal machinery for the promotion of regional security did not preclude co-ordination and tacit co-operation. Lastly, differences between approaches to the Arab-Israeli Middle East question narrowed rather than widened over time.[54]

The 'duopolistic' equilibrium defined the code of conduct for regional interaction and deterred utopian experiments. Deterrence was not so much enforced by military measures, but rather by diplomatic means, 'behind the curtain' negotiation and brinkmanship. Determined by the Saudi/Iranian consensus, the preference for diplomacy over massive military force tamed the virulence of assertive powers, de-legitimising efforts to alter the governing status quo. The successful containment of Iraq's territorial claims against Kuwait supports that argument. After the Ba'thist coup in

February 1963 which terminated the military regime of General Abdel-Karim Qassim, who had declared Kuwait part of the country's southern province of Basra, Iraq continued to challenge the sovereignty of the Emirate both rhetorically and by taking offensive action. In 1973, Iraqi forces occupied Kuwaiti border outposts, demanding control over the Kuwaiti islands Warbah and Bubiyan in exchange for recognising the country's sovereignty. The fact that Iraq had to retreat and did not launch an invasion of its southern neighbour at that stage was certainly not because the small Emirate was able to defend itself militarily – rather, Iraq was deterred because Kuwait received 'both official and private assurances of support not only from nearby Arab states but also from Iran'.[55] Facing 'diplomatic deterrence' Iraq was forced to adjust its foreign policy according to the regional realities, which did not allow for alterations to the Saudi/Iranian order. In further compliance with that order, Iraq agreed to delineate the Shatt al-Arab according to Iranian demands and established diplomatic relations with Sultan Qabus of Oman, whose downfall during the Dhofar rebellion the country had previously supported via its alliance with the Marxist Democratic Republic of South Yemen. Iraqi aspirations were hence deterred due to the Saudi/Iranian lead and because revolutionary Arab socialism espoused by the Ba'thist regime did not appeal to the monarchies of the Gulf.[56] Without regional and global legitimation of its self-bestowed revolutionary role, Iraq was 'socialised' in the regional system. The political-cultural determinations of this system altered the country's foreign-policy disposition from revisionist power after the revolution in 1958 to a moderate actor after the Algiers Agreement in 1975. In the latter part of the 1970s and up until the invasion of Iran, Iraq's implicit acceptance of the regional order brought the country back into the mainstream of Persian Gulf politics, without however changing the state's aspiration to assert a leadership role in the future.

So far so good. But does all this mean that the relatively co-operative relations were reflective of a strong security order? Certainly not. That would be an idealist distortion of what essentially remained a rump international society. The communitarian norms were not translated into formal security institutions and littoral states continued to operate within a territorial imperfect, quasi-Westphalian regional system. That the territorial map was far from being consolidated was exemplified by border disputes and occasional skirmishes between virtually all littoral states, most notably however between Iraq and Kuwait, Saudi Arabia and Qatar and Iran and the United Arab Emirates. Infant institutionalisation of nation-state structures, on the other side, undercut the authority of the ruling governments and their ability to enforce the state's monopoly of violence domestically. The period since the ending of the 'age of empires' in the Persian Gulf – Ottoman on the Arab side and Qajar in Iran – had been too short for the creation of symbiotic state identities and effective governmental bureaucracies to sustain them. Out of the chaos, national elites had to create new realities. 'Nations do not make states and nationalisms' Eric Hobsbawm pertinently cautions 'but the other way round'.[57] Because of the non-existence of nation-state histories, the manufactured, imagined communities in Iraq, Qatar, the Trucial states (after 1971 the United Arab Emirates) and Bahrain were particularly hard put to develop state identities that would fit the Westphalian mould crafted by their imperial godfathers. Identity had become a 'scarce resource' and recourse to exclusionary historiography became the understandable, albeit conflict laden, reaction to the new realities.[58]

The relatively stable period between 1968 and 1978 should not be taken to imply that the moment of self-help anarchy was simply 'beamed' into the Persian Gulf by the victory of the Islamic revolution. The structures of conflict were already there, sometimes deeply embedded in the domestic political cultures of the ruling elites. We may conclude, however, that the norms and rudimentary institutions of the regional system in the 1970s were strong enough to balance the fragile regional society and keep a lid on utopian experiments. As long as the role identities of Iran and Saudi Arabia as the guardians of regional security were complementary and systemically legitimated, 'superpower' intrusions remained confined and challenging states such as Iraq had to subordinate their aspirations to the cultural status quo.

If regional states did not leap at the chance to forge a viable security architecture, there must have been inhibiting forces at play that require investigation. Why did the dominant states not take advantage of the momentum to integrate security co-operation during a period when regional and global politics were so conducive to this end? The answer, I think, lies in a parallel process to the inter-state consensus, specifically the 'negative externalities' generated by exclusive discourses of Persian and Arab state identities projected by Pahlavian Iran and Ba'thist Iraq. The identity politics of both states and its authoritarian enforcement in domestic politics constituted elite political cultures that were inconsistent with the exigencies of genuine security integration. At any given point of time in the stable period outlined earlier, Persian Gulf states *did* imagine that they could go to war with each other. This, students of Karl Deutsch would agree, negates the criteria for the emergence of a strong security community.

2.2.1   State-sponsored Iranianism and the metaphysical mendacity of Persian supremacy

By itself, the fact that the Pahlavi state had developed superior military power capabilities in the 1970s does not suffice to explain why Iran was perceived as a potentially hegemonic force by most Arab states. Turkey had comparable military capabilities, but the country was not considered an immediate threat. I would argue that the Pahlavi state aggravated the security dilemma amongst littoral, non-Persian states because of its insistence on an exclusionary and chauvinistic 'Iranianist' state identity. From the Arab perspective, 'Iranianism' appeared belligerent, 'making Iranian nationalism ideological expansionist, hegemonial and fanatical towards geographical, cultural or ethnic neighbours'.[59] Both Mohammad Reza Shah and his father Reza Khan nurtured the idea of Iranianism in order to legitimate the Pahlavi monarchy and to link their rule to ancient, pre-Islamic Persian empires. The Iranian 'self' was embedded into the romantic discourse about a superior 'Aryan' nation (*mellat-e aryan*), married to Indo-European heritage because of common linguistic roots and hence different from the 'Arab-Semitic other'.[60] Secular Iranian intellectuals who socialised during the Pahlavi period relied on this romantic conception of Iran's 'lingua franca' as the source of national identity and predominant characteristic of 'Iranianness':

> During the period in which we Iranians emerged from defeat and consternation [by the Muslim conquest] to the time when we could again stand on our own feet, we persevered as a people in two ways, indirectly and directly or, in other words, culturally and militarily. And after four hundred years [since the Muslim conquest] we achieved two results: defeat and victory. We suffered defeat in direct confrontation, in direct opposition and contest for political and social aims, for separatism from the Arab victors, from the Baghdad caliphate, and from the religion of Islam. But we achieved victory in the preservation of nationality and language. We maintained one nationality . . . our national identity, our Iranianness, through the blessing of language, by means of the vitality of Persian as a refuge. Despite political fragmentation into numerous geographical units and with Arab, Iranian and Turkic governments, Iran . . . was not dissimilar in those days from ancient Greece, or Germany and Italy until the second half of the nineteenth century. In all of these countries, one people and one national group with a common language existed with a degree of common culture alongside differences in government. They possessed cultural unity without political unity, unity in roots but fragmentation in branches and leaves.[61]

Iranian 'ultra-nationalism' demonstrates affinity with 'orientalist' views about the supremacy of the Indo-European peoples and the mediocrity of the Semitic race.[62] Late nineteenth-century figures such as Mirza Fath Ali Akhunzadeh or Mirza Aqa Khan Kermani were the forerunners of the Aryan *myth* adopted by the Pahlavi state and secular intellectuals.[63] Iranian nationalist discourse idealised the status of pre-Islamic Persian empires, whilst negating the Islamicisation of Iran by Muslim forces. The Shah's celebration of 2,500 years of Iranian empire in Persepolis in 1971 and his decision to abandon the Islamic solar *hegra* calendar in favour of an imperial one exemplify his adherence to the Iranianist *idea*. Nurtured by the dream of reviving ancient Persian grandeur and establishing the ultimate 'Great Civilisation' (*tamadon-e bozorg*), the Iranian self was presented as Aryan, tied to a notion of chauvinistic supremacy towards neighbouring nations and cultures.[64]

Translated into the external relations of Pahlavi Iran, that self-identification was anathema to genuinely communitarian relations in the Gulf. In line with the notion of superiority, the historic designation of the waterway separating Iran and the Arabian peninsula as the *Persian* Gulf (*Khalij-e Fars*) was literally understood as evidence for historically determined Persian pre-eminence.[65] As R.K. Ramazani observed during that period:

> Despite all the vicissitudes of its stormy existence in the past, contemporary Iran seems to perceive its role in the Persian Gulf as almost uninterrupted and as always active. Facts would not seem to support this perception, but the important point is that this belief influences Iran's behaviour today.[66]

The norms of Iranian nationalism disseminated by institutionalised Iranianism contributed to the misperception between Iran and the Arab states of the Persian Gulf. By virtue of its ideological precepts, Pahlavi Iran needed the Arab other in order to essentialise the Iranian self. Social psychologists would suggest that 'positive distinction' of the (Iranian-Aryan) 'in-group' *vis-à-vis* the (Arab-Semitic) 'out-group' was achieved by emphasising the superiority of the pre-Islamic Iranian heritage and undervaluing the Islamic identity of the Iranian populace. Within that ideational context, the Shah's aggressive military build-up under the patronage of the United States, claims to Bahrain that were dropped only after a plebiscite in the small sheikhdom voted against unification with Iran, the seizure of half of the Abu Musa island from Sharjah and the Greater and Lesser Tunbs from Ras al-Khaimah in 1971, confirmed the perception that the Iranian role as regional guardian could lead to an aggressive Iranianisation of the Gulf. The brand of Iranian nationalism espoused by the Shah, and more specifically, the reification of the insidious, metaphysical mendacity of racially coded Iranian supremacy, not only widened the gulf between the state elites of the region, it inhibited the formal translation of communitarian norms into a functioning security architecture.

2.2.2   The geopolitics of pan-Arabism: Arab vs. Ajam[67]

The adoption of European nationalist *Weltanschauung* in the Iranian context was comparable, albeit not similar, to the ideological evolution of Arab nationalism (*al qawmiyya al' arabiyya*). Whilst Iranian nationalism showed close affinity with French notions of Indo-European supremacy most forcefully elucidated by Ernest Renan,[68] the branch of Arab nationalism developed by Sati Khaldun al-Husri and institutionalised in the Ba'th (rebirth) party by Michel Aflaq was closer to the tradition of German romanticism.[69] Following Johann G. von Herder's romantic idea of *Kulturnation*, that is a cultural community transcending the confine of the state (later developed by Johann Gotlieb Fichte), al-Husri defended a culturalist interpretation of political community. According to that view, the 'Arab nation' was perceived as a cultural entity held together by a common national language and shared common folklore. In an essay in response to Ernest Renan's question *Qu'est-ce qu'une nation?* al-Husri suggested that Arabs were Arabs first and foremost due to the common linguistic bond. He argued, that because of their eternal kinship, Arabs were destined to fulfil a sacred and eternal mission as a resurgent nation. Denial of their identity means self-deception because every Arabic-speaking person was a member of the Arab nation, 'whether we will it or not, whether he admits it or not'.[70]

Michel Aflaq, the founder of the Ba'th party in the 1940s, affirmed Husri's idea of Arab nationhood, contending that 'Arabness' is primarily determined by the common Arabic language. Moreover, Aflaq sought a synthesis between the pan-Arabic utopia and socialism. This programme attracted followers from European educated circles in Syria and beyond, leading to the establishment of *al- Ba'th al- 'Arabi* (the Arab rebirth) in 1943 which joined forces with *al-Ihya' al-'Arabi* (the Arab revival) in 1947 and the Arab Socialist Party in 1953.[71] With the romantic notion of an 'Awakening of Arab consciousness' as the ultimate goal, the newly created Arab Ba'th

Socialist Party advocated a unified Arab 'superstate' stretching from the Atlantic Ocean in the West to the 'Arab' Gulf in the East.[72]

Similar to the transgression of Iranian nationalism which too often took the shape of a racist discourse about the constitution of 'Iranianness', the dissemination and institutionalisation of Arab nationalism dramatised the self-Other delineation between the Iranian and Arab peoples inhabiting the Gulf. By stressing the primacy of language as the source of common political identity of an imagined pan-Arab community, al-Husri and Aflaq not only separated the state from the nation, but also essentialised the 'Arabness' of Islam. According to Aflaq and Ba'thist ideology, Islam was a revolutionary Arab movement and constituted the true renewal of Arabism as the fate of the community. Consequently, both the religion and the Prophet Mohammad were treated as the prerogative of the Arab nation, rather than symbols of a heterogeneous Muslim world:

> The abstracted nationalist idea of the West is logical in its separation of nation-alism from religion. Religion entered Europe from [West Asia] and is therefore foreign to its nature and history.... Islam for the Arabs on the other hand is not merely a belief for the end of time, nor is it abstract moralisms; it is the highest expression of their universalist feelings and outlook on life. It is the strongest expression of the total unity of their personality, in which expression mixes in with feeling and thought, reflection with labour, and the self with fate. Islam is the most brilliant picture of their language and literature, and the grandest part of their national history.... *The relation of Islam with Arabism, therefore, is not the same as that of any other religion in relation to any other nationality.*[73]

In the tradition of the idea of *shu'ubiyya*, an ancient concept often used to depict anti-Arab conspiracies by movements that were deemed united in their hatred of 'Arabhood' (Turks, Communists, Iranians, Shiites etc.), the fortification of Islam as an Arab domain by implication ostracised the non-Arab peoples in the Gulf. Iran, as a non-Arab country, neither met the criteria of 'Arabness' nor could be considered akin due to common religious bonds because of the essentialisation of Islam as an Arab prerogative and the secular tenor of Arab nationalism itself. Hence, the more Arab nationalism became the prime narrative of state identity in the region, the more it identified non-Arabs as a peripheral minority *within* the Arab world.

The institutionalisation of pan-Arabism in Iraq – on the educational level imple-mented by al-Husri's educational posts between 1921 and 1941 and on the political level boosted by Aflaq's decision to side with the Iraqi Ba'th of Saddam Hussein against the Syrian Ba'th of Hafiz al-Asad in the late 1970s – constituted the Iraqi state as the primary agent of socialist Arab nationalism in the Persian Gulf. With the death of Nassir in 1970 and the demise of the Nassirite Arab Nationalist Movement (*Harakat al-Qawmiyyin al-'Arab*), Iraq's self-portrayal as the 'liberated Arab vanguard' served the purpose to legitimate the totalitarian rule of the Ba'th party domestically and claim the mandate for leadership of the Arab states externally. As part of the process of institutionalising pan-Arabic fervour and later as a means to sustain Iraq's pan-Arab credentials during the Iran–Iraq war, anti-Iranianism became the third pillar of Iraqi state ideology along with anti-Zionism and anti-imperialism. This is not an abstract observation derived from the exclusionary ideology immanent to any radical nationalist notion. The construction of the enemy-image was organised and pervasive. The idea of 'the Persian' as the chief nemesis of the 'Arab nation' became even embedded in the educational curricula of Ba'thist Iraq. In a survey about the image of Iranians in Arab schoolbooks, Talal Atrissi confirms the 'fascist' disposition of Iraqi Ba'thist education:

> The image of the Iranians (Persians) in the Iraqi schoolbooks is clear-cut.... The Iranian is always that mean racist Persian who conspired against the Arab nation, its unity and its language, as well as the Islamic Arab civilisation, since the era of the Orthodox Caliphs and until 'Saddam's glorious Qadisieh' [Iran–Iraq war].
>
> Each time the Persians are mentioned they are the invaders, an absolute evil that has to be deterred, being a constant danger that threatens the [Arab] nation and its fate. All the problems of Muslims and Arabs, all the sectarian conflicts and unrest, as well as the attempts to undermine their civilisation, may as well be, if we are to rely on these books, the product of Persian conspiracies.[74]

The modern phenomenon of nationalist discourse in Iran and Iraq was a source for mobilising the support of the populace and a symbol of legitimacy for the authoritarian regimes in power. The state identity building process projected exclusionary transnational loyalties into the relatively stable regional system, inhibiting efforts to translate the relatively co-operative *modus operandi* into a viable security architecture. In order to invent salient state identities, differences were accentuated and commonalities underplayed, hardening Self-Other categorisations between Iranians and Arabs. 'From an Arab perspective', it is typically argued 'the Persian mentality is influenced by strong nationalistic sentiment wrapped in chauvinistic Aryan feelings which the shah manipulated and fostered in the Iranian psyche'.[75] From an Iranian perspective, the fact that Arab nationalist discourse isolated the country as a 'peripheral minority' operating in what accordingly was called the 'Arab' Gulf sub-system, reinforced similar grievances.[76] In both contexts, nationalism served the function to meet specific political ends. For Iranian ultra-nationalists, representation of the 'Arab other' was perverted in order to herald Iranian distinctiveness and the country's 'natural' affinity with the 'West'. Joya Blondel Saad makes the link between Iranian nationalism, anti-Arabism and pro-'Westernism' explicit:

> For some Iranian nationalists, the Other has been not so much the West, but the Arabs and Islam. Identifying Iran with the West, as fellow 'Aryan' nations, allowed for the acceptance of Western modernisation and the importation of Western culture.... The myth of the common origin of Iranians, 'proved' by categories of race ('Aryan') and language (Indo-European), and the myth of the pre-Islamic Golden Age, allowed Iran to fit the Western national model.[77]

Arab nationalism, on the other side, was invoked as a political strategy to exclude Iran from the arena of inter-Arab politics, ideologically 'fortifying' the system against potential penetration by the assertive Shah. As an essentially secular idea and modern occurrence in West Asia, the translation of Western European, mainly German and French notions of nationalism contributed to the myth that Arab-Iranian relations have been perennially antagonistic. Parochial debates about the nomenclature of the Gulf and its designation as 'Persian' or 'Arab' became a symbol for the ideological warfare between two manifestations of nationalism(s), rooted in – and nurtured by – the same exclusionary political philosophy. This suggestion links our discussion to the question asked at the beginning of this chapter: Why did regional states not take advantage of the momentum to integrate security co-operation during the 1970s? First and foremost, this section proposes, due to the incompatibility of exclusionary ideologies of the state. Borrowing from social psychological terminology one might contend that the immanently relational process of identity formation promoted selective accentuation of inter-cultural differences, juxtaposing the 'in-group' against the 'out-group' in order both to create an image of the 'Self' and suggest positive distinction *vis-à-vis* the 'Other'. For both Iranians and Arabs that 'significant Other' was not necessarily only the 'West'. Rather, both appear to have attempted to externalise what was considered the 'Cain' of the Self: radical Arab nationalism attempted to 'externalise' the pan-Islamic, Turkish and Iranian elements in order to sustain a viable imagery of a common Arab *Volksgeist*, unattached to a religious identity and bonded by a common language; Iranian nationalism adopted by the Pahlavi state on the other side endeavoured to distance itself from the Islamic identity of Iran, hence externalising the 'Arab-Semitic other' from the 'Persian-Aryan self' in order to claim 'natural' affinity with the 'Western' world.

2.3 Revolution, war and the Iranian-Iraqi legitimacy contest

Whilst during the 1970s, co-operative norms were stronger than the pull of ideology projected by Iranian and Arab nationalist discourse, revolution in Iran constituted a reverse constellation. How did that process translate into inter-state relations? It has been argued that before the revolution in Iran, interaction in the Persian Gulf was determined by the Saudi/Iranian equilibrium. Despite the divisions generated by exclusionary narratives of state identity, the regional society was strong enough to balance out differences between its constituent members. That order was complementary to regional and global norms of appropriate behaviour, legitimating the role identities of its two principal guardians. Revolution in Iran crushed that order. By nature of its revolutionary zeal, the Iranian movement rejected the pre-existing system and transgressed the orthodox conduct of international diplomacy. Whereas the Shah pursued the role of regional 'gendarme' and was closely allied with the United States, the Islamic Republic of Iran vociferously opposed that role.

With the ascendancy to power of the revolutionary movement, the parameters of the twin-pillar system were subordinated to the uncompromising foreign-policy culture of the Islamic state.[78] The most central institution of this culture was encapsulated in the notion of *na sharghi na gharbi, jomhuri-ye eslami* (neither Eastern nor Western; only the Islamic Republic). This revolutionary rallying call prescribed a radical non-alignment policy for its agent and explains why revolutionary Iran articulated 'some of the most vociferous calls for political independence and cultural authenticity in the 'Third World'.[79] Concurrent with this revolutionary process and the detachment from the Cold War rationale, the role of Iran changed from *guardian of the status quo* under the patronage of the United States to *revisionist power.*[80] Consequently, Saudi Arabia and the smaller sheikhdoms of the Gulf remained the only actors wishing to preserve the regional equilibrium, whilst Iran opted out of that role, self-consciously isolating itself from the bipolar mechanisms of international society. With the two principal powers (Iran and Iraq) now pursuing revisionist roles and in the absence of a regional security order that would balance confrontational interaction, communitarian norms were subordinated, leading to a period of prolonged conflict that was to dominate regional foreign-policy calculations for over a decade.

Yet despite the unequivocal impact of the revolution on the Persian Gulf area and the wider Islamic worlds, it would be wrong to assume that events in Iran solely determined the ensuing unfolding of regional events. Even revolutions occur within a context of pre-existent and salient structures. The Iranian-Islamic movement is no exception. To explain the discrepancy between revolutionary aspiration and 'socialisation', one might return to Marx's note of caution that 'Men make their own history ... not under circumstances they themselves have chosen but under the given and inherited circumstances with which they are directly confronted.'[81] Once in power, the Iranian revolutionaries were immediately challenged by the rules and laws of international society and the realities of inter-state relations in the Persian Gulf. Perceptions, images, roles, collective memories, in short the 'stock' of shared knowledge accumulated from previous interaction was not simply washed away and continued to feed into the post-revolutionary process. International relations theorists would point to the fact that despite regression into a state of prolonged conflict and the *realpolitik* foreign policies it necessitated, functionally similar sovereign nation-states remained the central protagonists in a temporarily disrupted, yet functionally Westphalian, state-centred system.

This section discusses the modified ideational context between 1979 and 1988. The chronology of the revolution and the details of military strategy of the First Persian Gulf war have been discussed extensively elsewhere and will therefore play a secondary role.[82] What I am interested in is the impact of revolution and war on the cultural system in the Persian Gulf and in turn on the foreign-policy choices of the littoral states. Here, following a cultural genealogy requires screening of the modified state identities and the dominant ideational propositions that conditioned the decisions of the political elites during the specific period of time. Scholars dealing with the Iranian revolution and the Iran–Iraq war have produced numerous empirical studies of high quality and what follows is not designed to compete with their analyses. Rather more important for our purposes is to move beyond the apparently authoritative facts and offer alternative ideas that appreciate the antithetical impacts of ideational or cultural constructs.

Let me explain. The problem with the inculcation of facts is that it takes insufficient note of human beings and – by extension – nation-states as introjected agents of ideas, ideologies or other artefacts of culture. 'Introjection', a term central to the writings of the late critical theorist Herbert Marcuse, highlights the penetrative powers of culture.[83] It reveals that socialisation in cultural systems has not only mediating or causal impacts, but also *constitutive* effects.[84] In other, less formal words: governments and nation-states are both culture maker and culture taker. They produce their objective reality and are products of it. This explains why the cultural constitution of international societies is so virulently contested, because ultimately, the cultural system determines what is considered legitimate or anti-systemic (it also decides who is to be designated a freedom fighter or terrorist). The Westphalian culture of international society is, for example, radically opposed to transnational 'panisms', whether Arab, Islamic, African or otherwise. I think most modern wars have a lot to do with the question of legitimacy, the contested issue of what is permissible and what not. I would suggest that the Iran–Iraq war was a near-perfect example for such wars. It boiled down to a legitimacy contest between two ideological constructs: Iraqi pan-Arabism and Iranian-Islamism. The struggle for hegemony in the Persian Gulf, I would propose therefore, was primarily cultural. Programmed according to their respective state identities, regional states were entangled in a war for ideological primacy, with clashing narratives of state identities competing for dominance within a temporarily disrupted, embattled regional society. The following paragraphs trace this cataclysmic cultural transformation process in close relation to the empirical facts.

2.3.1   Islamic norm entrepreneurs: the impact of Iran's revolution

Revolution in Iran changed the state identity of the country from a monarchic-nationalist system to a revolutionary, Islamic-republican one. The equilibrium (*tavazon*) norm sustained by the Shah was abandoned in favour of 'Islamic revisionism' synthesised with the populist imagery of an universal struggle against imperialism. The self-attribution of a new state identity was embedded into the notion of a 'true and unique Islamic state', equipped with the legitimate transnational mandate for the export of the revolution (*sudur-e enghelab*). That the identity of the 'new Iran' was deemed 'unique' was enshrined in the preamble of the Islamic Republic's constitution, which emphasised that the 'basic characteristic of the Revolution, which distinguishes it from other movements that have taken place in Iran during the past hundred years, [was] its ideological and Islamic nature'.[85] Previous mass movements such as the Constitutional Revolution in 1906 and the nationalisation of the oil industry by Mohammad Mossadegh in 1951 'quickly fell into stagnation' due to departure from the 'true positions of Islam'.[86] Embedded in a third worldist and Shiite-Islamic discourse, revolution thus transformed the Iranian state into a vehicle for romantic revolutionism, destined to fulfil an eternal mission for the emancipation of the oppressed (*mostazafan*) people of the world. The opening announcement of Radio Tehran broadcast translated that call into revolutionary language, typical for the Iran of the late 1970s: 'In the Name of Almighty God crusher of tyrants and champion of the oppressed' it was triumphantly proclaimed '[t]his is the voice of right, the voice of the oppressed, this is the voice of the Islamic Republic of Iran'.

Reserving a special place for Muslims, but nonetheless addressing a broader audience, the broadcast continued: 'Muslims everywhere, we transmit our programs to you from Tehran, the bastion of the Islamic revolution, so that they will be a light for all oppressed people everywhere.' Repeating the role attribution of the Islamic Republic as the vanguard of a worldwide resurgence of Islam, the statement concluded by pledging 'to remain loyal' to the Islamic mission, 'the mission of right, justice and freedom'.[87]

The philosophical-theoretical context of the self-bestowed transnational, indeed universal, mandate of the Islamic Republic was rooted in Shiite political theory and its interpretation by Ayatollah Rouhollah Khomeini.[88] The leader of the revolution (*rahbar-e enghelab*) frequently employed the imagery of the millenary struggle between the 'oppressed' against the 'oppressors' in order to rally the masses behind the revolutionary cause. That Manichean *mostazafan-mostakbaran* dichotomy was central to the world-view of Khomeini, representing a modification of the traditional Islamic differentiation of world affairs in *dar al-Islam* (the abode of Islam or the place of peace) and *dar al-harb* (the abode of war or the place of non-believers).[89] Borrowing from anti-imperialistic terminology of the Iranian left and touching upon the country's third world populist and socialist *Zeitgeist* during the 1970s, Khomeini referred to a wider struggle, not only between Muslims and non-Muslims, but between justice and injustice.[90] According to that ideological dualism, the ongoing clash between the 'oppressed' who have been deprived of their political, cultural, natural and economic resources against the 'oppressors' who have subjugated the 'disinherited', is zero-sum in nature. Elevating the position of Islamic Iran to the highest 'moral highground', the aspiration to effect a total change of that 'unjust' system was rendered explicit. Confirming that goal, the preamble of the constitution of the Islamic Republic declared that the revolution aims to bring about the triumph of the *mostazafan* against the *mostakbaran*. Moreover, it is stated that the Constitution 'provides the necessary basis for ensuring the continuation of the Revolution at home and abroad'. Illustrated in accordance with the Quranic verse 'This your nation is a single nation, and I am your Lord, so worship Me (21:92)', it is further declared that the Constitution 'will strive, in concert with other Islamic and popular movements, to prepare the way for the formation of a single world community'.[91]

2.3.1.1 Pax Islamica vs. Westphalia: the challenge to international order

Despite contradictory sections in the Constitution where abstention from 'aggressive intervention in the internal affairs of other nations' is accentuated (see Article 154) and the overall anti-militaristic tenor during the early days of the Islamic Republic, the Iranian revolutionaries did as much as any revolutionary movement to propagate their message abroad.[92] Khomeini explicitly endorsed the export of the revolutionary idea, but also cautioned that 'this does not mean that we intend to export it by the bayonet. We want to call [*dawat*] everyone to Islam [and to] send our calling everywhere'.[93] Although covert support to 'liberation movements' in Iraq, Lebanon, Palestine and Afghanistan was sometimes openly justified, exporting the *idea* of the Islamic Republic without military aggrandisement was rather more central.[94]

Reliance on *dawat* (calling) and *tabligh* (propagation, advertisement, dissemination) hence substituted for the militaristic coercion periodically characteristic of the Shah's reign. In accordance with that disposition, the Islamic Republic cancelled the Shah's billion dollars defence contracts with the United States and Western Europe and abandoned Iranian military installations in Oman. Conscious of the appeal of the Islamic-republican model to the Muslim world and caught in a momentum of revolutionary 'ecstasy', Iran relied upon its ideological power transmitted by the charisma of Ayatollah Khomeini and transplanted by sympathising movements in the region and beyond.[95]

The occupation of the US embassy by the *daneshjuan-e musalmanan-e piramun-e khatt-e imam* (the Muslim Students following the line of the Imam) in November 1979 was the most explicit rejection of international 'norms of appropriate behaviour', and here specifically the institutions of international law. Denying diplomatic immunity to the over fifty US American embassy personnel was intended to symbolise the revolution's protest against imperialism, and specifically what was perceived to be an unjust and 'oppressively hierarchical world order'. The 'hitherto prevailing conventions of diplomatic immunity and representation' were considered 'worthy of attack', because of the legitimating force of revolution.[96] In other words, here and elsewhere, the long-term image and ideological symbolism of the revolution superseded crude, short-term cost-benefit calculations. Rejection of central tenets of international political culture was deemed conducive to appeal to other revolutionary movements, representing '[t]he Islamic Revolution of Iran [as] a new achievement in the ongoing struggle between the peoples and the oppressive superpowers'.[97] Ayatollah Khomeini condoned the occupation, because it reiterated Iran's revolutionary aspirations and symbolised the combatant-Islamic state identity he favoured.

Moreover, the hostage crisis was taken as an opportunity by the *khat-e imam* (the Imam's line) revolutionary wing of the Iranian fractions to encourage a process of internal radicalisation and subdue their liberal-left competitors organised around Prime Minister Mehdi Bazargan. The preferred state identity espoused by that faction was to be offensive, revolutionary and idealistic, rather than conservative, accommodating and status quo oriented. As the closest manifestation of the omnipotence of the United States whose government was deemed to be the prime agent of anti-Iranian conspiracies,[98] occupying the 'den of spies' (*lane-ye jasusan*) as the US embassy was called, was meant to reiterate the revolutionary, anti-imperialistic character of the Iranian movement. From the perspective of the students, the occupation symbolised the 'total' victory of the Islamic revolution, kindling 'flames of hope in the hearts of the enchained nations' and creating 'a legend of self-reliance and ideological steadfastness for a nation contending with imperialism'.[99] As Halliday observed:

> While the hostage affair and the campaign against the 'liberals' around Bazargan were designed to encourage a process of internal radicalisation, the seizure of the U.S. embassy also became a symbol of revolutionary Iran's defiance of the established patterns of diplomacy and of the United States, seen as the historic oppressor of Iran.[100]

A comparable rationale propelled Ayatollah Khomeini to pursue the second prominent challenge to the central tenets of international political culture. By issuing a religious verdict (*fatwa*) against Salman Rushdie and the publishers of *The Satanic Verses*, Khomeini negated the very basis of the Westphalian nation-state system, whereby the citizens of a sovereign state are only subject to the jurisdiction of territorial state law and, where applicable, to secular international law. From Ayatollah Khomeini's perspective, the extension of *sharia* law to someone who used to be part of the *umma*, had become an 'apostate' member of the Islamic community and who had insulted the Quran and the Prophet Mohammad was not only legitimate, but an obligation.[101] Khomeini felt mandated by his religious status as *marja-e taghlid* (source of emulation, highest Shiite religious rank) and legitimated by a popular revolution in the name of Islam, to position divine law above secular international law during periods when safeguarding the *maslahat* (interest) of the Islamic state and – by extension – the Muslim *umma* demanded political expediency. In both cases, hostage taking and the *fatwa* against Rushdie, Ayatollah Khomeini found it conducive to assert the Iranian state identity as the anti-imperialist, revolutionary-Islamic power house, because in both cases asserting that role identity was helpful to fence off domestic dissent and claim the leadership of the Muslim *umma* externally. Seeking acknowledgement and support for the primacy of the revolution's spiritual and political power, calculations were made on the basis of the *absolute* ideological appeal of the revolutionary idea, rather than the *relative* costs of confrontation. Ironically, the more international society turned against Iran, the more it confirmed the self-perception of the Iranian state as the leader of an 'oppressed' nation, facing the overwhelming force of the 'arrogant powers'. In the Iranian/Shiite context this imagery was very powerful. It related to the sufferings of Shiites at the hands of unjust rulers, and upon the martyrdom (*shahadat*) of Imam Hussein during the Battle of Karbala against the Umayyad monarch Yazid in AD 680:

> Imam Husayn was not to be killed again. Thus, he defeated Yazid [i.e. the Shah] in Iran last year. Imam Husayn, who is now leading a battle against a greater Yazid [i.e. imperialism], will also triumph, God willing. The revolutionary Imam Husayn in Iran, who is fighting imperialism, is not alone now. In addition to some 35,000,000 Iranians who bravely and devotedly rally around him, there are billions of Muslims and non-Muslims everywhere in Syria, Libya, Algeria, Lebanon, Palestine, Pakistan, Africa, the Omani liberation front, Eritrea, the Chilean resistance, the Chadian liberation movement, the Canary Islands' liberation movement, the Futami liberation movement, Spain, Korea and many other places as well as the entire Islamic world, and the oppressed all over the world, who all support Iran, the revolution and Imam Husayn, represented in leader Imam Ayatollah Khomeini.[102]

The anti-imperialist norm put forward by the Iranian revolutionaries, central as it was to the language and symbols of the Islamic Republic during the first decade of its existence became a dominant institution in revolutionary Iran.[103] Inextricably linked to the identity of the Islamic state, the rhetoric about the struggle of the 'oppressed' against the 'arrogant powers' soon broke the boundaries between political idiom and political action, explaining the Iranian belligerence towards the prevalent rules and institutions of international society. Consistent with 'Islamic leftist' concepts of a socialist nature and the prominent intellectual discourse about *gharbzadegi* ('westtoxification'), intrinsic to the works of popular pre-revolutionary intellectuals such as Jalal Al-e Ahmad and Ali Shariati, encroachment of the Islamic world by corrupting 'Western' concepts was deemed poisonous for the evolution of a just society and the emergence of the ultimate *homo Islamicus*.[104] In theory, regaining authenticity – in Shariati's terminology returning to the Self (*bazgasht be khishtan*) – and retaining independence required detachment from the bipolar international system which was perceived as 'dangerous for humanity'.[105] Alluding to the intellectual production of that mindset, Mehrzad Boroujerdi goes one step further, suggesting a causal link between the anti-imperialist, anti-'Westernisation' disposition of Iranian intellectuals and the challenges of revolutionary Iran to the international system. The eloquent paragraph deserves to be cited in full:

> [Iranian thinkers] believe in the telos of living a moral, sensible, passionate and authentic life. Authenticity is tantamount to taking hold of one's existence and traditions in a manner that is genuine, trustworthy, and sincere. To be 'authentic' is to embrace one's time and culture critically, and, yet to keep an eye on the overriding sense of loyalty and belonging. For the prototypical Iranian intellectual this has translated into a rejection of the apish imitation of the West on the grounds that mimicry and submission are fraudulent and counterfeit states of being. This explains why anti-Westernisation and anti-imperialism have become two of the fixed hallmarks of the modern Iranian intelligentsia's identity discourse. The formidable ideological permeation of the West and its (neo)colonial exploits lead many Iranian intellectuals as well as the common people of Iran, in search of indigenisation, authenticity, and freedom, to turn toward nativism and Islamicism. In their desire not to be a prolegomenon to Western philosophical texts or a nodal point in the Western imperialist maps, some of these intellectuals and social movements, alas, succumb to cultural xenophobia toward the West and adopt essentialist world-views. As a result, precarious policies (i.e. hostage taking, export of revolution, the death sentence against Salman Rushdie) should not come as a surprise.[106]

Boroujerdi suggests that anti-imperialism, cultural authenticity and independence constituted the central parameters of Iran's (state) identity discourse after the revolution because the three norms were deeply internalised by the revolutionary elites and an immediate factor of Iranian political culture. In turn this would suggest that it was due to this ideational mindset that the foreign-policy norm *na sharghi na gharbi, jomhur-ye eslami* (neither Eastern nor Western, only the Islamic Republic) entered the revolutionary programme, pitting the Islamic Republic against the established order of the Westphalian nation-state system. R.K. Ramazani agrees:

> The policies of the state of the faqih, aiming as they do at the eventual creation of...an Islamic world order, will inevitably entail confrontation between that

state and the superpowers. Such a conflict is inevitable because the superpowers have arrogated all power (*qudrat*) to themselves.... It is in the context of these basic ideas that the Iranian slogan 'neither East, nor West, only the Islamic republic'... should be understood, not the irrelevant notions of equidistance or non-alignment.... These ideas in effect accept the Western notion of power politics, whereas Khomeini's religious, millenarian, and idealistic view rejects the global role of both superpowers; they are both considered to be illegitimate players in the international system they dominate.[107]

Hence, once the revolutionary state had chosen anti-imperialism as an integral part of Iranian state identity, it acted upon that disposition by ending the country's membership of Cold War institutions such as CENTO (Central Treaty Organisation), challenging established norms of appropriate behaviour in the conduct of international affairs, turning into a passionate advocate of the Non Aligned Movement (NAM) and transforming its alliance with the United States into a relationship of enduring antagonism. The costs of these policies were taken, even if that meant that the country would be isolated, and labelled as a 'rogue' or 'outlawed' state by international society.

2.3.1.2   *The geopolitics of Iranian-Islam: revolution and Iran's 'significant Other'*

As a logical consequence of the Islamic nucleus of the Iranian revolution and the self-bestowed mandate for leadership of the Muslim world, the Persian Gulf states became the primary agent of the idea of an Islamic Republic. Whilst state-sponsored 'Iranianism' during the Pahlavi era limited interaction between Iran and the Arab states to the inter-state level, '[t]he Islamic Republic's downplaying of Persian nationalism and its promotion of the theme of Islamic universalism and Islamic brotherhood opened... the Arab masses to Iranian political influence'.[108] That intention was as much a by-product of 'genuine' revolutionary sentiment, as it was a rational calculation to acquire 'strategic depth' and enhance the communicative capabilities or geopolitical outreach of the Islamic movement. After all, it was also on the basis of the incompatibility of 'Iranianism' with regional constructs of identity that pre-revolutionary activists criticised the chosen nationalist identity of the Pahlavi state. In *Islam and Iran*, Ayatollah Muttahari, who was one of the most popular clerics of the Islamic left, argued:

> If it is decided that [the] basis in determining the limits of the Iranian nation is the Aryan factor, the ultimate end of that is proclivity towards the Western world. But this proclivity in our national and political mission involves submissions and consequences, the most serious being a severance with neighbouring Islamic nations that are not Aryan and an attachment to Europe and the West... [I]f we [would choose as] the foundation of our nation our intellectual, behavioural and social heritage over the past fourteen centuries, [however,] we would have a different mission and other costs... Therein, Arab, Turk, Indian, Indonesian and [Chinese] would become our friends, even kinsmen.[109]

The 'Islamisation' of the Iranian state identity opened up communicative channels with receptive political constituencies on the sub-state level, and here especially with Shiite circles in Afghanistan, Iraq, Kuwait, Bahrain and Southern Lebanon, who used the revolutionary impetus to struggle against marginalisation within their own national frameworks.[110] Interaction with the Persian Gulf states and the wider Muslim world was hence not conducted merely on the inter-*state* level, but transferred to the transnational, inter-*cultural* one. This transnational dynamic clashed with the orthodox nation-state principles of the international Westphalian system. Whilst inter-state diplomacy before the revolution had reiterated the institution of nation-state sovereignty, Iranian internationalism engendered transgression and sometimes negation of international rules (during post-revolutionary crisis as in the cases of the Hostage Crisis and the Rushdie *fatwa*).

In line with its pan-Islamic posture, the Islamic Republic rejected the regional status quo, challenging the legitimacy of the regimes in power. According to Khomeini, monarchic and secular-nationalist forms of governance (most notably in Saudi Arabia and Iraq respectively) were incompatible with the requirements of 'Islamic governance'. The opposition of Khomeini to the former institution became more virulent in the early 1970s. In condemnation of the Shah's opulent celebration of 2,500 years of Iranian imperial dynasties in Persepolis, he declared that monarchy is 'one of the most shameful and disgraceful reactionary manifestations'.[111] According to his view, struggling against monarchies was at the heart of religion and it was incumbent upon religious leaders – in the tradition of the prophets Abraham, Moses and Mohammad – to fight monarchic systems. Typical for his invigoration of Shiite imagery and symbols, Khomeini declared:

> The Lord of the Martyrs [Imam Hussein, grandson of the Prophet Mohammad] (peace be upon him) summoned the people to rise in revolt by means of sermon, preaching, and correspondence and caused them to rebel against a monarch. Imam Hasan (upon whom be peace) struggled against the king of his day.... This struggle and confrontation has continued without respite, and the great scholars of Islam have always fought against the tyrannical bandits who enslaved their peoples for the sake of their passions and squandered their country's wealth on trivial amusements.[112]

The anti-monarchic norm was central to the later stages of Khomeini's political theory and explains the belligerence of the Islamic Republic towards the ruling elites in Saudi Arabia, Jordan and Morocco during the first decade of the revolution. If 'Islam proclaims monarchy and hereditary succession wrong and invalid', Khomeini argued, abolishing 'the entire institution of monarchy' becomes the central task of a true Islamic government which is only legitimated by the legislation of God.[113] The norm of 'Islamic governance', as interpreted by Khomeini, was by definition the antithesis of the existing forms of rule in the Persian Gulf and beyond. In accordance with the ethical-moral nucleus of the theory, both the GCC monarchies and the secular-nationalistic government in Iraq were accused of having departed from the path of 'true Mohammadan Islam' and castigated to practice *Islam-e amrikai* – an Americanised perversion of the true tenets of the faith.

The rejection of monarchic rule as a legitimate form of governance was deeply rooted in Khomeini's theory of *velayat'e faqih* (governance of the supreme jurisprudent) and went beyond the calculations of short-term power politics. According to the central normative pillar of that theory put forward in *hukumat-e Islami* (Islamic Government), the *vali-e faqih* (the supreme jurisprudent) 'must possess excellence in morals and belief; he must be just and untainted by major sin'.[114] That 'Islamic' moral-system was heralded as the main attribute that guided the Prophet Mohammad during his leadership of the *umma*. Conversely, monarchic rule was considered as immanently decadent and hence inconceivable with the moral requirements of a Muslim state. After employing this powerful idea to undermine the rule of the Shah, Khomeini used similar accusations against the al-Saud family in Saudi Arabia, castigating them for the blatant ignorance of Islamic morality evident in their 'frivolous, shameless way of life, robbing funds from the people and squandering them, and engaging in gambling, drinking parties, and orgies'.[115]

The clash between Khomeini's state theory and the leadership of the al-Saud went deeper, however. In Saudi Arabia, the eighteenth century coalition between Mohammad ibn 'Abdal al-Wahhab and the local tribal ruler Abdal Aziz ibn Sa'ud led to the establishment of a (Wahhabi) Islamic state based on a monarchic system that transmuted into a conservative status quo oriented, pro-Western and hereditary state identity.[116] Conversely, Khomeinian Islam guided the Iranian movement into a revolutionary, idealistic, anti-imperialist and anti-monarchical direction.[117] The conflict hence turned into a rivalry between two contradicting narratives of state identity: Sunni-Wahhabi conservatism of the al-Saud on the one hand side and revolutionary, Shia internationalism of the Islamic Republic on the other.

In the second place, from the perspective of radical Wahhabi *ulema* (religious scholars), the Shia propensity for saint worship, shrine and grave cults, and veneration for Imams were considered abhorrent acts of *shirk* (polytheism). Indeed traditional Wahhabism viewed Shiites as 'the incarnation of infidelity, and... polytheists' making it the duty of believers 'to manifest enmity to the polytheists [who] were perceived as unbelievers (*kuffar*), and were therefore liable to the severest sanctions, including that of holy war (*jihad*).'[118] From the viewpoint of Ayatollah Khomeini on the other side, the conservatism and monarchic precept of Wahhabism were inherently contradictory to the teachings of Islam. Khomeini asserted that sovereignty was not merely a legal attribute enshrined in national and international law, it required popular and religious-moral legitimacy. By allying the Saudi state with the 'Great Satan' (the United States), indulging in an immoral and materialist lifestyle, and holding on to monarchic principles to legitimate the al-Saud tribal leadership, 'the government of Hejaz', as Khomeini referred to the Saudi leaders, had forfeited its legitimacy both as a state and as guardians of the two holy shrines (*al-Haramein al-Sharifein*) in Mecca and Medina. Nowhere was the challenge more serious than during the Muslim pilgrimages. After the revolution in Iran, the *hajj* to Mecca and Medina had become the main stage for political demonstrations by the followers of the Iranian model. Saudi authorities accused the Islamic Republic of fomenting unrest and that the demonstrators acted in ways contrary to the aims of pilgrimage. In accordance with his political interpretation of Islam, Khomeini countered that it was imperative to take the *hajj* as an occasion to politicise the Islamic masses. Hence, until the clashes of 1987 when around 400 people, including 270 Iranians were killed, Ayatollah Khomeini's uncompromising politicisation of Islamic symbols and tradition turned the pilgrimage into a stage for the dissemination of the idea of an Islamic Republic. Peculiarly, this was done on the territory of a sovereign nation-state, whose government itself was a target of the revolutionary message.

Next to anti-imperialism and anti-monarchism, anti-nationalism constituted the third central challenge to existent cultural forms in the Persian Gulf region and beyond. Whilst the former two guided Iran towards agitation against the United States and Saudi Arabia (and to a lesser extent the smaller Gulf monarchies) respectively, the third norm transmuted into opposition to the Ba'thist government in Iraq. In a message to the *hajj* pilgrims on 13 September 1980, nine days before the invasion of Iran by Iraqi forces and in the midst of escalating border skirmishes between the two countries, Khomeini linked the disuniting impact of nationalism on the Islamic *umma* to the Iraqi provocations.

> For years the government of Iraq has been busy promoting nationalism . . . setting the Muslims against each other as enemies. To love one's fatherland and its people and to protect its frontiers are both quite unobjectionable, but nationalism, involving hostility to other Muslim nations, is something quite different. It is contrary to the Noble Qur'an and the orders of the Most Noble Messenger. Nationalism that results in the creation of enmity between Muslims and splits the ranks of the believers is against Islam and the interests of the Muslims. It is a stratagem concocted by the foreigners who are disturbed by the spread of Islam.[119]

Nationalism, as distinct from 'taking pride of one's homeland' (*hobbe-e vatan*), was considered to be an obstacle to the ultimate goal of the Islamic revolution: the creation of a just world order under the communitarian aegis of Islam. The political philosophy of Ayatollah Khomeini and his idea of 'Islamic community' was meant to transcend social, racial, linguistic sectarianism and nation-state boundaries.[120] In essence that notion qualifies the 'pan' in pan-Islamic and constitutes the central tenet of Islamic political theory as interpreted by Ayatollah Khomeini and other advocates of 'political Islam'. Brought to a logical conclusion, Saddam Hussein's Iraq, as the main agent of Arab nationalism in the region, was a 'natural' target of Imam Khomeini's rhetoric, setting the framework for the ensuing process of conflict between the two countries.

2.3.2   *The system strikes back: the aftermath of the revolution and the Iran–Iraq war*

The seriousness of the challenge to existing cultural forms of state legitimisation in the Persian Gulf stemmed from the impetus the Iranian revolution gave to the pre-existent pan-Islamic *Zeitgeist* in the Muslim world. We will return to this point later. Suffice it to say at this stage that not least because of the Arab defeats against

Israel in 1967 and the frustration about failed pan-Arab experiments such as the United Arab Republic between Egypt and Syria or the Arab Union between Jordan and Iraq in 1958, political Islam had become the primary 'challenging agent' to existent narratives of state identity in the area. The Islamic Republic brought the collective power of an affluent nation-state in explicit connection to the pan-Islamic idea. As a consequence of that impulsion, regional security was not merely challenged 'horizontally' on the inter-state level, but even more acutely in its 'vertical' appearance, that is, regime security within states. Hence, organised domestic dissent such as the occupation of the Grand Mosque at Mecca by a radical Wahhabi group led by Juhayman al-Utaybi who demanded the ouster of the al-Saud family in November 1979 which was unrelated to events in Iran,[121] was exacerbated by Shia revolts in the oil rich eastern provinces of Saudi Arabia and in Iraq, Bahrain and Kuwait which drew their inspiration from the revolutionary impetus in the neighbouring country. The pan-Islamic norms and institutions that were now pushed to the forefront – by necessity of their immanently transnational constitution – defied traditional forms of international sovereignty and diplomacy, hence contradicting prevailing norms and institutions of regional and global political culture.

The identity politics of the Islamic Republic were aimed at portraying the country as the vanguard of the Islamic movements and the legitimate leader of the Muslim *umma*. As part of that effort and in order to avoid isolation of the revolution as a primarily Iranian event, the Islamic Republic endeavoured to narrow the gap between the two areas of potential ideational contention, namely the Iranian-Arab and Sunni-Shiite schisms. Whilst the former issue was dealt with by underplaying the symbols and language of Iranian nationalism, tackling the latter division was rather more tentative. Four measures were taken:[122] it was declared that official cursing of the first three caliphs Abu Bakr, Umar ibn al-Khattab and Uthman ibn Affan that had been in place since the Safavid dynasty was unlawful; canonical writings which included such vilification were banned from further publication; Iranian pilgrims were allowed to pray behind a Sunni imam in Mecca and Medina and events such as the *hafte-ye vahdat* (week of unity) and *vahdat-e eslami* (Islamic unity) were institutionalised as a means to facilitate intra-Islamic exchanges. Those measures, however, were much too tacit to elevate the role of the Islamic Republic out of the 'Shia-Iranian' context and translate the revolutionary impetus into a pan-Islamic mass movement. What was lacking was a decisive 'ecumenical' effort that would have homogenised relations between the two principal branches of Islam in a systematic manner.[123] The Islamic Republic was not in the position to implement such an effort, because the indigenous salience of the country's Iranian and Shiite identity could not be escaped. Both were intrinsic to the very idea of the Islamic Republic and were institutionalised accordingly, beginning with Khomeini's theory of the *velayat-e faqih* which was deeply rooted in Shiite political thought, to the decision to retain Twelver Shi'ism (*Ja'fari* school) as Iran's official state religion and the requirement of Iranian origin to qualify for the office of Presidency.[124] The new set of norms projected by the Islamic Republic was hence weaker than pre-existing shared knowledge inhibiting both the domestic Iranian political culture itself and the Persian Gulf cultural system – both reproduced and represented the country first and foremost as an Iranian/Shiite entity. Hojatoleslam Hasan Yusof Ashkevari, a theorist and proponent of 'Islamic Democracy' in Iran, describes the dilemma in following terms:

> *Velayat-e faqih* is a Sh'i concept of rule. The Sunnis outside of Iran, many of whom doubt that Shi'is are Muslims at all, will therefore never accept this principle. The suspicion with which Sunnis regard the pan-Islamic project of Iran's current government is being fuelled by that very same government, which made Shi'ism the religion of state and reserved all leading governmental positions for Shi'is, all in clear and incontrovertible contradiction to the message of the Islamic Revolution. If the government does not work toward Islamic unity within Iran, how could it do so beyond the country's borders?[125]

The discrepancy between self-perception as a representative pan-Islamic actor and the inherent Iranian/Shiite identity of the movement denied the Islamic Republic the sought after role as the avant-garde of an international Islamic movement. Employing theoretical terminology we may observe that the Iranian role remained a subjective self-understanding of the revolutionary state and did not turn into an objective, collectively constituted position or an accepted *role identity* of international structure.[126] The inhibiting norms and institutions of the international system did not accommodate the idea of a transnational Islamic Republic nor did it identify Iran as the vanguard of Islamic revivalism. The orbit of Iranian activity abroad hence remained confined to primarily Shiite circles with established links to the clerical elite in Iran.[127]

The Shiite identity of the revolution turned neighbouring Iraq into the primary agent for protest outside of Iran. At least three factors supported that development: the country's majority Shiite population was marginalised by the governing Sunni, Arab nationalist regime; Ayatollah Khomeini had developed a close association with the Iraqi *marja'e taghlid* (source of emulation) Ayatollah Seyyed Mohammad Baqir al-Sadr during his exile in Najaf; and third (and related to the former point), once in power, the revolutionary movement could employ the Shiite clerical network spawning from Qom and Mashhad in Iran to Karbala and Najaf in Iraq to co-ordinate mutual activities. Organised Shiite opposition in Iraq was spearheaded by the *Hizb al Da'wah al-Islamiyyah* (The Party of the Islamic Call) which had been engaged in anti-governmental campaigns since the party's establishment in the late 1960s. Al-Dawah's efforts were joined by new parties such as the *al-Mujahidun* (holy warriors) formed by Shiite religious intellectuals in 1979 and later by the Supreme Council for Islamic Revolution in Iraq (SCIRI) led by Ayatollah Baqir al-Hakim.[128] During 1978 and 1979 serious rioting spearheaded by the *al-Dawah* party turned into an assassination campaign against Ba'thist government officials including a bomb attack against Tariq Aziz. The Iraqi state responded by decapitating the Shiite movements and eroding their power base: after announcing in March 1980 that membership of the *al-Dawah* party was punishable by death, the government moved on to execute Ayatollah Baqir al-Sadr and his sister Bint-al Huda.[129] Another senior Shia cleric, Ayatollah Abu al-Qasim al-Khoi, was put under house arrest and during 1980 alone an estimated 40,000 Iraqi-Iranians were forcibly expelled to their country of origin.[130] Amidst that domestic situation and the demise of the restraining liberal-left government of Mehdi Bazargan in Iran, Saddam Hussein publicly abrogated the 1975 Algiers treaty. Five days later, on 22 September 1980, Iraqi troops moved beyond the Shatt al-Arab and invaded Iran.

The causes of the Iraqi invasion continue to be controversial. Whilst in terms of international law, the question of who started the war was settled belatedly by the UN report of 9 December 1991 (S/23273) – which only after Iraq's invasion of Kuwait refers to 'Iraq's *aggression* against Iran', the overall picture is far more complex. Three arguments dominate the discourse: first, Saddam Hussein took advantage of the favourable international climate that was conducive to a military attack against the newly established Islamic state in Iran.[131] Second, Iraq expected the support of the Iranian-Arab population living in the Iranian border province of Khuzestan. Third, the Ba'thist Iraqi regime felt threatened by the export of the Islamic revolution and decided to pre-empt further Shia uprisings in Baghdad and its southern provinces.[132] The latter aspect was rather more central to the Iraqi efforts to justify the invasion. From that perspective, by interfering in the internal affairs of Iraq, Iran had broken the terms of the Algiers Agreement. Saddam Hussein's speech in which he symbolically tore the document apart touched on that point:

> The Iranian rulers' attitude, since assuming office, has confirmed their violation of the relations of good neighbourliness and their non-commitment to the clauses of the March Accord [Algiers Agreement]. They, therefore, fully bear the legal and de facto responsibility of rendering this Accord null and void.[133]

Moreover, it was pointed out that the delineation of the Shat al-Arab in favour of Iran itself was forced upon the country during a period of Iranian supremacy and after a long-lasting covert war against the Iraqi government sponsored by the United States and Israel. Taken together with the continued Iranian occupation of the three Persian Gulf islands and the 'Persianisation' (*tafris*) of the south-western Iranian border province of Khuzestan – which continued to be referred to as 'occupied Arabistan' by Iraqi officials – Iraq believed to have a solid case to portray the invasion as a just cause.[134]

In this context, the fact that in retrospect the threat of the Iranian revolution was as much real as it was 'hyped-up' to legitimate war does not really matter. From the perspective of international society, the rhetoric and the occasional actions aimed at challenging international order on the basis of the most powerful narrative in West Asian politics, namely political Islam, was reason enough to immediately confront the 'anti-systemic' movement. In other words, by implicitly or explicitly rejecting the right to sovereignty of others, the Islamic Republic invited others to reject theirs. From the perspective of the Carter administration, it was hence just and legitimate to launch a military rescue mission to free the US hostages which tragically failed when the helicopters crashed in the Iranian desert area of Tabas in April 1980 because, by tolerating the seizure of the US embassy, Imam Khomeini had forfeited Iran's right to territorial sovereignty. It was against a comparable background that

Saddam Hussein rationalised the invasion of Iran. According to the Iraqi President – who had consolidated his rule over the Ba'th party and the Revolutionary Command Council (RCC) after the resignation of Ahmad Hassan al-Bakr in July 1979 – the subversive activities of the Iraqi Shiites inspired by Iran were reason enough to abrogate the Algiers Agreement of 1975 which called for mutual non-intervention in the internal affairs of the two countries.

That much for an interpretative account of the facts. But to what extent is it possible to move beyond the myriad causes mentioned thus far? Some questions remain only partially answered: why did Iraq not launch an invasion of Iran during the Shah period when there was a more immediate threat of Iranian interference in the country's affairs? Why launch a full-scale invasion of a larger and more resourceful neighbour? My claim is that the primary cause explaining the Iraqi decision to launch an invasion of Iran can be found by investigating the self-perception of the Iraqi state and its inter-relationship with international society. With regard to the former aspect it is suggested that the Iraqi leadership made its decision within the inter-subjective context of Arab nationalism, its anti-Iranian posture and the regime's internalised self-perception as the main pan-Arab force in the region. The Iraqi state embarked on the war with Iran, because it reproduced the country as the leading agent of Arab revivalism externally, whilst securing the dominance of the Arab-Sunni/Tikriti leadership internally. Both calculations merge on the pivotal issue of Iraqi state identity and its inter-relationship with the norms and roles generated by Ba'thist pan-Arabism and its anti-Iranian precepts.

2.3.2.1 Qadisiyyat Saddam: *Iraqi Ba'thism and the 'eastern flank' of the Arab world*

The way in which the exclusionary tenor of both Arab and Iranian nationalism impeded the institutionalisation of genuine security co-operation in the Persian Gulf has already been discussed, as has the manner in which the Ba'thist version of Arab nationalism developed into a profoundly anti-Iranian discourse in Iraq. In the following paragraphs, I will elaborate on that mindset and investigate how pan-Arab ideology and anti-Iranian sentiments have contributed to the decision to launch a full-scale invasion of Iran. It is suggested that the elite-driven construction of the anti-Iranian norm became a central component of the preferred state identity in Ba'thist Iraq. The invasion of Iran can not be merely reduced to strategic and economic factors. As far as the Iraqi leadership was concerned, the war confirmed the country as the guardian of the 'eastern flank' of the Arab state system and gave the Iraqi political elite the opportunity to capitalise upon a deeply internalised antagonism towards Persian political and cultural outreach in the Gulf and beyond.

Arabs and Iranians were perhaps more deeply intermingled and akin in Iraq, than in any other country of the Persian Gulf, requiring a concerted and systematic effort to externalise the 'Iranian Other' from the 'Iraqi-Arab self'. Central to this task was the accentuation of the 'racial' composition of Iran, which was pursued by referring to the country as Persia. Emphasising the 'Persian' character of Iran, including the

Persian language and heritage, such as the Iranian New Year (*Nowrouz*) which continues to be celebrated in Zoroastrian tradition to the present, was meant to historicise the conflict. Moreover, invoking the racial delineation was deemed instrumental to guarantee the allegiance of the Arab Shiites to the Iraqi state domestically and rally the Arab states behind Iraq externally. To achieve that dual goal, the myth was created that there has been a perennial conflict between the two peoples, and that the 'backstabbing Persians' had a history of collusion with Zionists and imperialists forces against the Arab nation.

In order to give the Iraqi Ba'thist campaign against Iran and Iraqis of Iranian origin a historical dimension, the challenge of 'the Persians' was projected back to the days of Cyrus the Great, who gave refuge to the Jews when they were persecuted by the Babylonian King Nebuchadnezzar in sixth century BC. Conspiracy theories about the historic collusion between Iranians and Jews were central to the attempt to foster a paranoiac attitude towards the Iranian presence in the region, forming the central thesis of two books published in 1980: *Al-Madaris al-Yahudiyya wa-l-Iraniyya fi-l-'Iraq* (Jewish and Iranian schools in Iraq) by Fadil al-Barrak and *Al-Harb al-sirriyya, khafaya al-dawr al-Isra'ili fi harb al-khalij* (The secret war: The mysterious role of Israel in the [First]Gulf War) by Sa'd al-Bazzaz.[135] The former, deals with the 'destructive' and 'dangerous' impact of Jewish and Iranian schools on the Iraqi society. The latter, outlines how Israel and Iran conspired to fight Iraq during the First Gulf War, with special reference to the destruction of the Iraqi nuclear reactor by Israeli Air Force in June 1981.[136] Representing Iranians as *ajam*, an inferior people within the dominance of Islam, which was deemed to be first and foremost an Arab domain, Iraqi Ba'thism also employed overtly racist propaganda, marketing pamphlets such as Khairallah Tulfah's, *Three Whom God Should Not Have Created: Persians, Jews and Flies.*

In line with the campaign to provide 'historic proof' of Iranian enmity towards the Arab nation, anti-Iranian newspaper articles, monographs and poetry gained a prominent place in Ba'thist Iraq. Books such as *Ta'rikh al-hiqd al-Farsi 'ala al-'Arab* (The history of Persian hatred of the Arabs), serials entitled *Judhur al-'ada al-Farsi li-l-umma al-'Arabiyya* (The roots of Persian hostility towards the Arab nation) and proverbs such as *Ma hann a'jami 'ala 'Arabi* (An *ajam* or Persian will not have mercy on an Arab), repeatedly depicted Iranians as cruel, merciless, the ultimate bearers of *shu'ubiyya* and possessed by a 'Persian destructive mentality' (*aqliyya takhribiyya*). The myth was created that hatred towards Arabs was an integral part of the Persian character, and that this racial attribute had not changed since the days of the Islamicisation of the Sassanian empire in the seventh century.[137]

Nowhere is the legacy of the cultural war between Iranian and Arab versions of nationalism so pertinent as in relation to the nomenclature of the Gulf. In 1977, the Iraqi Revolutionary Command Council established an 'Arab Gulf Office', under the direction of Saddam Hussein. The designation of the waterway as the Persian Gulf by Iran, it was argued, testified to the country's historic dream of regional hegemony.[138] Indeed, as discussed earlier, Iranian nationalism often conflated the historically evolved designation of the waterway as the Persian Gulf with 'natural' cultural and political pre-eminence in the area. This was especially true for the rule of the Pahlavis, whose insistence on Iran's pre-Islamic heritage fostered the myth that the Gulf has been a Persian lake ever since the Achaemenid Kings Darius and Cyrus established the first Iranian world empire. It is no wonder then that the 'Arab Gulf Office' in Iraq was established in 1977, during a period when state sponsored nationalism dominated the state identities in both countries. By confronting Pahlavi Iran on the basis of the naming of the Gulf, Ba'thist Iraq wanted to assert its status in the region and counter the chauvinism of Pahlavi nationalism. Likewise, by disseminating maps designating the Gulf as *Khaliji Basra* (the Gulf of Basra) or *al-Khalij al-'Arabi*, Iraq claimed a prominent role in the region by appealing to (Iraqi-centric) Arab nationalist and anti-Iranian sentiments. Indeed, that the campaign to rename the Gulf (initially popularised by Nassir) was at least partially successful, suggests that the weariness towards the Iranian presence in the region transcended the confines of Iraqi state propaganda and was to a certain extent shared by the other Arab states of the Gulf as well.

The development of the anti-Iranian norm constituted an integral part of the state identity of Ba'thist Iraq. The Iranian revolution itself was portrayed as part of a long history of Iranian efforts to dominate the Persian Gulf. The Ba'thist regime even described Ayatollah Khomeini himself as an infidel (*kafir*), and heretic (*taghut*), unfit to preach Islam which was portrayed as an exclusive domain of the Arab people. In order to foster the 'Islamic credentials' of the otherwise secular regime, the Ba'thist state underplayed its secular image, increasingly reverting to Islamic symbols and imagery instead. Central to this task was the decision to officially call the Iran–Iraq war *Saddam's Qadisiyya* or *Qadisiyyat Saddam*, projecting two precepts of Ba'thist Arab nationalism: the romantic mystification of the leadership ideal on the one hand side and suspicion and animosity towards Iranians on the other. The phrase, which was to be used in any official Iraqi correspondence, likened the war to the battle of *Qadisiyya* in AD 637. During that battle the armies of Sassanid Iran led by General Rustum which were fighting as a Zoroastrian-Persian force were defeated by a Muslim army under the command of Saad bin Abi Waqqas. The defeat led to the capture of the Sassanid capital Ctesiphon, causing the ending of Sassanid suzerainty in Iraq and opening up ancient Iran (or Persia) for the ensuing process of Islamicisation. Iraqi intelligence documents captured after the Second Persian Gulf war suggest that Saddam Hussein's identification with a comparable historical role and the regime's anti-Iranian disposition were indeed systematic.[139] Whilst most of the documents refer to the Iran–Iraq war as *Qadisiyyat Saddam*, Iranians are consistently referred to in derogatory terms as the 'Zionist Persians', *al-'adu al-ajami* (the illiterate or foreign enemy) , *al-'adu al-Irani* (the Iranian enemy) or *majus* (fire worshippers).[140] The official terminology is consistent with other institutional manifestations of anti-Iranianism and its invented linkage with the history of Iraq and the character of Saddam Hussein. Iraqi history books, for instance, gave the following explanation for the naming of the war as *Qadisiyyat Saddam*:

> It is the everlasting heroic epic that the Iraqi people fought to defend Iraq and the Arab nation; it is the battle in which the Iraqi people achieved victory against the racist Khomeinist Persian enemy. It was named Saddam's Qadisieh

after the victorious, by God's Will, leader Saddam Hussein, who led the marvelous heroic battles . . . just as leader Saad bin Abi Waqqas did in the first Qadisieh about 14 centuries ago.[141]

In a critique of the use and abuse of historical symbols to legitimate the war, Neguin Yavari rightly observes that '[n]ational, ethnic and sectarian pretexts were evoked to ground the conflict in history', which according to her was a strategy to rationalise the war 'to make it appear to be an organic outcome of past events or a final act in a long drama'.[142] But the effort to historicise Iraq's campaign was not sudden or merely in response to the revolution in Iran. Ba'thist Arab nationalist ideologues have singled out Iranians as a main source of resistance to Arab pre-eminence at least since the writings of al-Husri and Aflaq. The translation of this norm permeated the state identity of Ba'thist Iraq and reached all the way down into the terminology and symbolism employed by the regime, developing into an inextricable factor of the mindset of the Iraqi leadership. In turn this suggests that anti-Iranianism was as much an ideological tool to delineate the Iraqi-Arab self from the Iranian-Shiite other, as it was firmly rooted in the belief system of the Iraqi leadership. By attacking Iran, the regime did not only want to produce itself as the guardian of the Gulf, it acted on the premise of a deeply embedded resentment of Iranian cultural and political outreach in the Persian Gulf area and beyond. To clarify, this was not only an act of instrumental expediency in the sense that it was suddenly invoked to rally the support of Arab states in reaction to the exogenous effect of the Islamic revolution. System effects were interpreted and processed against the background of a pre-existing, deeply embedded 'paranoia' about Iranian expansionism. Why else pursuing a full-scale invasion during a period when the Iraqi state appeared to be relative secure? After all, at the time of the Iranian revolution the Iraqi state was both wealthier and stronger than any other state in the modern history of Iraq and largely uncompromised by internal unrest. The regime had already solved the Kurdish revolts in the north of the country by granting them a higher degree of autonomy and with the guarantee of the Shah to halt his support to the separatist movements in the mid-1970s. Shiite unrest on the other side was endemic and not merely determined by the Iranian-Islamic revolution (although exacerbated by events in Iran). Moreover, Shiite opposition was largely due to social deprivation and cultural subjugation, rather than primarily political and was put under control before the invasion of Iran.[143]

Conventional reasoning about the causes of the Iraq war that orients itself at the superficial Iraqi propaganda, rather than the deeper ideational structure of the Iraqi state appears to be flawed in many directions. At no stage during the tumultuous early days of the revolution was the fragile Islamic Republic in the position to launch an invasion against Iraq or to co-ordinate a systematic covert war as the Shah did. It was not the real threat from Iran that propelled the Iraqi state to launch the invasion. The Iraqi perception was framed by Ba'thist Arab nationalism and its paranoia about Iranian designs in the Persian Gulf and executed on the basis of opportunistic misperceptions about the nature of the revolution itself. The Ba'thist mindset signalled to Iraqi decision-makers that the Iranian revolution might turn into an irrevocable campaign aimed at 'Persianising' the Gulf. According to that perception, the revolution was only one effort in the long line of Iranian strategies to master the Arab world. Before Iraq would turn its attention to Palestine, the country would rid the Arab states once and for all from that historical challenge to the eastern flank of the nation.

The disposition of Saddam Hussein's Iraq during the time when the decision for the war is thought to have been made (according to Ofra Bengio in April 1980) was encapsulated in Khairallah Talfah's writings. According to him: 'Many People say that Palestine must be dealt with first. That is true – and yet I say: Iran is a dagger in the heart of the Arabs, therefore it must be removed so that the Arabs can regain their health . . . . As the old proverb has it: 'He who lives with us is the worst thief.'[144] Whereas Zionism and imperialism were distant threats that needed careful, long-term planning to be dealt with, Iran was perceived as the eternal, immediate 'enemy from within'. With the international climate conducive for the war, Ba'thist anti-Iranianism broke the border between political self-indoctrination and action. Regional experts agree, valuing the causal effects of Iraq's Ba'thist state identity higher than the effects of Iranian threats or purely economic or territorial cost-benefit calculations:

> *Qadisiyyat Saddam* captures a mood that prevailed in Ba'thist circles at the start of the fighting, a mood that had nothing to do with rancour over possessions, competition for economic assets, greed for territory, or alleged Iranian intentions. The regime was brimming over with self-confidence . . . it was armed to the teeth and capable of those great things that were given to it by 'history' and everything that the pan-Arabism of the Ba'th stood for. The time was ripe for the Ba'th to take externally the kind of decisive action they had already taken internally, to signify to the outside the rising preeminence of Iraqi Ba'thism in regional and Arab affairs. Ba'thist motives were singularly political, derivative ultimately from deeply held ideological tenets to which they had given ample proof of their commitment. . . . [E]conomic, material, and strategic benefits . . . come afterwards, as a consequence of the extension of Ba'thist power the imperative for which originated elsewhere.[145]

Sociological theory informs us that the essential factor of the world that humans create is socially constructed *meaning*. Needing to order their environment, humans infuse their own interpretations into reality. The individual rationalises his or her behaviour by attaching subjective meaning to all action taken. Acts are hence made on the basis of *intentional* consciousness of something. These meanings become objectified in the 'artefacts' of culture, that is belief systems, norms, roles, ideologies, moral codes, institutions and so forth. The significance of this notion of culture for our case is that by reifying, institutionalising, ideologising Ba'thist Arab nationalism and anti-Iranianism as central narratives of Iraqi state identity, the meanings of these self-attributed precepts became reabsorbed into the Iraqi regime's consciousness as subjectively plausible representations of reality, morally sanctioned codes of collective behaviour, rules of social discourse and a general plot for the conduct of foreign affairs. The internalisation process acquired the disposition to enact the (role) identity preference. Given that a persistent failure to act on identity needs would have compromised the Iraqi aspiration to lead the Arab world, the Iraqi state chose to reproduce its Arab nationalist identity by attacking Iran. In other words, the regime wanted to demonstrate its Ba'thist Arab nationalist credentials by acting upon one of its central norms – anti-Iranianism. That the perception of the surrounding realities was flawed is secondary. It was the subjective definition of the surrounding reality that determined Iraq's perception, not the objective viewpoint. Thus, we may infer that the Iraqi leadership did 'know' that the Iranian-Arab population of Khusestan would welcome the Iraqi troops as liberators. That they did not and indeed fought the Iraqi troops vigorously, was due to their treachery and 'Persianised' mentality. Likewise, Saddam Hussein 'knew' that the Iranian army would collapse, the same way the Sassanian army collapsed during the Battle of Qadissiya. That the Iranian army resisted and launched its own attacks into Iraqi territory was due to Zionist and imperialist collusion.[146] In short: the former Iraqi President implemented his decisions within the context of an 'alien' reality which explains his gross misperceptions during and after the conflict.

Denying the Iraqi mindset would not only show ignorance of human motives, belief systems and the ability to build up salient enemy images, but also undervalue decades of research into the social construction of reality by cultural theorists and social psychologists.[147] Ordering the environment and by extension constructing reality is a natural function of human behaviour.[148] In the most extreme case – and we would argue that this would be an adequate psychological 'profile' of the Iraqi regime's mindset at the beginning of hostilities with Iran – the invented reality is perceived as having a quality in and of itself. Hence, what was in fact a product of Ba'thist Arab nationalist theory had been reified to the extent that it appeared to have a reality of its own. Acting within this self-consciously chosen 'ideational habitat', the Iraqi regime was alienated from objective reality, forgetting that the world it lived in had been produced by itself and that this 'alien world' might not correspond with reality if viewed from an objective perspective. That Saddam Hussein tailored his actions according to this alien reality three times (against Iran, Kuwait and the US/UK alliance), only reiterates the salience of the ideational belief system that framed the existence of the Iraqi Ba'thist polity and explains its gross misperceptions during the three wars.

2.3.2.2   Social engineering and Iraq's war role

The following paragraphs benefit from the conclusions of the previous section. It is a central tenet of sociological theory that perceptions, representations of reality and identities are not constructed in isolation. States are not operating in 'encapsulated habitats'. It is not possible to act decisively upon a specific identity or role without perceiving a minimal degree of external recognition.[149] The Iraqi state viewed itself as the main agent of pan-Arabism at least since the Ba'thist coup in 1968. But this subjective self-understanding was not confirmed by the members of the regional system. This contradiction, in turn, prevented that the self-perception as the dominant Arab nationalist power was turned into as traditionally positioned role identity.

Revolution in Iran altered that constellation. In the reshuffling of the regional legitimacy norms, the way the Iraqi state viewed itself was approximated by the way it was addressed. Indeed, it can be argued that Iraq became the agent for containment of the revolution because of two reasons: it felt legitimated in its self-perception as the leader of the Arab world and it was confirmed as the suitable vehicle to preserve regional order. The interest of international society to strangle the Iranian revolution in the cradle required the social recognition of the role of an agent who was capable and willing to pursue that aim. Aware of the anti-Iranian precepts of Iraqi Ba'thism and the sensitivities of Iranian-Iraq relations, the GCC states and the United States felt that Saddam Hussein's regime was the ideal candidate to play out that role.[150]

To open a parenthesis here, it is not suggested that the Gulf states accepted the Iraqi regime's self-perception as the vanguard of pan-Arabism or even shared its anti-Iranian sentiments. They did not. Rather, I would suggest that after the demise of the Pahlavi state as the regional status quo power, both regional and global-international society provided enough explicit and implicit incentives to signal to the Iraqi state that its regional role was elevated to a higher status and by extension, that launching an inter-state war against Iran will be accommodated. English-School theorists would argue that this reveals the tendency of 'anarchical societies' to tolerate war as a means to enforce regional order and control the repercussions as a threat to the stability of the system itself.[151] From this perspective, international society condoned war against the anti-systemic force because it was felt that the sovereignty principle as the most fundamental fact of international political culture was threatened. On the other side, by supervising the war, international society made also sure that no party gains an absolute victory which would upset the regional balance of power.

2.3.2.2.1   THE REGION AND SADDAM'S MOMENT OF HUBRIS

Let us return to the empirical facts. Underestimating the salience of the pan-Arab aspirations of the Iraqi regime, the Gulf monarchies had already reacted positively to the tactical moderation of Iraqi behaviour in the period after 1975. In February 1979, Saudi Arabia and Iraq signed a security agreement which committed Iraq to defend the former in the case of war. Simultaneously, high level diplomatic exchanges between the two countries and Iraq and Rais al-Khaimah, Oman and Kuwait became frequent enough to bring Iraq out of isolation and into the limelight of inter-Arab politics.[152] From the perspective of Iraq, the recognition gained from the diplomatic exchanges was reason enough to believe that an invasion of Iran would be supported. Ehteshami and Nonneman go even one step further, speculating that the Iraqi decision to take military action gained approval beforehand:

> [I]t is very likely that Saudi Arabia at least had given the green light.... All six, [Saudi Arabia, Kuwait, Oman, Qatar, Bahrain and the UAE] we believe, showed varying degrees of support for Iraq's initiative, after having come reluctantly to the conclusion that there appeared to be no effective alternative. Iran was not thought to be able to put up a serious battle, and the consensus was that a *Blitzkrieg* could cut the revolutionaries down to size.[153]

The minimal argument that can be deduced is that regional society signalled that an invasion of Iran will be tolerated. That social engineering of the Iraqi war role has been largely underplayed in the literature about the causes and consequences of the Iran–Iraq war. Focusing upon the 'systemic approval' of the Iraqi war role, however, reveals convincing evidence that Iraqi state identity, external confirmation and the decision to go to war can be causally related. In other words, the argument that I put forward is that the Iraqi regime was convinced that military confrontation will be tolerated because international society did not suggest otherwise. Processed within the framework of Iraqi Ba'thist Arab nationalism, external signals were interpreted as a green light – if not carte blanche by the Ba'thist regime, precipitating the escalation of violence during and after the war. The fact that Iraq managed to organise the high degree of political, economic and moral support both in the Arab world (apart from Libya and Syria) and in the Western hemisphere, appears to prove that the anticipation of the Iraqi regime was at least partially accurate. In turn, this does also suggest that the signals before the war must have been quite strong indeed. The Iraqi war role was hence socially constructed, in that it existed only in relation to the international system – the role-*taking* side could never function without the role-*constituting* side. After I have investigated the properties of the former, I will now turn my attention to that role-*constituting* side, by reviewing the international collusion with Iraq during the war. I build the case along two systemic positions: regional and global.

The initial reaction of the oil monarchies to hostilities between Iran and Iraq has been touched upon earlier. Apart from Dubai and Sharjah, which continued to have cordial relations with the Islamic Republic, primarily because of their cultural affiliation with Iran and economic interests, the other sheikhdoms were either directly or indirectly involved in the Iraqi war effort.[154] That support got even more forceful after the failure of the Iraqi *Blitz* and the Iranian counter-offensive into Iraqi territory in 1982. One year later, Saudi Arabia and Kuwait agreed to forward the profits of oil production in the Khafji oil field, located in the neutral zone between Saudi Arabia and Kuwait, to the Iraqi government.[155] In addition, the two countries provided Iraq with loans ranging from an estimated US$ 35 billion to US$ 50 billion, most of them not necessarily meant to be repaid.[156] The financial contribution of Saudi Arabia and Kuwait was complemented by the opening up of their ports for the shipment of products bound to the Iraqi market and the selling of oil on behalf of the Iraqi government. On top of these measures, the cash flow to Baghdad was further enhanced by a pipeline running from Iraq to Saudi Arabia. The Saudi state arguably even offered to finance the rebuilding of an Iraqi nuclear reactor, destroyed in a pre-emptive strike by Israeli warplanes in June 1981.[157]

During the 'tanker war' period intensifying in 1984 and the 'war of the cities' beginning in the spring of 1985 – both parts of the Iraqi strategy to internationalise the war by attacking Iranian oil installations and targeting Iranian cities in order to demoralise the country's army – regional collusion with Iraq remained strong. Kuwait supported Saddam Hussein directly by transhipping arms and supplies via its port overland to Iraq, thus circumventing the naval supremacy of Iran in the Persian Gulf. At this stage of the war and faced with a relentless Iranian army, the Persian Gulf monarchies were also willing to take direct military action against

Iran, exemplified by the shooting down of an Iranian fighter jet in violation of Saudi controlled airspace by Saudi aircraft in June 1984.[158]

The particularities of the support to the Iraqi war effort may be disputed, the regional disposition to take sides may not. The sketch of regional collusion with Iraq provided here should not mislead however – the support was not unequivocal. Concurrent with the quasi-alliance of Saudi Arabia and Kuwait with Iraq, the Gulf monarchies were continuously engaged in containing the economic calamities and military spill-over of the war. Apart from sustained efforts to appease Iran, they also refrained from formalising their relationship with Saddam Hussein. After all – in a move to confirm their autonomy from both regional powers and to reiterate their distinct state identities as conservative Arab monarchies governed by family and tribal rule – the six states established the Gulf Co-operation Council (GCC) leaving both Iran *and* Iraq out. Neither can the bias be primarily explained on the basis of pan-Arab solidarity with Iraq, because the state identities of the Persian Gulf monarchies are not consistent with Arab nationalism. From the perspective of regional states, pan-Arabism was a secondary issue during the First Persian Gulf War, as is clear not only from the decision to create the GCC without granting Iraq membership, but also from the fact that 'Arab' Syria and Libya sided with 'non-Arab' Iran.

Conversely, from the perspective of the Iraqi regime, the support of the country's war efforts was perceived as a boost to its claim to regional power – and more specifically – its self-bestowed role as the leader of the Arab world. The external confirmation and support from regional states was processed against the background of the Arab nationalist and anti-Iranian meta-narrative of Iraqi Ba'thist state identity. From that viewpoint, supporting the war effort was considered only 'natural' – indeed a rational response of Arab states against the threat to the eastern flank of the Arab nation. According to Saddam Hussein:

All Gulf countries are aware of Iran's ambitions in targeting them.... They know that had it not been for Iraq, they would have been taken as prisoners to the lands of the Persians...I think they know that, and if they do not, then that is an even graver problem.[159]

It has become a truism that the oil monarchies had balance of power calculations in mind when they supported Iraq as the lesser threat against what was perceived to be the larger, most immediate danger. The primary *Angst* of Saudi Arabia and the other GCC states was and continues to be a unilateral configuration in the Persian Gulf. This was not the way the support was interpreted by the Iraqi state, however. Iraq portrayed *and* perceived itself as defender of the Persian Gulf states against the revolutionary tide from Iran. This view was not only reinforced by the support granted to the Iraqi war effort by the Gulf states before and after the invasion, but also by the acquiescent reaction of the wider international society.

2.3.2.2.2   INTERNATIONAL SOCIETY AND SADDAM'S CARTE BLANCHE

The constitutive effects on the Iraqi war role, deriving from the support by the wider international community had been perhaps even more decisive than the collusion on the regional level. Since the ouster of the Iraqi monarchy in 1958, no Iraqi leader had enjoyed more international support than Saddam Hussein did during the war with Iran. The first international reaction to the conflict is emblematic for the pattern of behaviour that followed: after six days of hostilities, on 28 September 1980, the UN Security council unanimously adopted Resolution 479, calling for an immediate cessation of hostilities without, however, naming Iraq as the invading force, or calling for the country's withdrawal from Iranian territory (the call to return to internationally recognised boundaries came only after Iranian advances into Iraqi territory as a result of the counteroffensive in mid-1982).[160] In essence then, Resolution 479 and the final Resolution 598 adopted after nearly eight years of fighting were similar with regard to the question of who started the war. Both failed to name Iraq as the invading party.

Complacency was not only limited to the terminology of Security Council resolutions, there was also calculated accommodation regarding Iraqi chemical and biological warfare against Iran. The complaints from the Iranian side about this can be traced back to November 1980. It took the international community, including the most prominent non-governmental organisations (NGOs), at least three and a half years to investigate the allegations systematically. A report by the Stockholm International Peace and Research Institute (SIPRI) dated May 1984 testifies to that:

> Three and a quarter years [after the first Iranian complaints in November 1980], by which time the outside world was listening more seriously to such charges, the Iranian Foreign Minister told the Conference on Disarmament in Geneva that there had been at least 49 instances of Iraqi chemical-warfare attack in 40 border regions, and that the documented dead totalled 109 people, with hundreds more wounded.[161]

The same report indicated that after visiting several hospitals in Tehran, the International Committee of the Red Cross (ICRC) confirmed that 'substances prohibited by international law' were employed during hostilities (7 March 1984). The confirmation by the United Nations came in the same month, with a report by the Secretary General, condemning the use of chemical weapons, without however, naming Iraq as the perpetrating party (see below).[162] During the period of the 'tanker war' and the 'war of the cities', both initiated by the Iraqi state in violation of the 1925 Geneva Conventions, the same pattern of 'calculated negligence' towards both Iraqi modes of warfare and the identification of the invading force could be observed.[163] Even the final Resolution 598 which ended the war after it was accepted by Ayatollah Khomeini did only deplore 'the use of chemical weapons' and merely determined 'that there exists a breach of the peace as regards the conflict between Iran and Iraq', hence in both cases refraining from naming Iraq as the guilty party.[164]

Viewed from the perspective of the Iraqi leadership, international acquiescence accommodated the systematic employment of chemical and biological weapons against Iraq's own population and Iranian army units and civilians during and after the war. The regional and global complacency contributed to the perception of the

Iraqi regime that they have been granted a 'free rider' role, creating the paradox that by using 'Iraq to wear Iran down',[165] the co-operative norms and institutions of international society itself were rendered useless, manipulated to function according to the overarching *leitmotif* to prevent Iranian advances. In turn, this compromised the authority of the international community to act as a restraining force during the war. Intercepted communication by Saddam Hussein's cousin Ali Hassan al-Majid, infamously called 'Chemical Ali' after the *al-Anfal* (spoils of war) campaign against Iraqi-Kurdish militia and Iranian forces operating in the Halabja area between February and September 1988, indicates the degree of disregard that Ba'thist officials had developed *vis-à-vis* international norms at the end of the Iran–Iraq war:

> Jalal Talabani asked me to open a special channel of communication with him.[166] That evening I went to Suleimaniyeh and hit them with the special ammunition. That was my answer. We continued the deportations [of the Kurds]. I told the *mustashars*[167] that they might say that they like their villages and that they won't leave. I said I cannot let your village stay because I will attack it with chemical weapons. Then you and your family will die. You must leave right now. Because I cannot tell you the same day that I am going to attack with chemical weapons. I will kill them all with chemical weapons. Who is going to say anything? The international community? F . . . them! The international community and those who listen to them.[168]

In many ways the international bias in favour of Iraq mirrored the strategies and policies of the United States and the Soviet Union.[169] The former, with whom Iraq had signed a 'Treaty of Co-operation and Friendship' in 1972 and who actively assisted Iraq during the country's military build-up in the latter half of the 1960s and the 1970s, was embroiled in Afghanistan and pursued a reactive balancing strategy in the Persian Gulf.[170] Conversely, the role of the United States was more proactive. Declassified documents reveal that the US government, and here especially the Reagan administration, contravened the official policy of neutrality in order to prevent an Iranian victory.[171] There is also enough evidence to presume that the support was more significant than previously thought.[172] Whereas the United States saw the relationship primarily within the context of the Iran–Iraq war and the balance of power in the Persian Gulf, the Iraqi regime interpreted the sudden twist towards a quasi-strategic partnership as an implicit approval of its claim to regional supremacy.

From the outset of the war the US government provided Iraq with intelligence information about Iranian force deployments and movements from the US Airborne Warning and Control Aircraft (AWACS) that had been stationed in Saudi Arabia and was operated by the Pentagon.[173] After the ending of the 'Hostage crisis', the change of US administrations from Carter to Reagan and Iranian advances on the battlefield, intelligence sharing was complemented with diplomatic, financial and military assistance. On the diplomatic front, the United States pursued an active policy of reconciliation with Iraq, removing the country from the State Departments' list of 'state sponsors of terrorism' in February 1982, followed by the official resumption of diplomatic ties in November 1984. Economic assistance ranged from authorisation of dual use equipment, such as the sale of helicopters which were capable of being converted to military use, and generous loans provided by the US Export-Import Bank (Eximbank) and other financial institutions. In a speech presented to the US House of Representatives by Henry Gonzalez (D-Texas) on 27 July 1992, it was shown that '[b]etween 1983 and the invasion of Kuwait in 1990, Iraq received $5 billion in CCC [US Department of Agriculture's Commodity Credit Corporation] guarantees that allowed them to purchase United States agricultural products on credit'.[174] In October of the same year, the US Committee on Banking, Housing and Urban Affairs held hearings which were later confirmed by the 'Riegle Report', revealing that the United States had not only exported agricultural products but also 'chemical, biological, nuclear, and missile-system equipment to Iraq that was converted to military use in Iraq's chemical, biological, and nuclear weapons program', which were in turn also used against the US soldiers in the Second Persian Gulf War.[175]

In 25 May 1994, the aforementioned investigation conducted by Senator Riegle showed that the US government approved sales of a wide-range of chemical and biological materials to Iraq, including components of mustard gas, anthrax, Clostridium Botulinum, Histoplasma Capsulatum, Brucella Melitensis and Clostridium Perfringens.[176] In an affidavit to a US District Court in Florida, National Security Staff Member Howard Teicher revealed that the US collision with Iraq went beyond mere economic and diplomatic assistance:

> Pursuant to the secret NSDD,[177] the United States actively supported the Iraqi war effort by supplying the Iraqis with billions of dollars of credits, by providing U.S. military intelligence and advice to the Iraqis, and by clearly monitoring third country arms sales to Iraq to make sure that Iraq had the military weaponry required. The United States also provided strategic operational advice to the Iraqis to better use their forces in combat. For example, in 1986, President Reagan sent a secret message to Saddam Hussein telling him that Iraq should step up its air war and bombing of Iran. This message was delivered by Vice President Bush who communicated it to Egyptian President Mubarak, who in turn passed the message to Saddam Hussein. Similar strategic operational military advice was passed to Saddam Hussein through various meetings with European and Middle Eastern heads of state where the strategic operational advice was communicated.[178]

Further declassified documents provide an insight about the spectrum of US support to Iraq. In that regard, a State Department Information Memorandum dated 7 October 1983, defined the financial, diplomatic and military means needed to qualify a 'tilt' towards the country, concluding that the 'policy of strict neutrality has already been modified, except for arms sales, since Iran's forces crossed into Iraq in the summer of 1982', adding that the 'steps we have taken toward the conflict since then have progressively favoured Iraq'.[179]

From the perspective of the Iraqi regime the US tilt was a confirmation of its elevated regional role. During the various diplomatic encounters repeated attention was given to inter-Arab politics (the situation in Lebanon, Syrian expansionism, the reintegration of Egypt, the Israeli-PLO 'peace process' etc.). By alluding to these conflicts, the Iraqi regime presented itself as a pivotal power in the Arab world at the expense of Syria and Libya whose leadership was described as radical, revisionist and irrational by Iraqi officials. The diplomatic exchanges were also used to present the nature of the Iraqi regime as moderate, pragmatic, modern, without ideological 'complexes', and acting 'within the context of five thousand years of Mesopotamian civilisation'.[180] Due to the reawakened historic weight of Iraq under the leadership of the Ba'th party, it was argued, the country's role as a force for stabilisation was indispensable: 'What...would have happened to the states of the Gulf and Arabian peninsula' Saddam Hussein asked during a meeting with Donald Rumsfeld in Baghdad in December 1983, 'if Iraq had not stood fast [against Iran]? No one would have been able to put out the fire. Zionism was in fact encouraging it to burn'.[181]

Nothing convinced the Iraqi leadership more of its newly acquired primacy than the international silence about the use of chemical and biological weapons. In a State Department memo to the then Secretary of State Shultz in November 1983, it was confirmed that the United States knew 'that Iraq has acquired a CW production capability, primarily from Western firms, including possibly a U.S. foreign subsidiary' and that it appears that Iraq uses chemical weapons almost on a daily basis.[182] Further intelligence suggested that 'as long ago as July 1982, Iraq used tear gas and skin irritants against *invading* Iranian forces quite effectively' and that 'in October 1982, unspecified foreign officers fired lethal chemical weapons at the orders of Saddam during battles in the Mandali area'.[183]

Before Donald Rumsfeld returned to Iraq in late March 1984 for a second official visit, the United States, for the first time during the war, had publicly condemned the use of chemical weapons. The press statement whilst acknowledging that the 'United States has concluded that the available evidence substantiates Iran's charges that Iraq has used chemical weapons',[184] also condemned the Iranian insistence on the removal of the Ba'thist regime. Historically valuable if viewed in a comparative perspective to the events that have surrounded the US led invasion of Iraq in March 2003, the US government named Iran as the invading force (presumably because of the successful offensive in mid-1982 and thereafter), declaring that the 'United States finds the present Iranian regime's intransigent refusal to deviate from its avowed objective of eliminating the legitimate government of neighbouring Iraq to be inconsistent with the accepted norms of behaviour among nations and the moral and religious basis which it claims'.[185]

From the Iraqi perspective, the complacency of the Reagan administration was reason enough to presume that employment of chemical weapons would not cause a serious damage to the country's international reputation. The degree of carelessness was indicative for the degree of comfort. In this spirit, the Iraqi government, expecting a major offensive by Iranian forces, had issued a public statement that 'the invaders should know that for every harmful insect there is an insecticide capable of annihilating it whatever the number and Iraq possesses this annihilation insecticide'.[186] Asked whether or not Iraqi use of chemical weapons will affect the US-Iraqi diplomatic and economic relations at a State Department Press Briefing in March 1984, the department's spokesman replied: 'No. I am not aware of any change in our position. We're interested in being involved in a closer dialogue with Iraq.'[187]

The position of Iraq found comparable US support in the United Nations. Hence, when the Iranian government submitted a draft resolution asking for UN condemnation of the chemical warfare by Iraq, the US delegate was instructed to lobby for a general motion of 'no decision' on the resolution. At a meeting between the Iraqi interest section head Nizar Hamdoon and the then Deputy Assistant Secretary of State James Placke on 29 March 1984, the former spelled out what the Iraqi government expected from the UN resolution. Hamdoon stressed that his country favoured a Security Council presidential statement to a resolution, reference to former resolutions on the war, progress towards termination of the conflict, and no mentioning of responsibility regarding the employment of chemical weapons. One day after the meeting, the Security Council issued the aforementioned presidential statement, condemning the use of chemical weapons without naming Iraq as the offending party. A State Department memorandum from 30 March 1984 acknowledged the successful diplomatic 'spin' in support of Iraq, noting that the 'statement... contains all three elements Hamdoon wanted'.[188]

The actions during the latter half of the war such as the US attacks on Iranian oil platforms during the 'tanker war' period and the accidental shooting down of an Iranian Air Bus aircraft by the *USS Vincennes* which killed 290 civilians, only reconfirmed the Iraqi position.[189] The Iraqi regime even got away with an apology and payment of US$ 27.3 million for hitting the *USS Stark* which killed thirty-seven US navy personnel and wounded twenty-one.[190] The Reagan administration made sure that the support to Iraq was systematic and pervasive. This is not to say that the United States did not reserve open channels with the Iranian government. After all, it was not knowledge about Iraqi war crimes that proved disastrous for the Reagan administration but the much publicised Iran-Contra Affair.[191] Important for our line of argument is that, by granting support to the Iraqi state, US policy presented the Ba'thist regime as the guarantor of the regional status quo, lending to it a prominent role in regional affairs. This was largely complementary to the way the Iraqi regime wanted to present its invasion, 'sacrificing' Iraq by pre-empting the threat of the Iranian revolution on behalf of the Arab world and the 'West' before it gathered strength. '[Y]ou [were] not the ones who protected your friends during the war with Iran', Saddam Hussein pointed out during a conversation with US Ambassador April Glaspie in the build-up to the Second Persian Gulf War. 'I assure you, had the Iranians overrun the region, the American troops would not have stopped them, except by the use of nuclear weapons. I do not want to belittle you' the Iraqi President went on '[b]ut I hold this view by looking at the geography and nature of American society.... Yours is a society which cannot accept 10,000 dead in one battle'.[192]

Because of the systemically legitimated role and the diplomatic-political cover and military-economic collusion it brought with it, the Iraqi state felt empowered to assert its claim to regional leadership. That the United States had balance of power considerations in mind does not contradict our argument. What is central is that by supporting the Iraqi leadership, the United States gave the regime the opportunity to act upon its self-perception as the leading power in the Persian Gulf. This was the exact opposite constellation to the *Second* Gulf War, when the US war role was systemically legitimated and the Iraqi one was not. Role identities are never merely constituted in the encapsulated habitat of the nation-state. In order to effectively enact a certain role identity, social recognition is crucial. During the Iran–Iraq war, international society granted that approval to the Iraqi leadership. Without the regional and global recognition, the Iraqi state would have never been able to act upon its war role, nor follow the campaign of unrestrained warfare. It was against that background that the regime could pursue its genocidal 'Anfal' campaign against its own Kurdish population and Iranian army units operating in the area, culminating in the gassing of the Northern Iraqi town of Halabja which killed at least 4,000 to 5,000 people in March 1988. International society did not only not intervene previously, it provided the Iraqi regime with the means to implement its policies.

2.4   The changed parameters of regional relations

This chapter set out the task to investigate the sources of conflict in the Persian Gulf primarily during 1971 and 1988. In the first place, this goal was pursued by juxta-posing regional relations before and after the revolution and investigating the shift from a status quo regional system to a revolutionary one. Examining pre-revolutionary regional interaction, it has been argued that despite the relative order sustained by the complementary roles of Saudi Arabia and Iran which received global-systemic legitimisation under the 'twin-pillar' norm, exclusionary identity politics inhibited the institutionalisation of a viable regional security architecture in the Persian Gulf. In the absence of territorial security and in order to shape salient 'Westphalian' nation-state identities, inventing nationalist historiography had a dual purpose: consolidating state authority over the populace on the one hand side and formulating a codified program for external relations on the other. In other words, Persian Gulf states invented 'territories of identities' in order to structure their external environ-ment. Being Arab suggested some sort of solidarity with Arab causes, being 'Aryan' or speaking an 'Indo-European' language suggested identification with the 'West'. Because of the inherently exclusionary character of the nationalist discourses, whether in its Arab or Iranian version, mutual suspicions were aggravated and the emergence of a genuine security community during a period where regional and global parameters were conducive to that end was not achieved.

In the second place, the revolution in Iran and its impact on the regional system were discussed. It was observed that the anti-imperialist, anti-monarchic and anti-nationalistic norms of the revolution were anathema to established forms of governance and inter-state behaviour in the region and beyond. Iran saw herself as the embodiment of a new Islamic *Zeitgeist*, destined to function as the 'Trojan Horse' for the spread of Islamic revolution. Regional shared knowledge accumulated during several millennia of previous interaction, however, identified the country as an Iranian and Shiite state. Culture appeared as a 'self-fulfilling prophecy', reiterating and reproducing Iran's identity in those two directions and hence impeding the state's aspiration to lead a representative pan-Islamic movement. Efforts to 'pre-empt' the isolation of the revolution as a primarily Iranian event did not contribute much to yield a different outcome, limiting the outreach of the revolution to constituents with already pre-existent links to the clerical elite. Hence, whilst the Shah's role was complementary to the regional consensus and legitimated under the 'twin-pillar' norm, the Islamic Republic failed to export its revolution because its state identity was neither confirmed nor legitimated by international society.

Third, the transformation of the regional role attributions triggered a regional legitimacy contest that culminated into inter-state war. From the perspective of international society, Iraq's invasion of Iran was meant to strangle the Islamic revolution in the cradle. By allocating the war role to Iraq, the country was empowered to contain the transnational appeal of the anti-systemic movement as a means to retain the regional status quo. The Iraqi state on the other side, acted according to its preferred Arab nationalist role conception and an internalised weariness regarding the Iranian presence in the Gulf, and interpreted the support given to its invasion as an implicit approval of its prominent role in regional affairs.

In order to bring the discussion about the war to its logical conclusion, let me return to the argument expressed at the beginning of this chapter. We may observe that the First Persian Gulf War was not merely a 'war of position' or a war that does not challenge the legitimacy of a particular cultural form of authority (in our case US impe-rialism, monarchic rule in Saudi Arabia, Ba'thism in Iraq) – it was a 'clash of legitimacy principles' with potentially system transforming qualities or 'a contest over what form of rule constitutes the most viable, competitive unit in the international system'.[193] The political elites of both states saw the war as an opportunity to produce their respective state identities and considered a victorious outcome as imperative for the transnational appeal of their underlying ideologies. In retrospect that ideational dimension does explain the viciousness in the conduct of the war. Because it was directly linked to the very identity of the parties involved and because their legitimisation was at stake (including the co-belligerents such as Saudi Arabia or Kuwait), losing the war would have eventually led to the destruction of the defeated state. Neither Ba'thist Iraq nor revolutionary Iran was willing to allow for such an event.[194]

War was not only a manifestation of disorder in a temporarily disrupted 'anarchical society', however, it had also long-term *constitutive* dimensions, affecting both the domestic contexts of the interacting agents and the properties of the regional cultural system as a whole: first, by engaging in war with Iran, and generating the high degree of international support, the Iraqi state constituted itself as a prominent Arab actor. And second, by fighting off a revolutionary movement with an explicitly pan-Islamic mission, the Iraqi state identity itself was reconstructed. As far as the political elite in Iraq was concerned, countering the ideological challenge from Iran and mobilising the Iraqi masses for war required positioning the foundations of the Iraqi state identity on an Iraqi-centric version of Arab nationalism and the persona of Saddam Hussein and adding Islamic symbols to the rhetoric of the leadership. The modified internal constitution was not only conducive to counter the appeal of the Iranian revolutionaries, it strengthened the power of the Ba'thist state *vis-à-vis* internal opposition (i.e. Shiite and Kurdish movements), whilst diversifying its ideational appeal and claim to leadership in the Persian Gulf and beyond.

Whilst the process of war reiterated the very raison d'être of the Iraqi state, it took the movement in Iran out of the revolutionary context and brought it back into the 'real world' of international relations. By getting embroiled in the conflict with Iraq, the infant Islamic state was abruptly confronted with the determinations of international society. The new political elite had to translate a movement for domestic and international emancipation into a functioning state apparatus capable of conducting inter-state war. To do so, the Islamic Republic had to rely on the very institutions and norms of international culture it had previously endeavoured to overthrow, compromising the steadfast revolutionary chorus carrying the movement forward during the early days of the revolution. As E.H. Carr noted in his *Twenty Years' Crisis*, once 'utopian' movements assume power, theory tends to be discarded in favour of practice: the 'leftist' gravitates towards the 'right'.[195] In the Iranian case the containment of the revolutionary ideals was not a matter of choice, but caused by a systemically legitimated war. By having to revert to the symbols of state and nationalist imagery in order to organise the Iranian masses, the Islamic Republic lost much of its transnational momentum at quite an early stage of the movement. Divested from its pan-Islamic appeal, the war not only prevented Iran from constituting an inclusive Islamic state, but also represented the country through the altered regional 'truth conditions' after the revolution as the villain of the piece and a looming threat to the regional equilibrium – an image that the Iranian government has to struggle against to this date.

3 Westphalia and the anarchic Gulf society

The second Persian Gulf War and its aftermath

3.1 Introduction

Chapter 2 concluded with the contention that revolution in Iran altered the 'truth conditions' of international conduct in the Persian Gulf. How can this abstract claim best be developed? To elaborate what we mean by 'changed truth conditions' a simple comparison between regional perceptions of war before and after the revolution is helpful. Whilst during the former period an Iraqi attack on Pahlavi Iran would have been evaluated as an *aggression*, the same act was considered *legitimate* against the Islamic Republic of Iran. Attacking Iran before the ascendancy of Khomeini was impossible not necessarily only because of the superior military capabilities of the Pahlavi state, but because the country's privileged role as regional 'gendarme' was legitimated regionally and globally. The Ba'thist regime was deterred from an invasion of Iran because Iraqi decision-makers knew that a military assault during that period would have been immediately identified as a punishable aggression by international society. After all, the systemic backing of pre-revolutionary Iran was the dominant reason why the Shah felt empowered to pursue the delineation of the Shatt al-Arab along the thalweg, or seize the three Persian Gulf islands. It is well known that the former goal was pursued by a long-lasting covert war against the Ba'thist state via the Iraqi-Kurds and with substantial backing from the United States and Israel.[196] In a conversation with the US Ambassador April Glaspie in July 1990, Saddam Hussein indicated the helplessness of the Iraqi state *vis-à-vis* the Shah's requests, admitting that 'forced to choose between half of Shatt al-Arab or the whole of Iraq . . . we [gave] the Shatt al-Arab away, to keep the whole of Iraq in the shape we wish[ed] it to be'.[197] Power politics by the Pahlavi state yes, but Iranian power would have been one dimensional and ineffective if it had not been carried (not only backed up) by regional and global approval.

In the second place, the challenge to Iraqi security under the Shah was much more organised and straightforward than the agitation by revolutionary Iran which remained largely rhetorical. At no stage during the revolutionary turmoil that brought Iran's formerly strong military into disarray was the Islamic Republic in the position of launching a military invasion or co-ordinated covert war against any of the country's neighbours. Shia unrest in the Persian Gulf states was due to their marginalisation in their respective societies and was largely articulated along national lines.[198] The decisive factor that propelled the Iraqi state to consider war in the post-revolutionary regional system and not during the pre-revolutionary one was not the extent of Iranian provocations. The central reason was that Iraqi decision-makers anticipated that the former would have identified the Iraqi attack as an aggression and interference, whilst the latter portrayed it as legitimate – a 'rationale' response against an external threat.

To propose that the same act of aggression would have been evaluated differently by international society has causal and constitutive significance for our argument. Causally, it relates to the observation that different beliefs create different interests and incentives, which will in turn affect foreign-policy behaviour. But the difference between the pre- and post-revolutionary systems has also constitutive dimensions. What counts as 'aggression' in one case and 'self-defence' or 'intervention' in the other, is determined by the 'truth conditions' or shared knowledge (i.e. culture) that are prevalent among the constituent members of an international society.[199] What would have made an invasion of Iran during the Shah period 'illegitimate' was not the act of war itself or not even the protest of the Iranian state, but the cultural context it would have occurred in. Shared knowledge during the pre-revolutionary period 'told' the Iraqi regime that inter-state war against one of the pillars of the regional system was untenable. The same act after the demise of the Shah against the same country was permitted and supported. In other words, there is a case to argue that the dominant (international) political culture of international society determines if inter-state war is legitimate or not. This dimension of the contemporary international system refers to an inherently relational process, and would be neglected by a purely materialist interpretation of world politics.

This chapter benefits from that theoretical assertion. It will be argued that the single most decisive factor that determined Iraq's decision to attack Kuwait was the Ba'thist perception that international society would let the country get away with another invasion. The relative power capabilities at the disposal of the Iraqi state have always put the country in a better position *vis-à-vis* its smaller neighbours to the south. The reason why after 1961 when General Abdel-Karim Qassim prepared an invasion of Kuwait, Iraq did not launch another attempt to annex the Emirate was not because the country did not have the material capabilities to do so, it was because the Iraqi state knew that such an act would be rejected *in toto* by international society. That perception changed after the revolution in Iran and the events during the Iran–Iraq war. The international support to the Iraqi war effort conveyed the message to the Ba'thist state that it can assert the country's supremacy in the Persian Gulf by seeking systemically accommodated military aggression. This follows from what has been observed in Chapter 2 with regard to the social construction of the Iraqi war role in the war with Iran. Interpreted against the background of the Ba'thist identity of the regime, Iraqi decision-makers acted upon the premise that the country's war role during the Iran–Iraq war legitimated its assertive behaviour thereafter, including the right to invade Kuwait.

In the second place, the fact that Iraq was expelled from Kuwait, had to endure over eleven years of sanctions, was left with circumscribed territorial sovereignty and eventually that the Ba'thist state was crushed altogether in the Third Persian Gulf

War (see Chapter 4) proves that the regulating powers of international society were strong enough to balance out revolution, two inter-state wars and numerous domestic crisis. In the final analysis, it will be argued that the structure of international politics of the postwar Persian Gulf provides striking similarities with relations during the pre-revolutionary period.

3.2   Umm Kul al-Ma'arik (mother of all battles) 1990–1991

3.2.1   *International society and the Second Gulf War: clouded lenses in the desert storm*

On 2 August 1990, some 140,000 Iraqi troops and 1,800 tanks, spearheaded by two Iraqi Republican Guard armoured divisions invaded Kuwait. Immediately after the invasion, the Iraqi state announced the appointment of Colonel Ala Hussein Ali as the head of a nine-man 'Provisional Free Kuwait Government'. Less than a week later on 8 August, the transitional government was dissolved and Saddam Hussein announced the annexation of Kuwait, incorporating the Emirate's area as the nineteenth province of Iraq. The international reaction was swift, following the invasion there was a five months period of crisis diplomacy, marked by the passing of several UN Resolutions, calling for the immediate withdrawal of Iraqi forces from Kuwait. The Iraqi state remained defiant. On 17 January 1991 an international coalition led by the United States began an air war against Iraq, followed by a one-hundred-hour long land offensive at the end of February. After an air war phase of 38 days and 4 days of ground combat, Iraqi troops were driven out of Kuwait, southern Iraq was occupied, a UN sanctions regime was installed and the tribal rule of the Al-Sabah dynasty was restored.[200]

To many decision-makers in the Persian Gulf and beyond, the Iraqi invasion of the country's steadfast ally during the First Persian Gulf War came as a surprise. Saddam Hussein himself reassured regional states on two occasions: in a conversation with Egyptian President Hosni Mubarak, who arrived in Baghdad on 24 July 1990 in order to mediate between the country and Kuwait, declaring that '[a]s long as discussions last between Iraq and Kuwait, I won't use force. I won't intervene with force before I have exhausted all the possibilities for negotiation'.[201] And one day later (that is one week before invading Kuwait) in his talk with the then US Ambassador April Glaspie, indicating that Iraq will not do 'anything' against Kuwait until a meeting between the countries.[202]

Although there continued to be considerable suspicion towards Iraq, proven by the fact that the Gulf Co-operation Council (GCC) persistently turned down Iraqi requests for a Iraqi-GCC security pact in the Persian Gulf, there appeared to be a general consensus that the country did not pose an immediate threat to the security of the Gulf monarchies. Reassuring Iraqi initiatives such as the 'Arab National Charter' of 1980,[203] which was designed to formalise the mutual acceptance of sovereignty in the Arab state system, were taken as reason enough to believe that the Iraqi state identity had shifted from a socialist revolutionary version of *al qawmiyya al' arabiya*

(Arab nationalism) which had an expansionist outlook to the notion of *al wataniyya al' Iraqiya* (Iraqi patriotism) which was rather more inward looking. Adeed Dawisha observes that '[t]hroughout the 1970s, the regime embarked on a political and cultural program designed to create a continuous link between modern Iraq and the ancient civilisations that had resided in the same land'. The shift arguably explains why the Iraqi leaders decided 'to gradually abandon their aggressively revolutionary and expansionist policies in the Arab world' and adopt 'a largely non-interventionist stance' instead.[204] Having provided the Iraqi state with the diplomatic, economic and political support during the First Persian Gulf War, and having relied upon gestures such as Iraq's non-aggression pact with Saudi Arabia in 1989, the GCC states felt reassured that an era of co-operative relations in the Persian Gulf was possible.[205] Perceived as the 'West's opportunity'[206] after the demise of the Shah, the United States shared that view, believing that Saddam Hussein could be transformed into a 'minimally usefully [*sic*] member of the international community', a role that was deemed conducive to opening up the country to American business.[207]

Indeed, after the ending of the First Persian Gulf War and right up until the invasion of Kuwait in August 1990, Iraq continued to benefit from the support of the US government. The Bush administration built upon the policy of the Reagan years, aiming at cultivating Saddam Hussein as a potentially moderate leader, willing to guarantee the regional status quo. When the then US Ambassador to Baghdad, April Glaspie met with Saddam on 25 July 1990 a week before the invasion of Kuwait, an Iraqi transcript of the conversation shows that she assured him that Bush 'wanted better and deeper relations' and that the US President 'is an intelligent man' who does not want 'to declare an economic war against Iraq'.[208] Glaspie also used a cautious tone regarding the Kuwait crisis, indicating to Saddam that the United States had 'no opinion on the Arab-Arab conflicts, like [his] border disagreement with Kuwait'.[209] One and a half month before that meeting on 12 April 1990, Glaspie and five US Senators were even more overt in their support to Saddam Hussein. During the conversation with Hussein, Senator Howard Metzenbaum who identified himself as a 'Jew and a staunch supporter of Israel' called the Iraqi leader a 'strong and intelligent man' who can be 'a very influential force for peace in the Middle East'.[210] These diplomatic overtures were complemented with considerable financial and military assistance. The aforementioned investigations led by Henry Gonzalez which were presented to the US House of Representative in July 1992 revealed the extent of the Bush administration's collusion with Iraq, concluding that

> the highest levels of the Bush administration, including the President himself, had specific knowledge of Iraq's military industrialisation plans, and despite that knowledge, the President mandated the policy of coddling Saddam Hussein as spelled out in National Security Directive 26 (NSD-26) issued in October 1989. This policy was not changed until after the Iraqi invasion of Kuwait, by which time the Bush administration had sent Saddam Hussein billions of dollars in United States financial assistance, technology and useful military intelligence information.[211]

In the words of one analyst 'Saddam was less a Hitler than he was Frankenstein's monster, with the U.S. playing the role of Dr Frankenstein.... It was in fact only after the invasion of Kuwait...that Washington did a 180 degree turn and instead of covering for Saddam, began to castigate him as an Arab Hitler'.[212]

The miscalculations regarding the intentions of Saddam Hussein were based on the supposition that the secular-nationalist ideology of the Iraqi regime could be manipulated to the advantage of US interests in the region, underestimating the salience of the anti-imperialist and Ba'thist-Arabist identity of the Iraqi state and the 'megalomania' of Saddam Hussein himself. The Soviet Union and regional states planned their strategies according to a similar misperception, willing to support and appease Iraq in order to guarantee the regional status quo. It was only two weeks into the Second Persian Gulf War, when Mikhail Gorbachov acknowledged that building up the arsenal of the Iraqi army may have had adverse effects on regional stability. Announcing the termination of the Iraqi–Soviet relationship, Gorbachov conceded that

> [f]or us to have acted otherwise would have been unacceptable, since the act of aggression was committed with the help of our weapons, which we agreed to sell to Iraq only to maintain its defence capability rather than to seize foreign territories and whole countries.[213]

US officials echoed that view, lamenting in retrospect that '[e]verybody was wrong in their assessment of Saddam' and that '[e]verybody in the Arab world told us that the best way to deal with Saddam was to develop a set of economic and commercial dealings that would have the effect of moderating his behaviour. History will demonstrate that this was a miscalculation'.[214]

That the nature of the Iraqi regime had not significantly changed (to the better) must have been clear from Saddam Hussein's handling of domestic dissent. The hospitable international environment allowed the Iraqi state to pursue organised violent campaigns to suppress the country's minorities and salvage the totalitarian rule of the regime's Sunni/Arab/Tikriti (Saddam's hometown) nucleus. Even more severe than the systematic suppression of the Iraqi Shia population in the south was the campaign against Kurdish opposition in the north of the country. Termed *al-Anfal* (spoils of war), the attacks against the Kurds consisted of a concerted series of eight military offensives between late February and early 1988. According to Human Rights Watch, as part of the campaign 'at least sixty villages, as well as the town of Halabja, were attacked with mustard gas, nerve gas, or a combination of the two'.[215] In the case of Halabja, when chemical weapons were employed against Kurdish civilians and Iranian soldiers operating in the area, independent estimates suggest that at least 4,000 people were killed.[216] There is no doubt that the international community was aware of what was going on inside Iraq. Airlifted by Iranian military personnel, international journalists provided detailed coverage of the chemical attacks in Halabja.[217] Moreover, a published Iraqi army communiqué dated 19 March 1988 provided enough references to the Anfal campaign to presume the scale of the operation. The communiqué stated

> Like all covetous invaders, the Zionist Khomeinyite forces relied on some of those who betrayed the homeland and people in the northern area of Iraq.... Among their shameful acts was facilitating the missions of the invading forces in entering in the Halabja border villages in the Suleimaniyeh Governorate.... Our forces attacked the headquarters of the rebellion led by traitor Jalal Talabani, the agent to the Iranian regime, the enemy of the Arabs and Kurds.... The commander of the force guarding the rebellion headquarters, and a number of traitors and misguided elements, were captured.... Many were killed and others escaped in shame.... This is a struggle admired by the entire world, the struggle of leader Saddam Hussein's people, Arabs and Kurds, who placed themselves in the service of the homeland and gave their love and faithfulness to their great leader, the symbol of their victory and title of their prosperity. Our people have rejected from their ranks all traitors who sold themselves cheaply to the covetous foreign enemy.[218]

The fact that the Iraqi handling of domestic dissent was not explicitly condemned by international society in the period between the First and Second Gulf War suggests that the hope of turning Iraq into a 'pro-Western' regional status quo power superseded the realities on the ground.

The international overtures to Saddam Hussein and the tacit affirmation of an eminent Iraqi role after the ending of the Iran–Iraq war lowered the threshold for another military conflict in the Persian Gulf. With its complacency towards Iraqi war crimes and the sustained support to the Iraqi state, international society unwillingly allowed for a second inter-state war in the region. Saddam Hussein did not decide to invade Kuwait because international support and mobilisation of the Iraqi populace led to a massive increase of the country's military capabilities. After all, the number of Iraqi soldiers had swelled from 190,000 in 1979–1980 to 1 million in 1987–1988 with a similar drastic growth in the number of tanks from 1,900 to 6,310, combat aircraft from 339 to over 500 and armoured fighting vehicles from 1,500 to 4,000.[219] In comparison to its southern neighbour, the Iraqi state had always commanded superior military capabilities. The Iraqi regime knew also that whether Iraq had 1 million soldiers or 3,000 tanks more or less did not change its inferior military position *vis-à-vis* the United States. The reason why Saddam Hussein launched the invasion was not based on military calculations, it was driven by the supposition that there would be no decisive response to the invasion. International society had not acted upon Iranian requests, nor had it done much to contain Iraq's use of chemical weapons. Why should it act now on behalf of Kuwait? After all, as Saddam Hussein pointed out on several occasions, it was Iraq that protected the 'oil people'[220] against the 'unknown flood' of Iranian revolutionism, something the United States would not have been capable of 'except by the use of nuclear weapons'.[221] Strengthened in its pan-Arab claim after the war against Iran and still committed to the anti-imperialist and anti-Zionist ideology of socialist Arabism, the Iraqi decision to attack Kuwait was hence driven by the perception that the country will face an acquiescent Arab world and a supine international society.

Explanations of the causes of the Kuwait war which rightly point towards the economic incentives of the Iraqi state or the country's aim to gain better access to Persian Gulf waters need to be framed by an ideational context which determined the long-term strategic goals of the Ba'thist state and the inter-subjective context Iraqi decision-makers were acting in. Halliday accurately observes that 'throughout the [Kuwait] crisis there was virtually no discussion in the media or the serious press of what kind of country Iraq was, what its long-run political strategies were, and, not least of the history and ideology of its ruling body, the Arab Ba'th Socialist Party'.[222] He further contends that failure to appreciate that factor is comparable to neglecting communism as an ideological driving force behind the foreign policy of the Soviet Union. Hence, his implicit call for an ideational explanation of the causes and consequences of the crisis, noting that the

> nature of Ba'thism, with its dramatic idea of the Arab nation, its cult of war as the purgative fire, its glorification of *sharaf* or honour, its obsession with the strong man, the knight or *faris* on horseback, who will deliver the Arab nation, and its explicit valorisation of *al-qiswa* (harshness) as a tool of government control, tells us much about [the Kuwait war] and its outcome.[223]

The logical conclusion of Halliday's argument needs to be that there exists a causal link between the subjective self-perception of the Iraqi regime (since 1979 inextricably related to the persona of Saddam Hussein), the definition of interest, the perception of external determinants and the Iraqi decision to go to war against Kuwait. Naturally, it is not suggested that the Iraqi regime blindly followed an abstract notion of Arab nationalism. Rather, Iraqi state interests were defined against the background of the invented and internalised identity of the Ba'thist regime. In other words, without any knowledge about what kind of role the Iraqi state envisaged for the country, we will not be able to comprehensively explain the grand foreign-policy design the regime was pursuing. The argument is that at any given period of time – at least since the ascendancy to power of Saddam Hussein in 1979 – the Iraqi state was acting upon the premise that the country was capable of being the uniting force in the Arab world and playing a prominent role in world politics. The very raison d'être of the Iraqi state was explicitly linked to the pan-Arabist project. Breaching the 'borderline between the political idiom and political action',[224] the country was pushed towards acting out what was constantly reproduced as the primary source of identity and legitimisation of the Iraqi regime during a period when systemic factors appeared to be conducive to that end.

A cultural methodology informs us in this context that actors need to define the situation before they can choose a course of action. The definition of the situation will be based on 'their own identities and interests, which reflect beliefs about who they are in such situations; and what they think others will do, which reflect beliefs about their identities and interests'.[225] Applied to our case this could mean two things. First, the Iraqi decision to invade Kuwait was based on the Iraqi Ba'thist state identity which informed Iraqi leaders about the strategic interests to be pursued (i.e. Arab unity, Iraqi pre-eminence in the Gulf and so on) and second, the Iraqi state thought that the other Arab states might support its leadership role and supposed that the wider international community might acquiesce to diplomatic brinkmanship and military force. Part of the latter aspect of this 'ideational transmission belt' (i.e. the systemic signals) have been addressed above. In order to further investigate how system effects were processed at the unit-level, we need to proceed with addressing the 'mindset' of the Iraqi regime with a special focus upon the period between the Iran–Iraq and the Kuwait war. This will be helpful to address the Iraqi perception of its environment and will eventually give us indications about the Iraqi behaviour during the ensuing international response.

3.2.2 Self-fulfilling prophecy? Iraqi state identity and the decision to attack Kuwait

Analysing Saddam Hussein's speeches and diplomatic correspondence with the Arab League and regional leaders between the end of the Iran–Iraq war in 1988 and the invasion of Kuwait in August 1990, the analyst cannot help but recognise three recurrent schemes and imageries that encapsulate the mindset of the Iraqi regime after its war with Iran. First, because Iraq gave 'rivers of blood' (*anhar al-damm*) to secure the 'eastern gateway' (*al-bawwabah al-sharqiyyah*) of the 'Arab homeland' against the revolutionary movement in Iran which threatened to 'Persianise' the whole of the 'Arab' Gulf, the Gulf monarchies were materially and morally indebted to the Iraqi nation. Second, because of the sacrifice of Iraq, the country's leadership had a legitimate claim to lead the Arab *umma*. And finally, by acquiring that status, Iraq was at the forefront of the struggle for the liberation of Palestine and the 'natural' bulwark against Zionist, imperialist and Iranian penetration of the Arab state system.[226]

The strong Arab nationalist content of those assertions points towards the continued relevance of revolutionary Ba'thist ideology for the self-legitimisation of the Iraqi state and represents the motivational drives for the country's foreign policy. Through its war against Iran, the Iraqi state constituted itself as the primary Arab actor, reinforcing the regime's view that the country was the main agent for pan-Arab unification. The postwar correspondence between Saddam Hussein and Iranian President Ali-Akbar Hashemi Rafsanjani reflects the Iraqi foreign-policy disposition, indicating that state expediency was sometimes less important than intransigent ideological self-legitimation.[227] Negotiations about concrete issues such as exchanges of prisoners of war (POWs), reparations, sovereignty, war responsibilities or territorial integrity appeared to be secondary to dramatic discussions about the supremacy of the core values of both states. The six letters of Saddam Hussein (which were answered with four letters by the Iranian President) constantly equated Iraq's role with the cause of Arabism, depicting the war between the two countries as a conflict between the Arab *umma* and Iran. In addition, as exemplified in his first letter to Rafsanjani dated 21 April 1990, Hussein also repeatedly referred to his other most favourite ideological schemes, pointing out that Iraq was under threat from Zionism and imperialism, with the 'objective . . . to leave the hands of the Zionist regime open to corrupt the world so that it can suppress whoever becomes an obstacle to falsehood'. The same 'evil forces' Hussein asserted 'shall surely try to restart the armed and bloody conflict between Iran . . . and the Arab *umma*'.[228]

Pointing towards his affinity with the strong exclusionary element of Arab nationalism, Saddam Hussein in his fifth letter to Rafsanjani – dated 3 August 1990, that is one day after the occupation of Kuwait – presented the invasion of the Emirate as a transitory event 'related to relations between Arabs', implicitly signalling that Iran (as a non-Arab country) should stay out of the conflict. Here and elsewhere, the choice of language and symbols indicates that Saddam Hussein invoked Arab nationalism as an expedient strategy to exclude the non-Arab competitor (in this case Iran) from inter-Arab affairs. But the story does not end here. Both Saddam Hussein himself and the Ba'thist regime identified with the causes of pan-Arabism, whilst exploiting its mobilising and legitimating force for the interests of the state. Arab nationalism was a logical choice of the available menu of state identities, because it simultaneously granted legitimation to the Tikriti-Arab-Sunni elite surrounding Saddam Hussein and fenced off potential power sharing with Iraq's minority non-Arab Kurds or Turkomen and majority non-Sunni Shiites. To that utilitarian choice, we need to add the constitutive 'corollary': exactly *because* Ba'thist Arab nationalism was directly tied to the very legitimation of the Iraqi state, it also constituted the central role identity the regime was identifying with. As much as France does not detach the French state from the imagery of 'la grande nation' (not that they would want to), the Iraqi state never really abandoned the idea of *al qawmiyya al' arabiya* (Arab nationalism). This role attribution exercised pressures due to the 'logic' of pan-Arabism, that is, 'that frontiers merely divide a political community that should be united'.[229] For reasons of state, the reification of the pan-Arabist idea could be reconstructed or reinterpreted but never really abandoned *in toto*. Total detachment would have taken away the central legitimating agent of the Iraqi state – the very raison d'être of the Ba'thist regime.

Let me add a theoretical mnemonic. Cultural theorists suggest that 'while a certain degree of role discrepancy is socially permitted and psychologically bearable, there are strong social and psychological pressures to achieve a level of consistency in the roles individuals play and in the identities they therefore assume.'[230] This is immediately relevant to the Iraqi case. Whilst during some periods Iraq distanced itself from the pan-Arab idea, the constant identification and reference to Ba'thist ideology and Arab nationalist imagery reified the role identity Iraqi leaders wanted to assume. The Arab nationalist identity informed the Iraqi state that the institution of Westphalian sovereignty was imposed on the Arabs in an imperialist plot aimed at splitting the Arab *umma*. By invading both Iran and Kuwait in the name of Arabism, Saddam Hussein pushed the country into the direction of undoing the colonial boundaries which segregated the united Arab territory. This endeavour was presented as a historical cause that the country was destined to fulfil because of Baghdad's heritage as the capital of the Abbasid caliphate and the centre for all Arabs.[231]

The announcement of the annexation of Kuwait by the Iraqi Revolutionary Command Council (RCC) on 8 August 1990 exemplifies the relevance of the dual discourse of Iraqi state identity – pan-Arab on the one hand side and Iraq-centred on the other. The declaration is permeated by the usual allusions to the catastrophic effects of Western colonialism and its 'partition of the Arab homeland' which was a plot to 'make all [Arab] states weak' and to 'prevent these states from closing ranks and demonstrating a unified stance'.[232] Iraq is viewed as the legitimate force to undo the partition of the homeland, returning the *fir* (branch, i.e. Kuwait) to *al-Kul wa al-asl* ('the whole and the origin', that is, Iraq) 'in a comprehensive, eternal and inseparable merger unity'. The immediate, strategic argument is presented at a later stage, indicating that by separating Iraq from the 'origin and well spring', colonialism 'kept Iraq away from the [Persian Gulf] waters to prevent it from acquiring part of its tactical and strategic capabilities'.[233] From the Iraqi perspective then, *al-wihda al-indimajiyya* (the pan-Arab unification of Iraq and Kuwait) was legitimate, a step in the direction of Arab unity with the removal of a boundary that was considered to be an artefact of Western colonialism. Alluding to the culture of thought carrying that disposition, Kanan Makiya argued:

> Bizarre as it may seem, the Iraqi annexation of Kuwait was genuinely seen by the Ba'thi[st] state, and by the majority of Arab intellectuals, as an extension of the total amount of freedom available to the Arab people. The anti-imperialist rhetoric of both Pan-Arabism and Palestinian nationalism revolves around the idea of 'freedom from' either imperialism or Zionism, as the case may be, toward unity of an artificially fragmented whole (the Arab world) or a yet-to-be-created state (a future Palestine in the Occupied Territories, for instance). Freedom lovers everywhere should support the annexation of Kuwait [as] a 'national act'...for this reason.[234]

From that perspective, the invasion of Kuwait was legitimated not only because it was in the Iraqi/Arab/Islamic interest but because it was a campaign to attain justice and freedom from domination. In the radio address of the Iraqi Revolutionary Command Council headed by Saddam Hussein on 15 February 1991, the self-legitimation of the Iraqi regime as a force for freedom and international emancipation, observed by Makyia, join the other three ideational schemes we have discussed earlier:

> O glorious Iraqis, O dear Arabs, O faithful Muslims, O free men and honourable persons throughout the world. The aggression that has been launched on Iraq, the courageous, proud, holy warrior, faithful, and patient country, is unprecedented in history. The entire history of mankind never records such an alliance in which the United States as well as two big powers participated...against the holy warrior, courageous, and patient Iraq, whose population does not exceed eighteen million people. It is an evil, rancorous, malicious, and atheistic alliance against the bastion of faith and principles, against the centre of freedom where the call for justice and fairness is made.[235]

The statement is clearly not only addressed to the Iraqi, Arab, Muslim constituencies of the Ba'thist regime, the impression is created that Iraq is fighting on behalf of all freedom loving people against the 'evil' imperialist-Zionist forces. The invasion of Kuwait becomes a heroic act against an 'invented and illegal state' and the 'mother of all battles' the stage where the Iraqi regime acts out its legitimate role as the force of good vs. evil.

Historically, it is of course true that Kuwait was an invented state in that the Emirates boundaries were drawn by British colonial strategist. Moreover, Kuwait *was* a sub-district of the southern Iraqi province of Basra in Ottoman times, which was presented as justification for challenging Kuwaiti sovereignty on several occasions, whether under the rule of the nationalist King Ghazi (1935–1939) or General Abdel Karim Quassim (1958–1963) who considered an invasion of Kuwait after the declaration of Kuwaiti independence from British rule in June 1961. By inventing a personal genealogy linking himself to historical Muslim figures and Iraq to ancient civilisations, Saddam Hussein wanted to dilute the fact that Iraq shared the same colonial predicament with Kuwait (and indeed other former colonies). After all, Iraq itself was artificially constructed, carved out of the territory of the Ottoman Empire by merging three provinces with different ethnic and cultural compositions. Choosing pan-Arabism as an integral part of Iraqi state identity served the function to invent an artificial historiography, reflecting the way the Iraqi regime wanted to view itself and conducive to mobilise popular support in the Arab world. To underscore the importance of this aspect further, let me relate it back to our earlier discussion of Arab nationalist theory as propounded by Michel Aflaq and Sati al-Husri. By emphasising the idea of Arab unification, Aflaq and al-Husri implicitly reiterated the importance of the state as the vehicle for the self-realisation of the Arab nation based on cultural and linguistic cohesion. Nazih Ayubi goes even one step further, arguing that Aflaq gave precedence to the (Ba'thist) party over the state. Ayubi suggests that '[n]ot only [was] the formation of the Pan-Arabist party a measure of the conscious and productive existence of the Arab nation but the party is, more specifically, the nation in miniature.'[236] In other words, in Ba'thist nationalist ideology the state is seen through the prism of the party and its goal to bring about a 'single Arab nation with an eternal mission' or in Aflaq's words 'the party must be a smaller version of the pure healthy and elevated nation that it wishes to resurrect.'[237]

The accentuation of an ongoing struggle to attain unity, in theory without the provision of long periods of pragmatist consolidation, may explain the salience of the pan-Arab push in Iraqi foreign-policy behaviour. The ideological foundations of Ba'thism did not really accommodate long-term utilitarian 'time outs' in the endeavour to bring about Arab unity. Aflaq reiterated this point, declaring that the 'Ba'th is a historical movement [destined] to be active for centuries; it therefore sees in struggle [*nidal*] the fundamental basis of party [work] and the source of its ideas and revolutionary qualities.'[238] According to Aflaq, loosing the revolutionary élan would be tantamount to betrayal of the struggle for unity, which is a matter of life and death. In a study about the effects of political culture on Iraqi politics, Ofra Bengio argues:

> According to Ba'th doctrine, the struggle must go on because the Arabs in general, and the Iraqis in particular, have 'eternal' enemies. It distinguished between *nidal salbi* (negative struggle; i.e. against something) and *nidal ijabi*

(positive struggle; i.e. for the sake of something). The former term was used to refer to the party's activities up to its advent to power, the second to its actions while in power.[239]

The Iraqi state did not only identify itself with the Ba'thist notion of continuous struggle for the sake of unification, the Iraqi leader himself was fascinated by the idea of an 'Arab Bismarck' who would bring about unification through Prussian-style military prudence, an imagery cherished by al-Husri.[240] In Aflaq's writings the leadership ideal even attained fascist dimensions, in close affinity with the German notion of *Führer* (leader):

> The People everywhere are unable to understand any idea truly and quickly. That is why they look to living individuals in whom the idea is vested. It is to these individuals, and only to the extent of their moral worth and enthusiasm, that one looks to measure the value of an espoused idea.
>
> So if a group of educated, active and moral youth were to unite powerfully, according to a fierce discipline, and in accordance with a hierarchy of grades, this in itself is enough to guarantee their influence over the people. *The holiness that these people endow upon their leader is in reality a sanctification of the idea which they wish to support and spread.* To the extent that the personalities of these followers are strong and have moral value, the idea's chances of success will be that much greater.[241]

Ba'thist Arab nationalist world-view defended an image of the leader as the embodiment of the collective will and spirit of the people. The mission of the people is a priori defined by the common goal to attain unity. In turn, the authority of the 'essential leader' is supported and organised by the totalitarian and hierarchical organisation of the party. Since Saddam Hussein's presidency in 1979, Iraqi national identity was constructed to follow that dual narrative: celebrating the leadership of Saddam Hussein on the one hand side and the Arabist mission of the Ba'th party on the other. The former dimension was pursued by a concerted effort to present the Iraqi President as the 'indispensable leader'. Adopting the romantic, moralistic view of the 'just leadership' principle introduced by Aflaq (see earlier), Saddam Hussein himself distinguished between the responsibilities and persona of *qa'id* (leader) and *hakim* (ruler). According to him, leading requires that 'you must give those you lead the feeling that you are just, even if circumstances require you to act with a heavy hand'.[242] A person who is perceived to be unjust could hence be a ruler, but not a leader who is dependent upon the people's 'extraordinary affinity [with him] and their constant loyalty'.[243]

The Iraqi propaganda machine put every effort into linking the metaphysical ideal of the ultimate Arab leader to the persona of Saddam Hussein, representing him as *al qa'id al-darura* (the leader by necessity) and his leadership as *darura wataniyya* (a national necessity). Hussein himself preferred to liken his role to historic figures such as Ali bin Abi Talib, the son-in-law of the Prophet Mohammad, al-Mansur, the second Abbassid caliph or Saladin who fought against the European crusaders in the twelfth century. Not that the choices were made at random. Invoking the myth of linkages with these figures served the function to symbolise and further specific interests of the state: choosing Ali bin Abi Talib as reference for identification was meant to appeal to the Shia population of Iraq and to counter the influence of the revolutionary movement in Iran, accentuating the 'Arabness' of Shi'ism in contrast of the 'Iranianness' of Ayatollah Khomeini and the Islamic Republic. Alluding to al-Mansur, who expanded the Abbasid territory to the north and east and who built Baghdad and made it into the legendary capital of the caliphate, served the purpose to pontificate the centrality of Iraq in the history of the Arabs. And identifying with Saladin, who was an ethnic Kurd supposedly from Saddam Hussein's hometown Tikrit, was thought to symbolise the potential for Arab-Kurdish unity and the steadfastness of Saddam Hussein in the face of the 'imperialist crusaders' of the contemporary age (i.e. Israel and the United States).

Viewed from the perspective of Ba'thism and its propensity for ideal leadership and missionary Arabism, systemic developments provided impulses and incentives to attain the sought after role as the centre of gravity in the region. A central systemic opportunity to reach that strategic goal, emanated from the expulsion of Egypt from the Arab League after Anwar Sadat's separate peace deal with Israel in 1979, ostracising the main contender for Arab leadership and opening up the position for Iraq. This reshuffling in inter-Arab politics coincided with the revolution in Iran and the Presidency of Saddam Hussein. By confronting revolutionary Iranian Islam, Saddam Hussein generated massive support from key regional actors including Egypt, Saudi Arabia, the Palestine Liberation Organisation (PLO) and Jordan, further enhancing the regional position of the regime. Between the ending of the war against Iran and the invasion of Kuwait, the Iraqi state acted according to this prominent position, by bringing Egypt back into the mainstream of Arab politics under the *Majlis al-ta'awun al-'Arabi* (Arab Co-operation Council) established together with Jordan and Yemen in February 1989. Viewed from the subjective perspective of the Iraqi state, the political prestige gained by those developments provided enough incentives to imagine an acquiescent, if not supportive reaction to an invasion of Kuwait. Given the support by the PLO and the late King Hussein of Jordan and the 'mass pro-Saddam Hussein demonstrations that took place throughout the Arab world',[244] the Iraqi state was at least partially accurate in its anticipation of regional reactions.

On the basis of the preceding discussion, it is proposed that from the perspective of Saddam Hussein and the Iraqi regime the symbolism of the attack as a mission to seal the Iraqi role as the motor for the realisation of the pan-Arab idea, superseded the cost-benefit calculations and, once realised, the potential consequences of facing military retribution itself. As soon as Kuwait was annexed, it was ideological power the Iraqi state was capitalising on, not military might. Bassam Tibi agrees: 'Saddam Hussein had counted on a war like the Suez War – one in which he might fail militarily, but win politically.'[245] Why else did the regime not concede to US demands, when it still had the opportunity to do so? Certainly not because Saddam Hussein assumed that he or even alliances with other regional states would fend off an Allied attack. The Iraqi state was aware of the potential consequences of the invasion once international society pointed out that in the case of Kuwait '[p]rinciple cannot be compromised'.[246] At that stage, it was clear that the country was facing a resolute alliance of 28 countries providing military units, authorised to enforce the 12 UN Security Council resolutions by military means if necessary. Indeed, as the first war of the post-bipolar world order, 'Operation Desert Storm' was one of the few modern wars with a high degree of systemic legitimacy. It was backed by the UN, there was NATO involvement, tacit support from the Soviet Union and massive financial, diplomatic and military backing from the EU and the GCC states. Then Iraqi Foreign Minister Tariq Aziz addressed the suggestion that the leadership of the country did not know what is going on around them directly. Responding to former Secretary of State James Baker's allegation that the Iraqi leadership miscalculated the situation, Aziz pointed out:

> We know what the deployment of your forces in the region means; we know what the resolutions you imposed on the Security Council mean; and we know all the facts about the situation – the political facts, the military facts, and the other facts.[247]

There is hence not much doubt that the Iraqi state knew what was coming. In turn, this would suggest that once the leadership decided to embark upon its Kuwait endeavour, sustaining the invasion as a symbol of the Iraqi role as the motor of the pan-Arab project in the face of overwhelming opposition was more rational than conceding to US demands. Saddam Hussein alluded to this determination in his conversation with US Ambassador Glaspie before the war:

> You can come to Iraq with aircraft and missiles but do not push us to the point where we cease to care. And when we feel that you want to injure our pride and take away the Iraqis' chance of a high standard of living, then we will cease to care and death will be the choice for us. Then we would not care if you fired 100 missiles for each missile we fired. Because without pride life would have no value.[248]

Short-term propaganda campaigns against Kuwait and others, alluding to the Emirates and UAE's overproduction in OPEC, Kuwait's annexation of parts of the Rumaila oilfield or the country's and Saudi Arabia's insistence on the repayment of loans granted during the Iran–Iraq war, need to be seen within the meta-narratives of Iraqi foreign-policy culture. The grand foreign-policy strategies of the country's leadership were ideologically and institutionally programmed to be consistent with the idea of Arab unification under Iraqi (Saddam Hussein's) leadership. Questioning the authority of Iraq was synonymous with betraying the Arab cause. Putting economic pressure on the country was 'in fact a kind of war against Iraq'.[249] Even a scholar such as Fouad Ajami, who portrays Arabism as a utilitarian idea exploited by self-interested leaders, implicitly concedes that structural shared knowledge about the ideal of Arab unification and the imagery of a strong Arab leader were central to the Iraqi drive for war. In the introduction of his investigation into the 'Arab Predicament' he describes that culture in vivid terms:

> The Arab world . . . would draw back in horror from Saddam Hussein after his cruel conquest of Kuwait in the summer of 1990. But the Iraqi upstart had not emerged out of a void. *He had emerged out of the political culture of populist Arab*

nationalism, out of its sins of omission and commission. He had been hailed and embraced when he did the work of containing the Iranian Revolution.... No alarm bells had gone off as the Iraqi upstart swaggered on his home turf and in the Arab councils of power. He was 'the sword of the Arabs', it was said of him by his admirers.... He had contained the threat from the east – Iran's threat. In time, he held out the promise that he would head west, toward the Mediterranean, to deal with Israel.

The dictator who rose in Baghdad annexed the dreams and resentments of the 'Arab national movement'. Large numbers of Arabs had insisted that their borders were contrived, that they were 'lines in the sand' imposed by foreign powers. Homage had been paid in the Arab historical narrative to the great tale of German unification and to Otto von Bismarck, who had built with 'blood and iron' a great power out of feuding principalities. The Iraqi leader who had warded off the Iranians would step forth to claim the mantle of an Arab Bismarck. The role with which the popular imagination had vested Gamal Abdul Nasser was now Saddam Hussein's. But Saddam waded beyond his depth when he overran Kuwait in the summer of 1990.[250]

Both the self-perception of Saddam Hussein and the very raison d'être of the Iraqi state were constituted in accordance with the ideology described by Ajami. Other than proposing that the Iraqi behaviour was irrational or an act of insanity, the centrality of the cultural driving forces, encapsulated in the idea of Arab unification and the romantic mystification of Saddam Hussein's leadership role, is hard to deny.

3.2.3   *The power of Westphalia reconstituted*

If the Second Persian Gulf War was a conflict in the name of pan-Arabism, it was also its Waterloo. The irony was, that the more Iraq identified with Arab nationalism, the more it was discredited as a programme for foreign-policy formation. The Persian Gulf monarchies and international society knew that the constitutive struggle in this war was ideational, with the protagonists taking on roles that were tailored to their self-perception and appeal of their respective camps: 'pan-Arabist missionaries' on the one side and 'Westphalian disciples' on the other. Analysts and politicians who made the case for US action agreed, indicating that the 'rationale for our no-concessions, no-compromise policy was that anything that made Saddam Hussein appear to have gained anything from his attack on Kuwait would make him a hero in the eyes of the Arab world, and a future menace'.[251] The reason why both sides defined their roles in absolute terms, without resorting to absolute violence (WMD warfare for instance) can be attributed to the 'configurative' nature of the war. According to John Ruggie, the main characteristic of a configurative war is that the adversaries accept each others' sovereignty and fight over strategic and/or territorial advantage instead.[252] 'Operation Desert Storm' would squarely fall into this category because the conflict was primarily aimed at reconstituting the *status quo ante* in the Persian Gulf, rather than altering the territorial map. In turn, this exemplifies the interest of the dominant powers in the international system to defend the institution of sovereignty.

The United States made this point clear on many occasions. According to George Bush the war aim was 'not the conquest of Iraq. It [was] the liberation of Kuwait'.[253] The same rationale, that is the defence of the nation-state order, propelled the United States to support Iraq in its war against Iran. Put simply, both cases represented the relative systemic rejection of Iranian-Islamic and Iraqi-Ba'thist challenges to the Westphalian culture of the international system. Because the challenges were directly linked to the raison d'être and grand ideas of the political elites in Iran and Iraq, they were pervasive and serious, demanding overwhelming measures by international society. The Iranian-Islamic and Iraqi-Ba'thist challenge hence caused the regional regression into a temporal moment of conflict and war, without eventuating in a pervasive transformation of the quasi-Westphalian character of the system itself.

If we continue analysing the period between 1979 and 1991 in one analytical narrative we find further evidence for the salience of the 'logic of Westphalia', that is the resilience of sovereignty as the central institution of international political culture in the face of anti-systemic challenges. With revolution, two inter-state wars, transnational political violence, acute inter and intra security dilemmas and instances of unrestrained warfare, the Persian Gulf during 1979 and 1991 appeared to be the archetypal perennial conflict formation. Political realists would point to these variables and identify the region as a typical example for a 'securitised' anarchy, where the 'war of all against all' and 'kill or be killed' mentality ruled the everyday life of the nation-states. Realists associate this state of affairs with 'Hobbesian' systems of anarchy, where structures of enmity constitute the dominant category of international relations.[254] This appeared to be the regional predicament during the two Gulf Wars between 1980–1988 and 1990–1991. The very attack on the dominant mode of legitimacy in the Persian Gulf by Iranian revolutionism and Iraqi pan-Arabism propelled regional status quo states (the GCC) and international society (most notably the United States) to adopt self-help measures in order to counter the threat to the foundations of the regional order. Moreover, from the perspective of regional society, revolution in Iran exacerbated the fears and insecurities of the other system members to the degree that unrestrained warfare against Iran was accommodated during the country's invasion by Iraq. International society identified the Islamic Republic as a threat, granting *jus ad bellum*, the right to go to war, to Iraq, without providing for standards of *jus in bello*, the right conduct of war itself. The mode of warfare during the Iran–Iraq war, as a conflict over what form of rule constitutes the most viable, competitive unit in the Persian Gulf and beyond, was neither effectively restrained nor explicitly condemned by regional and international society. The 'configurative' war against Iraq in 1991 on the other side came closer to the *jus in bello* norm. Whilst the shooting of retreating Iraqi combatants on the road to Basra and the Iraqi firing of SCUD missiles into Israeli and Saudi Arabian territory may be isolated as incidents of escalation, Iraq refrained from using chemical or biological weapons and the United States attempted to adhere to international norms by avoiding the killing of non-combatants.

These incidents of self-help aside, the structure of regional Gulf politics between 1979 and 1991 does not provide conclusive evidence for a realist interpretation of anarchy in the Persian Gulf. Whilst war was accepted and deemed legitimate as a means to reinstate the status quo, the two inter-state wars were simultaneously controlled and supervised, not in relation to the number of people killed but rather the 'killing' of states.[255] In both wars central ideologies of regional political culture, namely revolutionary Islam and irredentist Arabism, were pitted against global international political culture and its fundamental interest in retaining the status quo. In both cases, international society vehemently and violently upheld the sovereignty principle against the challenging force. In other words, international society was not interested in a total victory of any party in the two conflicts. That logic propelled the GCC states to 'omnibalance' against exogenous and indigenous threats to regime survival against both Iran *and* Iraq during the First Gulf War.[256] The Gulf monarchies supported Saddam Hussein in order to quell the Iranian revolution without, however, favouring a total victory of either one of the parties.

A comparable pattern was evident in the behaviour of the Reagan administration, which openly tilted towards Saddam Hussein at a stage when Iran threatened to overrun Iraqi forces, whilst also providing arms to the Islamic Republic when it was necessary for matters of state expediency. Equally, the US led intervention in Kuwait was meant to reconfigure the equilibrium rather than redraw the map, proven by the fact that the alliance acted as passive bystanders when the Shiites and Kurds were massacred after their uprisings against Saddam Hussein in the aftermath of the Kuwait war. The strategic reason why the US government committed itself neither to an active regime change campaign nor an effective support for the popular revolts against the Iraqi regime, in the aftermath of the cease-fire on 28 February 1991, was that it wanted to avoid a potential 'Balkanisation' of Iraq with the establishment of autonomous Kurdish and Shiite entities in the North and South of the country. Hence, even the victors could not resist the pressures exercised by the institution of sovereignty. In the final analysis, the Bush administration had to subordinate their interest in ousting the Ba'thist regime to the higher interest of preserving the regional (territorial) equilibrium. During both Gulf wars then, the prevalent mentality was not 'kill or be killed' or 'war of all against all'. Neither conflict altered the map of the Persian Gulf and both conflicts were conducted by sovereign nation-states working within established rules, norms and institutions of international society.

3.3   Plus ça change, plus c'est la même chose?

The preceding theoretical discussion of the dynamics in the Persian Gulf during 1979–1991 concluded with the assertion that the period of crisis neither altered the map of the Persian Gulf nor fundamentally changed the dynamics of the cultural system. This supports the argument, it was suggested, that the 'logic of Westphalia' defeated the logic of self-help anarchy. In other words, the anarchical society in the post-crisis Persian Gulf continued to function according to the fundamental rules and institutions of international society. International life in that system was not governed by the image of the Other as a life-threatening enemy, but as a rival with whom states compete for legitimacy, reputation, power and identity. In short: the kill or be killed logic attributed by IR theorist to Hobbes was superseded by the live-and-let-live logic associated with John Locke.[257]

Revolution and inter-state war did not usurp and nullify pre-existing structures in the Persian Gulf. Neither did the regional systemic parameters regress into a momentous stage of rebirth, envisaged by Islamic Iran and Ba'thist Iraq as the historic opportunity to re-craft the Gulf in their respective Islamist or Arabist self-images. The internal structure of the Persian Gulf in the 1990s looked much the same as the Persian Gulf in the 1970s. What follows builds upon this assertion, moving on to investigate how the regional system stabilised itself. That Persian Gulf states returned to the convergence on sovereignty, it will be argued, was due to the re-emergence of a state-centric national identity in Iran after the death of Imam Khomeini in June 1989 and the gradual demise of transnational pan-Arab pressures on (Arab) regional states. Regional order was not re-established due to the determinations of unipolarity, but because of the shift in the identity of the Iranian state on the one hand side and the reassertion of sovereignty norms over transnational pan-Arabist or Islamist loyalties on the other. The modifications were hence both intra-regional, caused by a shift in the cultural preferences of the system itself, and externally determined, caused by the pressures towards isomorphism by global structures.

3.3.1   *The decline of the pan-Arab idea*

It has become a truism that the ability of the Iraqi state to project pan-Arabism as an effective foreign-policy programme diminished due to the 'total defeat' in the Second Gulf War and the circumscribed Iraqi sovereignty thereafter. After all, the Iraqi state had to concede to three serious limitations to its sovereignty: first, the redrawing of the southern frontier in favour of Kuwait according to UN Resolution 833. This resolution was passed unanimously by the Security Council on 27 May 1993 and was implemented by the United Nations Iraq-Kuwait Boundary Demarcation Commission (UNIKBDC), shifting the 200 kilometres frontier line between Iraq and Kuwait northward by 600 metres in favour of Kuwait. As a result, Iraq lost six of the oil wells in the disputed Rumaila oilfield and a significant portion of the Umm Qasr naval base.[258] Second, the establishment of the United Nations Special Committee on Iraq (UNSCOM) and the acceptance of Resolution 687 and 715. The two resolutions provided UNSCOM with the mandate to dismantle the Iraqi WMD capabilities and the elimination of the Iraqi long-range missiles, including future monitoring and verification of the country's non-acquisition of these weapons. And finally, the establishment of the Northern and Southern No-Fly Zones, which constituted the most serious limitation of Iraqi sovereignty. The two no-fly zones were guarded by US/UK air force in order to protect the Shiite enclaves in the Southern marsh areas adjacent to the border with Iran and the Iraqi-Kurdish population in the North. The provision of a 'safe haven' for the Kurds agreed between Iraq and the United Nations on 18 April 1991, even led to the establishment of a quasi-autonomous Kurdish entity, with elections in 1992 and the formation of a Kurdish government thereafter.

The erosion of Iraqi state power was not only due to the obvious loss of sovereignty in the domestic realm, however. By attacking Kuwait, Iraq had also significantly weakened the appeal of pan-Arabism as an ideational system independent from its Iraqi agent. By conducting a major invasion against another Arab country, Iraq had broken the golden rule of inter-Arab relations. Never before had there been a full-scale invasion of one Arab state by another (neither did modern history provide evidence for major Iranian-Arab combat, before the Iran–Iraq war). Despite many conflicts during the past fifty years, including border skirmishes between Algeria and Morocco, Saudi Arabia and Qatar or Libya and Egypt, there has never before been a full-scale invasion, occupation and annexation of one Arab country by another. Documents such as the Arab League Pact (Article 5) or the Iraqi Arab National Charter explicitly supported the sovereignty principle in the conduct of inter-Arab relations. The majority of Arab states favoured that principle as the basis for regional order, and the Gulf War gave impetus to this trend.[259] In fact, by attacking Kuwait, Saddam Hussein achieved the very opposite of what he intended – the primacy of the state and its national interest over transnational loyalties, with each government favouring *raison d'état* over *raison de la nation*.

When Saddam Hussein invaded Kuwait he reinforced an existent trend amongst Arab leaders. Fatigued by the decades of inter-Arab 'cacophony' about the desired regional order and recurrent failures to find a common denominator in the dealings with Israel and the 'Western' world, Arab elites grew increasingly weary of further pan-Arab experiments. Rather than referring to utopian and romantic notions of unity, decision-makers now publicly advocated realism in the conduct of regional affairs.[260] That pan-Arabism could be relatively easily discarded as a source for the formation of foreign policies was largely due to the matured institutionalisation process of formal state structures. However artificial in their origins, by the time of the Second Gulf War, Arab nation-states had become realities 'each with a ganglion of interacting loyalties and interests and careers'.[261] Whilst the new nation-states periodically identified with pan-Arab and Islamic sources of identity in order to legitimate themselves, the process of institutionalising state structures also required forging allegiances between the populace and the regimes themselves. The late Albert Hourani observed in this context that the construction of the post-colonial Arab state required creating and maintaining a state-centric group solidarity (*asabiyya*). In Algeria, Tunisia and Iraq, solidarity was build around affiliation with the party; in Saudi Arabia, Kuwait, Oman, the UAE, Bahrain and Qatar, around tribal leadership of the ruling families; and in Syria and Egypt, solidarity had a militaristic-political character, 'that of a group of politicians who were held together by links established in early life and strengthened by a common experience'.[262]

The corrosion of Arab nationalism allowed for new initiatives in the conduct of regional affairs. With the new-found realism, representations of the Other, (whether Israeli or Iranian) softened, opening up new avenues for dialogue. From the perspective of the Iranian government, the exclusionary precepts of Arab nationalism were the primary factors why a regional security architecture based on Islamic principles had not been realised. Iranian leaders repeatedly stressed that the primary identity of the Gulf was Islamic, neither exclusively Persian nor Arab. Hence, whenever states or a group of states invoked Arab nationalism as a source of state identity, Iran felt vulnerable. Of course, one might rightly point to the fact that Ba'thist Syria had very close relations with Iran all through the war with Iraq and thereafter. But this does not contradict our argument. Hafez al-Assad's regime was hostile to its Ba'thist competitor in Iraq (and vice versa) and was not part of the Persian Gulf equation. Neither did the country enter into alliances with the Gulf states to extend its influence in that direction. When Syria attempted to do so after the Second Gulf War with the 'Damascus Declaration', the post-revolutionary Iranian state changed its attitude and vehemently protested its exclusion from the security agreement.

In fact, the 'Damascus Declaration' or 'six plus two formula', including the six GCC states plus Egypt and Syria drafted on 6 March 1991, is a good example that even state-centred inter-Arab projects became increasingly unattractive because of two principal fears: overexposure to the pressures for pan-Arab unification and Iranian antagonism towards exclusive alignments in the Persian Gulf. At the heart of the 'Damascus Declaration' was the formation of a 26,000 person force that would consist of 10,000 Saudi Arabians, 3,000 Egyptians, 3,000 Syrians and 10,000 troops from the other five GCC states.[263] In return for the security guarantees by Egypt and Syria, the GCC states formally committed themselves to cover the expenses and contribute to the economic development of the two non-littoral states. The Saudi newspaper *Al-Sharq al'-Awsat* wrote at that time that the inclusion of Syria and Egypt was intended to provide 'the nucleus of an Arab peacekeeping force for guaranteeing the security and safety of the Arab states in the Gulf region'.[264] Echoing the short revival of pan-Arab nostalgia, Egypt – itself rehabilitated into mainstream Arab politics by Iraq after the war against Iran – saw the initiative as an opportunity to fill the vacuum left by the containment of Iraq and present the country as the natural candidate for Arab leadership:

> Gulf security is primarily an Arab issue.... Egypt is the region's largest and most influential country. Pan-Arab security is an integral whole. What affects Gulf security necessarily affects the security of all Arab countries, notably Egypt. How then, can one imagine that security arrangements or structure can be established in the region without Egypt playing a role [and] indeed a prominent one?[265]

Paradoxically, despite pursuing the alliance in the name of closer inter-Arab co-operation, it was the very threat of overexposing the state to pan-Arab pressures, that contributed to the early demise of the six-plus-two formula.[266] In the volatile security situation after the Second Gulf War, Saudi Arabia and Kuwait were concerned about the consequences of having Egyptian and Syrian troops on their soil because of the potential threat to the legitimacy of the Al-Saud/Al-Sabah rule respectively. Moreover, the Saudi state was aware that hosting Egyptian and Syrian troops in the case of future domestic alterations to the rule of Hosni Mubarak in Egypt and Hafez al-Assad in Syria might prove threatening to the domestic security of the monarchy itself.[267] From the perspective of the smaller GCC states then, even state-centred inter-Arab projects were considered potentially destabilising. Consequently, Egypt withdrew its 38,000 troops from the region in May 1992 followed by Syria's withdrawal one month later. The Egyptian daily *Al-Ahram* commented during that time: 'We have to acknowledge the apprehensions of the people of the Gulf, or at least some of them, who fear an Arab presence in the Gulf, because the past is not very encouraging.'[268]

The decision to abandon the six-plus-two formula was catalysed by the opposition of the Iranian government. The Gulf monarchies knew that the more the Arab identity of the Gulf was pushed to the forefront, the more resistance came from Iran. The Iranian state repeatedly made clear that it was vehemently opposed to the inclusion of two non-littoral states and the exclusion of itself as the largest country in the Persian Gulf.[269] The six-plus-two parties were aware of the sensitivities attached to sidelining Iran and attempted to reassure the country's leaders by granting them 'observer status'. This symbolic gesture, however, did little to appease the Iranian leadership who continued to articulate a 'regional patriotism' in relation to the Gulf, insisting on the expulsion of *all* extra-regional forces. Faced with the threat of 'dual marginalisation' due to the US containment policy and the six-plus-two formula, the post-Khomeinian Iranian state considered it necessary to reassert its regional position through offensive action. It was within this context that the Rafsanjani administration decided to take a heavy-handed approach towards the island dispute by denying access 'to non-UAE nationals working in the southern, Sharjah-administered part of the Abu Musa island'.[270] Despite all the emotional cacophony surrounding this issue, the action taken was a symbolic snub, signalling that Iran will not accept being sidelined in regional issues. The offensive opposition which was coupled with demurring rhetoric from Tehran, and the reluctance of the GCC states to get sucked into yet another pan-Arab failure, were the two factors contributing to the early demise of the Damascus Declaration, pushing the GCC states towards bilateral agreements with France, the United States and the United Kingdom instead.

In general then, the Second Gulf War gave impetus to the reorganisation of the Arab state system, reflecting a shift from Arab nationalism to the centrality of sovereignty. This modification was evident during the negotiations between Israel and Palestine, which paved the way to the Oslo agreement. With the pressures of pan-Arabism receding, the romantic ideal for reunification of the whole of Palestine with the Arab nation was buried in favour of compromise with the state of Israel and a general state-centric posture in the conduct of inter-Arab affairs. This was true for both 'hesitant' states such as Syria and rather more accommodating actors such as the oil monarchies in the Persian Gulf. Militarily weak, ideologically conservative and struggling with external and internal threats to regime security, the Gulf monarchies – never really in the forefront of pan-Arab action – now considered even tacit inter-Arab projects potentially destabilising. Hence, the GCC saw itself more and more as a localised *Khaliji* (Gulf) entity,[271] and turned towards security guarantees from 'distant others' deemed to be less threatening to the internal sovereignty and security of the state. The 'intimacy' of the Arab selves, social psychologists would suggest, was rejected in favour of the distance of the 'Western others'. Hence, in contradiction to the Council's charter of 26 February 1981, stipulating that 'the region's security and stability are the responsibility of its peoples and countries' and that the organisation calls for 'keeping the entire region free of...the presence of military fleets and foreign bases',[272] the GCC states chose to open up their territory to large numbers of foreign troops. Agreements were signed on a bilateral basis between the

United States on the one hand side and Kuwait, Bahrain, Oman, the UAE and Qatar on the other. The ten-year bilateral military co-operation agreements among those states were complemented with memorandums on security and/or defence co-operation: the United Kingdom signed an agreement with Kuwait; France concluded bilateral treaties with the UAE and Qatar.[273] Under the most far reaching of these agreements, that between the United States and Kuwait, the United States was authorised to store weaponry and military equipment in Kuwait, conduct joint manoeuvres and exercises with the Kuwaiti defence forces and call for logistic support in the event of military confrontations in the Persian Gulf, including access to the Kuwaiti ports and airfields.[274]

3.3.2 The post-revolutionary Iranian state

The second development that contributed to the return of state-centric policies in the Persian Gulf followed from the changes in the internal constitution of the Iranian state after the death of Ayatollah Khomeini in June 1989. With the death of the Imam, the Islamic Republic did not only lose its charismatic leadership and part of its revolutionary appeal, but also its major source of religious and revolutionary legitimacy. Eleven years earlier, days before the return of Khomeini to Tehran, it was Michel Foucault who most prominently cogitated about the political role of the revolutionary leader:

> No head of state, no political leader, even with the support of all the media in his country, can claim today to be the object of so personal and so intense an affection. This attachment is, no doubt, the result of three *things*: Khomeini is *not there*. For fifteen years he has lived in an exile that he himself does not want to leave until the Shah is gone. Khomeini *says nothing*, nothing except no – no to the Shah, to the regime, and to dependency. Finally, Khomeini *is not a politician*. There will be no Khomeini party, there will be no Khomeini government. Khomeini is the point of fixation for a collective will.[275]

Like many, both within and outside of Iran, Foucault underestimated the centrality of Khomeini to events after the success of the revolution. The very fact that he 'was the point of fixation for a collective will' gave him a degree of informal power that made his role indispensable for the state-building process of the Islamic Republic. In turn, the centralisation of the state around his authority made the revolutionary leader irreplaceable, leaving 'an ambiguous foreign-policy legacy for his successors; as his personal authority had been indisputable, his dictates had overridden competing perceptions of national interest or national identity, and his governance was marked by a tendency to mediate among the fractious interests of the divisive political elite'.[276]

The absence of Ayatollah Khomeini necessitated a reorientation of Iranian foreign policies towards accommodation and hence a modified role conception for the external relations of the country. Under the dual leadership of Khomeini's successor as 'spiritual leader', Ayatollah Ali Khamenei, and the Presidency of Hojatoleslam Ali Akbar Hashemi Rafsanjani, the 'Iranian Second Republic'[277] refrained from interfering in the domestic affairs of regional states, focusing instead on reconstructing the war-ravaged economy and reconstituting Iran's regional influence. Analysts have rightly pointed out that after the reinterpretation of revolutionary Islamic internationalism as an effective foreign-policy programme, the post-Khomeinian Iranian state envisaged a regional role as a leading power – *primus inter pares* – for the country.[278] Reverting to symbols of Iranian nationalism 'dramatised' under the Shah, the Iranian Second Republic modified its regional posture, leading to the gradual deconstruction of revolutionary Islamic internationalism and the reemergence of an Iranian nationalist/Shia-Islamic disposition.[279] The pragmatic alterations to the country's state identity were in principle a restatement of the claim to state-centric, as well as ideological leadership in regional affairs. Formulas such as *harim-e amniyat* (security perimeter), *chatr-e amniyati* (security umbrella) and *amniyat-e dast-e jami* (collective security) were principally designed to put forward a 'region only patriotism' under Iranian supervision. The country's foreign-policy elites concurred that 'security of the Persian Gulf states rests solely with regional countries and Iran, which has the longest shore [and] shoulders the greatest part of the task of maintaining security of the region'.[280]

The Second Gulf War provided the opportunity for the Iranian state to apply its altered role conception to a serious crisis scenario in the country's immediate environment. Iran's passive reaction to the Kuwait conflict was aimed at avoiding any significant changes to the political geography of the region. When thirteen days after invading Kuwait, Saddam Hussein formally reaccepted the thalweg delineation of the Shatt al-Arab in order to initiate 'a new life filled with cooperation under the auspices of the principles of Islam', the Iranian state did not consider an 'anti-Western' alliance with Iraq.[281] Despite pressures from some conservative circles to that end, the overwhelming majority of public and elite opinion was opposed to any association with Saddam Hussein's regime. In the public imagination of the Islamic Republic, the Iran–Iraq war continued to be reproduced as *jangeh-tahmilli* ('the forced war') or *defahe-moghaddas* ('holy defence'), which by itself indicates the degree of emotions that were still attached to the eight-year conflict with the Ba'thist state.

Rather than forging an alliance with Saddam Hussein, Iran took the opportunity to reposition itself as the leading power in the Persian Gulf.[282] To that end, the restoration of the regional equilibrium, integration into the world economic system and increasing multilateral engagements were considered central. In that vein, Iran tempered its price policy in OPEC, cultivated its position in the United Nations, turned into an advocate of the Organisation of the Islamic Conference (OIC), and remained passive during the Shia uprisings in southern Iraq in 1992 and in Bahrain during 1994.[283]

The 'pro-consensus' posture of the Rafsanjani administration was immediately welcomed by regional actors. From the perspective of the GCC states, the return to a state centered foreign policy by the Iranian government was deemed conducive to stabilise regional affairs after a decade of revolution and wars. The empirical evidence is intrusive. Immediately after pursuing the policy of détente in accordance with the grand strategic preferences of the Iranian state, relations with the GCC in general and Saudi Arabia and Kuwait in particular strengthened. Diplomatic relations with Saudi

Arabia, severed in 1988, were re-established in March 1991, followed by a meeting between President Rafsanjani and King Fahd in Saudi Arabia one month later and Saudi Foreign Minister Prince Saud Al-Faisal's visit to Tehran in June 1991, the first visit of a high-ranking Saudi delegation since the revolution in 1979. The relation of Iran with Kuwait improved to a comparable high degree immediately after the end of the Iran–Iraq war and was strengthened by talks between Iranian Foreign Minister Ali Akbar Velayati in Kuwait shortly before the Second Persian Gulf War and reciprocated by the visit of Kuwaiti Foreign Minister Sheikh Ahmed al-Sabah to Tehran during the conflict. Here, the apologies of the Kuwaiti leaders for the support granted to Saddam Hussein during the Iran–Iraq war were of special significance to Iran.[284] This was a vindication for the Iranian leadership, in that the country's claim that it too had been a victim of the Iraqi aggression and that the international support to Iraq was 'morally wrong' had been (at least partially) acknowledged.[285]

The rapprochement between Iran and Saudi Arabia also paved the way for better contacts with the GCC. In this regard, Abdallah Bishara, the former Secretary General of the Council, declared during the Second Gulf war that good relations with Iran can be ensued in a 'period of "new pragmatism" in the Gulf'.[286] The re-iteration of sovereignty in the conduct of regional affairs was of particular importance to both sides. In that spirit, both Bishara and Iranian Foreign Minister Velayati accentuated dialogue and mutual understanding as new pillars of relations between the GCC and Iran on the sidelines of the UN General Assembly meetings in New York in late September 1991. According to the joint declaration, the 'new' Persian Gulf context would allow for peaceful settlement of territorial disputes, the mutual acceptance of sovereignty and encouragement of a Persian Gulf security architecture governed by the littoral states themselves.[287]

Whilst the dispute over the two Tunb islands and Abu Mussa impeded further rapprochement between the GCC states and Iran, the Rafsanjani administration was successful in bringing the country back into the regional security equation. The Second Gulf War and the demise of pan-Arabism were hence conducive to the Iranian effort to rebuild its relationship with the GCC member states. Conversely, however, the deployment of US American military troops reinforced Iranian fears of an emerging pax Americana in the Persian Gulf. From the Iranian perspective, Afrasiabi argued, the modified symmetries of interaction

> lent confidence to their expectation of playing a more meaningful role in managing the affairs of the region and, simultaneously, dispossessed them of this confidence by the gloomy prospect of the eclipse of Iranian power by the United States superpower and its allies in the region.[288]

3.3.3   *The determinations of the unipolar transition moment*

The transformation of the international system at the end of the Cold War provided the global context for the Second Gulf War and its aftermath. During the Iran–Iraq war, the United States refrained from deploying massive military force in the Persian Gulf because of the opposition of the Soviet Union, limiting its regional actions to containing a unipolar configuration in the Gulf. This was achieved by balancing the two principal regional powers, Iran and Iraq, against each other. In turn this provided the United States with the opportunity to assume the role of guardian of the status quo, forcing assertive powers to return to state-centred policies in the conduct of regional affairs.

With the transformation of the international system and the ensuing end of bipolarity, the United States government felt emboldened to assume a rather more proactive regional role. The Second Gulf War was central to this effort, providing the opportunity for the United States to position itself according to the new realities of the post-Cold War world order. By attacking Iraq, the United States did not only act according to the country's traditional aim to secure the free flow of oil from the Persian Gulf and avoid a unipolar configuration in the region, it took the opportunity to assume a new role identity as the only remaining superpower. The hope for global security, it was typically argued, could only be delivered by 'American strength and will – the strength and will to lead a unipolar world, unashamedly laying down the rules of world order and being prepared to enforce it'.[289] The Republican Bush administration embraced this new global outlook. When Iraq is broken, the President told the US Congress in his 1991 State of the Union Address, we 'will have sent an enduring warning to any dictator or despot, present or future, who contemplates outlaw aggression'. America, he envisioned, had to burden the share of delivering the 'New World Order', because '[a]mong the nations of the world, only the United States has had both the moral standing, and the means to back it up. We are the only nation on earth' Bush pointed out 'that could assemble the forces of peace'.[290]

In many ways the Second Gulf War was about the construction and reproduction of what it meant to be 'American' after the demise of communism as the chief nemesis of the 'Western' world. For four decades, the Cold War context provided the United States with a central ideological and discursive basis for shared identity. What Americans were (the leaders of the free world, democratic, respectful of human rights, Christian) was easily juxtaposed with what they were not (communist, dictatorial, atheist etc.).[291] The global recognition of this role was on its pinnacle after the fall of the Berlin wall and the adoption of capitalist and democratic systems by the former Warsaw Pact states. It was not at least this context which explains the high degree of legitimacy attached to the US war role against Iraq. 'Had such an invasion taken place during the Cold War' it is rightly argued 'there would have been no comparable global war'.[292]

From the perspective of US decision-makers, the Second Gulf War provided the suitable opportunity to reiterate the country's claim to global leadership in the absence of a serious military threat to US security. In order to assert that role, the image of an Other, prominent enough to be castigated and isolated enough to be persecuted, had to be invoked. After the invasion of Kuwait, Iraq fit exactly into this profile, with Saddam Hussein playing the role of the new Hitler and his Ba'th party likened to the Soviet politburo. Describing the mood generated by the end of the

Cold War and the imagery of an ensuing new world order, Noam Chomsky wrote during that time:

> The issue was raised to cosmic significance, with visions of a New World Order of peace and justice that lay before us if only the new Hitler could be stopped before he conquered the world – after having failed to overcome post-revolutionary Iran with its severely weakened military, even with the support of the U.S., U.S.S.R., Europe and the major Arab states.[293]

David Campbell was even more straightforward in his analysis, juxtaposing the Iraq experience of the United States in the Second Gulf War, with the country's engagement in Vietnam:

> For all the attempt to draw a contrast between the two experiences ... many of the features of the war in Vietnam resonated with the campaign against Iraq. Most notable in this regard was the reproduction of the myth of the frontier, in which territorial space becomes intertwined with ethical identity such that the fluid boundary and persistent struggle between 'civilisation' and 'barbarism' is rendered in terms of geopolitical conflict. Just as enemy territory in Vietnam was referred to as 'Indian territory', so too was the same said of Iraq. . . . The Gulf conflict and the discourse of moral certitude that ratified it can thus be seen as another instance of the orientalist and long-held disposition in the United States to seek regeneration of the self through violence. In this context, George Bush's postwar reflection that 'America rediscovered itself during Desert Storm' takes on additional significance. Indeed, this understanding of the conflict seemed to satisfy a widely felt desire.[294]

The cardinal mistake of the Iraqi state, that is, launching a full-scale invasion of another country that was considered 'friendly' by international standards, was taken as an opportunity by 'neo-conservative' circles in the United States to produce a new image for itself as the guardian of world peace.[295] International society empowered the United States to enact this role, because within the context of the Second Gulf War the mission to reconstitute the status quo and fight against the Iraqi dictator was considered just and legitimate causes for war. The US role was hence carried forward by international political culture and its propensity for state-centrism and the perseverance of nation-state sovereignty. Notwithstanding the new world order rhetoric followed by the Bush White House and propounded by neo-conservative ideologues, 'Operation Desert Storm' was not designed to conquer Iraq, nor even to crush the Iraqi state.[296] Rather, putting forward the world order norm was meant to symbolise a benchmark for dissent in the post-Cold war international system. The impression was created that deviation from the rules and norms of appropriate behaviour enshrined in the international political culture of the 'new' global system, will only be tolerated to the extent that US interests are not compromised. The new world order norm was hence the forerunner of the norm of 'preventive intervention', formally accepted as the US national security strategy in the aftermath of 11 September 2001, which turned out to be central to the US/UK invasion of Iraq in March 2003. In many ways then, the Second Gulf War was the precipitant of a neo-conservative current in US politics. From the perspective of this generation of decision-makers, the post-Cold War role identity of the United States had to be militarily offensive, idealistic and self-conscious about the newly gained eminence after the demise of the Soviet Union. It was not at least the victory against Iraq that provided for the 'psychological ease' to pursue that role:

> If the US was to retain hegemony, the US public had to support a globalist role but with the end of the Soviet threat, the US military-industrial complex needed a new mission to justify continued military spending. This new mission would be a Pax Americana, the defence of the liberal world order emerging from the defeat of communism against the remaining threat of Third World – especially Islamic – pariah states. Moreover, the Pentagon was determined that the war would be fought with the unrestrained application of its massive firepower and new high-tech military capabilities. Only if fought in this way would a war assure the American public that international policing could be cheap and incur minimal casualties. The Iraqi invasion posed a perfect opportunity to banish the Vietnam syndrome at home.[297]

In policy terms the new constitution of the US role conception required substitution of a *Pax Americana* for an intra-regional order in the Persian Gulf. Viewed within this context, the postwar dual strategy of the Bush administration makes sense: by signing bilateral security agreements with the GCC states, the country tied the security needs of the Gulf monarchies directly to its own presence in the Gulf. Second, by containing the two principal powers, Iran and Iraq, the United States secured its privileged role, making sure that its position will not be challenged by an antagonistic actor. Thus, in contrast to the UN phrased patent for the 'promotion of international security and peace in the Persian Gulf area' invoked in the wake of the Iraqi invasion of Kuwait, the United States reverted to its traditional block-building policy, attempting to isolate Iran and Iraq whilst promoting 'friendly' powers such as Saudi Arabia or the other smaller Persian Gulf states. By failing to propose an *inclusive* regional security order, however, US policies contributed to the sense of insecurity in the region. As a result, Iran felt isolated and asserted its regional position through offensive action (the Abu Mussa incident); the oil market fluctuated, creating popular socio-economic dissent; the United States and its allies resorted to flooding the region with arms, triggering a regional arms race that put even more pressure on the crisis-ridden economies; and perhaps most importantly, Saddam Hussein remained in charge of the Iraqi state apparatus and felt undeterred to reconstitute his domestic power position through coercive action.[298] In retrospect even staunch advocates of the war such as Margaret Thatcher had to agree with the assessment of the analysts, conceding that the lack of an inclusive postwar strategy led to a sense of self-inflicted helplessness in the face of the ensuing postwar crisis in Iraq and the overall volatile situation in the Gulf region itself:

> I don't see how the West can .... make him [Saddam Hussein] surrender. There
> is a balance of power...between Iraq and Iran....Now, just look, there is
> the aggressor, Saddam Hussein, still in power. There is the President of the
> United States, no longer in power. There is the Prime Minister of Britain who
> did quite a lot to get things there, no longer in power. I wonder who won?[299]

3.4   The new old Gulf and the full cycle of regional politics

This chapter opened with the assertion that revolution in Iran had altered the 'truth
conditions' in the Persian Gulf. What amounted to aggression in the modified
regional system, it was argued, was not determined by the act itself, but by the
representation of the act in international society. In relation to the First Gulf War,
societal approval contributed to the social construction of the Iraqi war role. In order
to provide the Iraqi state with the minimal legitimation to pursue its invasion
against Iran, it was pointed out, the aggression had to be represented as an act of
'self-defence'. This was achieved by supporting the Iraqi war role internationally and
denouncing the Iranian revolution as inherently radical and hegemonic.

Strengthened by the systemic support generated during the Iran–Iraq war, Saddam
Hussein felt emboldened to attempt a second invasion, this time against Kuwait.
International support for the Iraqi war role during the Iran–Iraq war conveyed the
message to the Ba'thist state that it could assert the country's supremacy in the Persian
Gulf by a combination of military aggression and diplomatic brinkmanship. System
effects were interpreted against the background of the Ba'thist/Arab nationalist
identity of the Iraqi state. By attacking Iran and Kuwait in the name of Arabism, the
Iraqi regime acted according to its deeply internalised pan-Arabist motivational
drives. The very raison d'être of the regime was tied to that ideal, exercising pressures
on the Iraqi state to enact its self-designated role in order to retain its prominence in
the Arab world.

In the second place it was observed, that the 'quasi-Westphalian' posture of the
anarchical Gulf society was reinforced after the Kuwait war by three transformations
in the prevailing regional political cultures: the decline of pan-Arabism as an effective
foreign-policy programme; the return to state-centrism of the post-revolutionary
Iranian state and the presence of the United States as a status quo power. Hence, after
a decade of revolution, two inter-state wars and numerous domestic crisis, the structure
of the regional society remained essentially the same, with striking similarities to the
parameters characteristic for the pre-revolutionary period.

That the state of affairs after the 'decade of ideational belligerence' followed the
same rules and conditions that it had throughout the modern existence of the Persian
Gulf (notwithstanding changes in actors), is supported by a theoretical assessment of
international life in the postwar Gulf. Essentially, rivalry continued to determine
regional perceptions, guiding the system (and the United States as a new actor)

towards recurrent periods of domestic and inter-state crisis, similar to regional politics during the 1970s. The Iranian escalation of the island issue, the intrusion into Iraqi territory by Turkey in pursuance of Kurdish rebels and Iran against the 'Peoples Mojahedin' movement (MKO), border skirmishes on the Arabian peninsula and the carving up of Iraq into Northern and Southern no-fly zones constituted new sources of conflict, without however, threatening the very existence of the nation-states involved. International life in the Persian Gulf continued to have its occasional 'shoot outs,' without bringing about the annihilation of any actor. In contrast to the period of self-help where security was either scarce or virtually non-existent, the mutually accepted right to existence provided respite from life-threatening conflicts.

With the emergence of state-centric policies and the relative decline of transnational loyalties, regional states had access to a larger pool of security. The orientation of formerly revisionist powers towards preserving the status quo reconstituted sovereignty as an institution, softening the security dilemma amongst regional states. In turn, the hardening of the sovereignty principle opened up space for positive-sum rather than zero-sum calculations, because accommodating foreign policies were rewarded by international society. Accordingly, the post-revolutionary Iranian state tempered its price policy in OPEC and distanced itself from the *fatwa* against Salman Rushdie. Both policies were immediately conducive to a repositioning of the Iranian republic. The former brought about better relations with the GCC states and the latter led to the re-establishment of full diplomatic relations with most states of the EU. In general then, the foreign-policy tendencies of Iran and the other Persian Gulf states followed a similar pattern to that of the 1970s. In both systems – pre-revolutionary and post-revolutionary – regional states aimed at preserving the territorial status quo, reinforcing the institution of sovereignty and exercising restraint in the use of force. These policies strengthened the Gulf society, without however transmuting it into an inclusive discourse about a communitarian regional security architecture.

4   Whither the leviathan

Sources of co-operation and
conflict in the 'post-romantic'
Persian Gulf

4.1   Introduction

In the conclusion to Chapter 3 it was asserted that the anarchical society in the
Persian Gulf remained fragile. Whilst the demise of transnational loyalties
(pan-Arabism, Iranian revolutionism) and the presence of the United States as a
status quo power diminished the likelihood of an all out regional war, regional states
reserved – and periodically exercised – the right to use violence to advance their
interests. Since culture and identities consist of relatively orderly, internalised sets of
classifications which allow states to interpret international life, the fact that the past
had an impact on the present should not be surprising. Once the rival cultural
formation was in place, actors in the Persian Gulf had a shared knowledge that they
were rivals which helped constitute their identities and interests. In turn, regional
states acted upon their internalised identities in ways that confirmed to the 'Other'
that they were a threat, reproducing the regional culture of anarchy. This said, the
tendency towards cultural reproduction does not leave us with the a-historical
determinism of neo-realist theory (i.e. eternal self-help Anarchy). Cultures are not
monolithic systems, immune to external and internal transformations.

> Cognitive beliefs about the world are constantly tested by actual events. While
> failures and surprises can be reinterpreted so that they do not contradict existing
> norms and beliefs, they also create pressures that can lead to a reevaluation and
> modification of the culture.[300]

In other words, whilst culture is not invariably reproducible, neither are structural
properties constituting cultural systems resistant to change.

Building upon the argument about the resilience and elasticity of culture, this
chapter investigates emergent sources of conflict and co-operation in the Persian
Gulf. It is argued that after the Second Gulf War, regional interaction revealed both
processes of reification of the regional culture of anarchy and contestation of its
underlying properties. On the one hand side, anarchy was contested because appre-
hension of ideological state identities and the adoption of democratic principles in
the domestic realm instead, created new incentives for co-operative policies amongst
regional actors. The most significant step towards 'religious democracy' was pursued

in Iran, with the ascendancy to power of Mohammad Khatami paving the way for internal reforms and external co-operation. This does not mean, however, that regional relations were devoid of conflict. Identity politics continued to be fought out on an exclusionary basis, with regional actors subscribing to roles that were conservative enough to retain the status quo but not amicable enough to guarantee genuine security integration. Comparable to regional relations before the revolution in Iran in 1979 then, regional states successfully stabilised inter-state relations, whilst failing to institute communitarianism as the dominant mode of regional interaction.

On the other hand, tensions were exacerbated by the re-constitution of the US state identity after the Cold War and the increasing prominence of a neo-conservative current in US politics. The influence of neo-conservatism pushed the country into the role of global hegemon – a self-attribution that was inherently contradictory to the international political culture in the Persian Gulf and beyond. By assuming the role of unipolar actor, US policies provoked resistance, exacerbating the 'legitimacy dilemmas' of regional states whose external security was directly associated with the United States (i.e. the GCC states but most notably Saudi Arabia). With the legitimation of the GCC states compromised and without popular mechanisms of state approval, the security vacuum was exploited by 'neo-fundamentalist' transnational networks which targeted weak regional states, internationalising their agenda and basing their popular support on the shared animosity towards the presence of 'foreign' troops in Saudi Arabia and elsewhere. After the Second Gulf War there was hence a divergent trend in the international politics of the region. Whilst asserting the role of global leviathan by the United States contradicted the ideational structure dominating the Persian Gulf system, hence creating friction, regional actors adopted less confrontational foreign policies than they did before, instead embarking on creating mutual trust and partnerships.

4.2   Sources of co-operation: beyond rivalry?

Since Immanuel Kant's famous 'democratic peace' thesis, political scientists have empirically validated the causal relationship between domestic democratisation and restraint in the use of force against another democracy. Cultural essentialism, however, has sometimes hampered investigating the correlation between democratisation and restraint in the external use of force in regions that were considered to be inherently anti-democratic and conflict ridden. The Persian Gulf is a case in point. From the perspective of most external analysts, the region continues to represent the archetypal conflict formation, with few mechanisms for the prevention of the use of force in international relations. Realist theory would point to the enduring security dilemma, balance of power considerations and the self-interest of regional states to explain the sources of conflict. With a simple overview of regional relations after the Second Gulf War, realists would find ample evidence to support the core concepts of their theory: Civil War in the North of Iraq during 1994 and 1996 between the Kurdish Democratic Party (KDP) of Massoud Barzani and the Patriotic Union of Kurdistan (PUK) led by Jalal Talebani; and unresolved border disputes between

Qatar and Bahrain over the Hawar islands, the Dibal and Jarada shoals and the status of the Qatari coastal settlement of Zubara, the dispute over the sovereignty of the islands of Qaru and Umm-al Maradim between Saudi Arabia and Kuwait and the Qatari-Saudi conflict over the demarcation of their borders, which culminated into minor border clashes in 1992.

Contrary to what (neo)realist theory would predict however, those occurrences of conflict and the improved relative power position of the Iranian state after the defeat of Saddam Hussein did not lead to escalation of insecurities amongst regional states. This was largely due to domestic changes and not balance of power strategies. Since the latter half of the 1990s there was an observable trend towards more public participation in most Gulf societies, concomitantly accompanied by less confrontational policies in international affairs. The most far-reaching reforms were accomplished in Iran, instituting the transformation of the Iranian state from a *theocratic* Islamic republic to a *democratic* Islamic republic which is evolving to this date. Political reform was not confined to the Iranian context, however. Bahrain, Kuwait, Oman and even Saudi Arabia experimented with new modes of public participation as well. The minimum argument that can be suggested is that the idea of 'democracy' – undefined, abstract, unspecified as it is handled – has entered the political jargon in the Persian Gulf and has hence a presence in the political discourse of the elites in power. Whether it is termed 'Islamic democracy' or 'liberal authoritarianism' is perhaps dependent upon which literature and intellectual context we refer to in order to legitimate our labels. The important aspect for our case is that the democracy norm, with its myriad forms of interpretations, has occupied a prominent place in the discourse amongst political and socio-economic elites in the Persian Gulf. Symbolic gestures as the official congratulations offered by Iranian President Mohammad Khatami to the Bahraini monarch Sheikh Hamad after the parliamentary elections in that country or the exchanges between Kuwaiti and Iranian parliamentary delegations suggest that there is a political identification with the idea of 'democracy' which goes beyond mere rhetoric for domestic consumption.

4.2.1 Enter Islamic democracy: pluralistic reform in the Persian Gulf

The case of Iran is symptomatic for the tide of reform in the Persian Gulf. Since the democratic movement in the country secured the election victory of the reformist President Mohammad Khatami on 23 May 1997, followed by the success of the 'Second Khordad Movement' (named after the date Khatami won the presidential election) in the parliamentary (*majlis*) elections on 18 February 2000, and the re-election of Khatami in 2001, the ideas of civil society, pluralism, democracy and empowerment have occupied the policy manuals of the majority of political parties in the country.[301] The composition of the reform movement is emblematic for its growing appeal. In the contemporary political landscape of Iran it encompasses 'technocrats', the 'nouveau riche', the Islamic left (an aggregation of lay intellectuals and religious nationalists) and progressive clerics.[302] In addition, numerous organised and influential opposition groups and individuals operate in the grey area between state and civil society, including the 'Iranian Freedom Movement' headed by Ibrahim Yazdi, lay intellectuals such as Abdolkarim Souroush, oppositional clerics such as Mohsen Kadivar or Abdollah Nouri and high-ranking religious authorities such as Grand Ayatollah Hossein Ali Montazeri.[303] The majority of these groups and individuals criticise the government on Islamic grounds, advocating reform within the boundaries of the existent constitution.

Despite the ongoing struggle about the extent and meaning of reforms and the idea of an 'Islamic democracy' which has stymied the democratisation process and led to repeated rioting and demonstrations against the state, it is hard to deny that the changes in contemporary Iran are nothing less than structural, long term and pervasive. 'Having freed themselves from the cordon of previously luminous ideologies' Mehrzad Boroujerdi observes 'many of Iran's intellectuals are now busy articulating serious and sophisticated criticisms of such autochthonous and quotidian features of Iranian political life as authoritarianism, censorship, clientalism, cult of personality, etatism, fanaticism, influence peddling, partisanship, and violence'.[304] The objective observer can not help but to notice that the idea of a 'religious democracy' has become an inextricable factor of Iranian political culture, cutting across the jargon and programmes of both 'conservatives' and 'reformers', concomitantly appearing as the dominant meta-narrative of societal activism and legitimating agent of the Iranian state.[305] Hence, democratising political Islam (or 'Islamicising' democracy depending from which perspective it is viewed) is as much a political phenomenon as it is an intellectual programme, occupying the paradigms of most contemporary Iranian philosophers and social scientists. As Robin Wright noted: 'Just as the Reformation was critical to the Age of Enlightenment and the birth of modern democracy in the West, so too have Iranian philosophers advanced a reformation within Islam that is critical to lasting political change.'[306]

Iran was not the only country in the Persian Gulf experimenting with political democratisation. Even the conservative monarchies who for centuries relied upon tribal affiliation (*asabyya*) to secure their political power felt the pressure to formalise the relationship between state and society. Challenged by recurrent domestic dissent, the GCC states implemented tentative measures to open up the political systems, allowing for public participation whilst institutionalising the rule of the state. In Bahrain, the ascendancy to power of Sheikh Hamad bin Isa al-Khalifa after the death of his father Sheikh Isa in 1998 led to the implementation of reforms in order to open up the political system and enhance the standing of the country's Shiite majority and ethnic and religious minorities. To that end, Hamad al-Khalifa appointed a Consultative Council in the beginning of 2000, including representatives from the Jewish, Christian and Indian community as well as four women. In December of the same year, the 'National Action Charter' advocated transforming Bahrain into a constitutional monarchy, formalising the rule of the al-Khalifa as a hereditary monarchy, whilst introducing a two chamber parliament with equal legislative rights. The first chamber, consisting of forty deputies would be elected and the second with the same number of deputies would be appointed by the King. Further suggestions included the separation of the legislature, executive and judiciary branches, equal treatment of all citizens in the courts of law, and the provision of a Constitutional Court and an

Audit Bureau independent from the government. On 14 February 2001, the 'National Action Charter' was approved with a nation-wide plebiscite. One year later, the proposals of the Charter were incorporated into the Bahraini constitution, followed by municipal elections on 9 May and 16 May 2002 and parliamentary elections on 24 October of the same year.

The other GCC states had comparable experiences with increased public participation in the political process. Kuwait held four consecutive parliamentary elections since 1992, leading to occasional stand-offs between the parliament dominated by conservative Islamic deputies and the al-Sabah monarchy over the relationship with the United States. Sultan Qabus of Oman established a new Consultative Council (*majlis-al shura*) in 1991 and a Council of State (*majlis al-dawla*) in 1997, preceded by a quasi-constitution or 'Basic Law', setting out (in theory at least) the freedom of press and of assembly and prohibition of discrimination of any kind as well as the definition of the executive rights of the state. Similar moves were pursued in Qatar, where a new constitution in 2002 provided for the establishment of an elected national parliament within the tribal rule of the al-Thani family. Even the Kingdom of Saudi Arabia allowed for periodical, confined political activism outside the monopoly of the al-Saud. Most recently, the relaxed atmosphere was taken as an opportunity by 104 intellectuals and activists to sign a petition, calling for the creation of a consultative (*shura*) council and formation of regional legislators by direct elections, independence of the judiciary, freedom of expression, assembly and human rights according to international standards and less restrictions on the involvement of women in public life.[307]

4.2.2 Harvesting the fruits of domestic change: towards a 'democratic peace?'[308]

These domestic democratisation processes contributed to the mutually reassuring predictions of behaviour amongst the GCC states and Iran. The constructive engagement between the Islamic Republic and the GCC states received a decisive impetus with the election of Mohammad Khatami as the fifth President of the Islamic Republic on 23 May 1997. The election of Khatami gave impetus to the critical reinterpretation of Iran's foreign policy strategies. Not that the revolutionary ideas such as third-world cooperation, Islamic communitarianism, anti-zionism and anti-imperialism were discarded in toto. But the adoption of pragmatic foreign policies to attain these long term ground strategic preferences reassured regional states opening up the path towards reconciliation.[309] The rotating chairmanship of the Organisation of the Islamic Conference (OIC) and its eighth session in Tehran on 9 December 1997 gave Khatami a well choreographed and effectively organised framework for the introduction of the Iranian dual policy calculus – democratisation at home and constructive engagement and dialogue abroad. In an intellectual discourse about the idea of an 'Islamic civil society' rooted in the concept of *Madinat ul-Nabi* (the City of the Prophet), Khatami elaborated:

> In the civil society that we espouse, although it is centred around the axis of Islamic thinking and culture, personal or group dictatorship or even the tyranny

of the majority and elimination of the minority has no place. In such a society, man, due to the very attribute of being human, is venerated and revered and his rights respected. Citizens of an Islamic civil society enjoy the right to determine their own destiny, supervise the governance and hold the government accountable. The government in such a society is the servant of the people and not their master, and in every eventuality, is accountable to the people whom God has entitled to determine their own destiny. Our civil society is not a society where only Muslims are entitled to rights and are considered citizens, Rather, all individuals are entitled to rights, within the framework of law and order. Defending such rights ranks among the important fundamental duties of the government.[310]

Given the quantitative and qualitative participation, especially from the Persian Gulf and non-Gulf Arab states (including a high-ranking delegation of the Palestinian National Authority led by Yassir Arafat) the Tehran session of the OIC not only upgraded the image of the Islamic Republic but enhanced the profile of the organisation as a whole.[311] Having secured the presence of a high-ranking Saudi delegation headed by Crown Prince Abdallah bin Abd' al-Aziz and deputy commander of the Saudi Arabian National Guard (SANG) Shaykh Abd al-Aziz al-Tuwayjiri – by itself a reorientation of Saudi policies away from the implicit approval of the US American policy of isolation – the momentum of pan-Islamic solidarity provided the desired scenario to expand upon the role of the Islamic countries and Iran in world politics:

> In the interdependent world of today where the security of different regions is indivisible, striving towards the promotion of mutual trust and the establishment of peace are considered a universal responsibility. Cultivation of confidence is the first and most appropriate strategic approach to ensuring security. Creating the necessary grounds for establishing mutual trust and alleviating or reducing security concerns should be placed at the top of bilateral relations between Muslim countries, and should be accorded a higher priority in the agenda of the Organisation of the Islamic Conference.[312]

The two interdependent concepts, namely the institutionalisation of an 'Islamic-democratically' legitimated domestic constituency and the projection of dialogue and détente abroad, constituted the meta-narrative for the political disposition of 'post-Second Khordad' Iran. Apart from having consolidated the selective reinterpretation of Iranian-Islamic utopianism already initiated by Rafsanjani, the shifting premise to state-centred multilateralism equipped the Iranian state with the necessary ideational impetus to enhance its communicative competency *vis-à-vis* the Gulf monarchies of the Persian Gulf (and beyond). Without compromising the grand strategic preferences of the state, the Khatami administration successfully managed the transition away from the country's image as an antagonistic actor to a pragmatic and constructive force for regional stability. Of particular significance from the perspective of the Iranian state was the diplomatic backing it secured with its modified posture, especially in relation to its continued stand-offs with the United States. The very fact that Iran was able to organise a major Islamic summit with the widespread international media coverage during the period of an apparently all-encompassing domination of the US dual containment calculus, was conducive to the country's campaign to expose the mediocrity of the approach. The immediate diplomatic success at the OIC which declared that it 'sympathises with the Islamic Republic of Iran' and castigated the Iran-Lybia Sanctions Act as 'against international law and norms, as null and void',[313] only contributed to the newly found comfort of the Iranian state.

After its injection into the regional security culture, the narratives of dialogue and co-operation translated into initiatives reciprocated by the primary addressees of the Iranian policies: the monarchies of the Persian Gulf. Bilateral relations with Kuwait, already growing steadily since the Second Persian Gulf War, were cemented during the OIC meeting in Tehran. The June 1998 visit of the Kuwaiti interior minister established the framework for the low-key security agreement signed on 2 October 2000 between the Iranian Interior Minister Abdolvahed Mousavi-Lari and his Kuwaiti counterpart Sheikh Mohammad Khaled al-Sabah in Kuwait City, establishing a co-operative framework for the prevention of drug smuggling, terrorism and organised crime.[314]

The relations between Saudi Arabia and Iran improved to a similar degree despite the rival ideational systems underlying the Wahhabi-Saudi state and the Shia-Iranian Islamic Republic. With hindsight, the representation of the post-revolutionary 'Iranian-Shia self' and the 'Saudi-Wahhabi other', redrawn in the process of the 'ideologisation' of state policies in the Persian Gulf after 1979, proved to leave enough room for critical deconstruction (and this despite the explicit condemnation of the al-Saud in Ayatollah Khomeini's will). Whilst the mix of revolutionary rhetoric, anarchic turmoil, national mobilisation for war and post-revolutionary state building during the first years of the Islamic Republic contracted the inter-state communicative power of the country, the reformist movement headed by Khatami reinvigorated state authority over the channels of foreign and security policy, empowering the government to divest the relationship with Saudi Arabia from its emotional demeanour.

It should be noted that the initiatives of the Iranian state were reciprocated due to the developing regionalist foreign-policy disposition of Saudi Arabia under the leadership of the country's de facto ruler Crown Prince Abdullah and the ambition of the Saudi state to selectively untie the country's policies from the United States. As a result, bilateral relations between Riyadh and Tehran, in a relatively short period of time, were transformed from insecurity and enmity to co-operation and consensus. The practical-policy manifestation of the new quality of interaction is multidimensional and extends into the sensitive realms of security, religion and political ideology. The rather more unproblematic issues of mutual benefit, that is, the approximation of economic strategies within OPEC and the implementation of a policy of equilibrium and stability in the Persian Gulf, were agreed upon on the sidelines of the visit of former President and Head of the Iranian Expediency Council Rafsanjani to Saudi Arabia in March 1998. Accompanied by Iranian Oil Minister Bijan Namdar-Zanganeh and a high-ranking business delegation, the March 1998 consultations with Saudi Oil Minister Ali Naimi created the framework for the co-ordination of relative production quotas within OPEC and an overall stabilisation of the oil market.[315]

The March 1998 negotiations between the two countries were expanded with a substantive agreement on joint investment in the technical, industrial and engineering fields, signed between the Saudi Petrochemical and Metal Industry Director and the Secretary General of the Iranian Chamber of Commerce in Tehran in May 1998.[316] The importance of the agreement, which extended beyond joint investment projects in the aforementioned sectors and entailed also clauses on environmental, consular, cultural, sport, communication and transport co-operation,[317] was further substantiated by the June 1998 visit of the Saudi Minister of Public Works and Housing Prince Mutaib ibn Abd al-Aziz and the participation of Saudi Arabia at the twenty-fourth International Trade Fair held in Tehran in October 1998.

The institutionalisation of economic co-operation, further strengthened by Iran's decision to suspend drilling operations in the offshore Dorra gas field whose maritime boundaries in the Persian Gulf are disputed by Saudi Arabia, Kuwait and the Islamic Republic,[318] was complemented by bilateral consultations in the sensitive realm of security. Confidence-building measures included the March 1998 visit of an Iranian warship at the port of Jeddah, a two-day visit to Iran in April 1999 by Saudi Foreign Minister Prince Saud Al-Faisal, followed by a five-day visit of Saudi Defence Minister Prince Sultan – the first visit of a Saudi defence minister to Iran since the revolution in 1979. During his consultations with King Fahd and Crown Prince Abdullah in Saudi Arabia in May 1999, President Khatami reiterated the intention of his government to establish a regional security framework that includes all the littoral states of the Persian Gulf. The official position of the government had been previously specified during the eighth seminar on 'Regional Approaches in the Persian Gulf' at the Institute for Political and International Studies, the research think tank of the Iranian Ministry of Foreign Affairs. Addressing the seminar on 24 February 1998, Foreign Minister Kamal Kharrazi re-stressed the need to implement an inclusive, collective security framework based on the notion of *amniyat-e daste-jami* (collective security) already suggested by the Rafsanjani administration:

> We have consistently stated that security in the Persian Gulf cannot be 'imported'.... Disputes and misunderstanding can, and must, be resolved through peaceful means, without resorting to coercive measures. The first step... is by building trust and evolving meaningful confidence-building measures.[319]

Within the framework of confidence-building measures, the Iranian state signalled its acceptance of the legitimacy of the al-Saud leadership in Saudi Arabia and the importance of the country for regional stability. The change of perception, whilst not absolute and irreversible, moved beyond mere rhetoric and symbolism. The signing of a low-key security agreement between Saudi Interior Minister Prince Nayef bin Abdul-Aziz and his Iranian counterpart Abdolvahed Mussavi-Lari in April 2001, on the first visit of a Saudi interior minister to Iran since the revolution in 1979, formalised the changed prospects of Saudi-Iranian relations.[320] Whilst encompassing 'low security' issues such as border surveillance and policing, money laundering, terrorism and drug trafficking, the agreement institutionalised the upgraded social, cultural and political exchange after Khatami's election and contributed to an overall stabilisation of relations between Iran and the GCC.[321]

At the same time that it was improving relations with Kuwait and Saudi Arabia, Iran upgraded bilateral relations with Oman, Qatar and Bahrain. The strategy of engagement followed a similar pattern, moving from economic co-operation to include security arrangements. With Oman, the Islamic Republic signed a security deal in a comparable format as the agreements with Saudi Arabia and Kuwait, whilst agreeing on joint development of an offshore gas field in disputed waters.[322] Relations with Bahrain exalted to a similar high level, leading to the signing of several agreements, including in the realm of mutual security. In sum, regional relations were stabilised to a degree that diplomatic consultations about the issues of concern and economic co-operation superseded coercive measures. By the end of the 1990s, Iran and the member states of the GCC had established a regional *modus operandi* that prevented coercive measures and antagonistic rhetoric. The consolidation of Khatami's position by the election success of the Second Khordad movement in the *majlis* (Iranian Parliament) elections in February 2000[323] and his re-election in 2001 added to the higher degree of security in inter-state relations and reassured the Gulf sheikhdoms that the strategy of the Khatami administration remained legitimated and hence sustainable, as long as the reformist movement remained able to sustain its domestic constituency in Iran.[324]

4.3   Sources of conflict: hegemonic penetration and regional resistance

One of the undervalued consequences of 'Operation Desert Storm' is the 'security transaction' that took place between the Persian Gulf region and the United States. By linking the security of the Gulf monarchies to its own, and by stationing large numbers of troops in these countries, the United States created a fundamental interdependence between its own security and the security of the region. Of course, the official proclamation of interdependence had already been made by President Carter in 1980 (and before that by Richard Nixon). In an effort to position the United States as the dominant external player in the region (deemed to be part of an 'Arc of Crisis' in Zbigniew Brzezinski's terminology), Carter declared in his State of the Union Address on 23 January 1980: 'An attempt by any outside force to gain control of the Persian Gulf region will be regarded as an assault on the vital interests of the United States of America. And such an assault will be repelled by any means necessary, including military force.'[325] The Second Gulf War was taken as an opportunity to solidify the US security engagement in the Persian Gulf. Never, since the withdrawal of the British in 1971, had there been a comparable degree of formalised security relationship between regional states and extra-regional powers. Initially, after revolution and two wars, that security interdependence was welcomed by the United States and the GCC states as a means to preserve the regional status quo, contain Iran and supervise the situation in Iraq.

However, the new constellation also created side effects. Interdependence is not reducible to homogenisation as 'globalists' sometimes suggest. Although it is often used to explain co-operative behaviour or globalisation effects, enemies can be as interdependent as friends, as shown by the conflicts between Iran and Iraq, Palestine and Israel and Irish Republicans and Britain. Keohane and Nye offer two dimensions of interdependence, 'sensitivity' and 'vulnerability'. 'Sensitivity interdependence is created by interactions within a framework of policies [and] assumes that the framework remains unchanged.'[326] Conversely, vulnerability interdependence refers to 'an actor's liability to suffer costs imposed by external events even after policies have been altered'.[327] In other words, sensitivity indicates the degree to which modifications in the properties (policies, identity, role, etc.) of one actor affect another actor and vice versa immediately and in the short term. Vulnerability, in contrast, measures the mutual dependence between two or more actors in the long run. Applied to our case this would mean that by linking the security of the GCC states to its own, the US elevated its sensitivity and vulnerability to events in the Persian Gulf to a higher level. The opposite constellation applies as well: by 'outsourcing' their security to the United States, the Gulf monarchies made the Persian Gulf system more receptive and vulnerable to changes in the posture of the United States. We will return to the former aspect later and will elucidate in the following the impact of the linkages on international politics in the Persian Gulf. This could be characterised as a focus on the 'outward flow' of interdependence – from the United States to the Persian Gulf area – before we turn our attention towards the 'inward flow – from the Persian Gulf to the United States.

4.3.1   *Outward interdependence: US state identity and*
'othering' after the demise of communism

How do we define a mission without a referential object? This rather simple question has manifold consequences for international politics. In the tradition of Marx and Hegel, Berger observed that man's constant urge for 'externalisation', that is the 'ongoing outpouring of human being into the world, both in the physical and the mental activity of men', is determined by biological factors, hence to be considered an act of anthropological necessity.[328] In order to be an acting being, man requires reference to society. After all, without an external reference, externalisation itself could not occur, because the differentiation between external and internal would not emerge in the first place. Juxtaposing the actor-society, internal-external relationship in inter-disciplinary terms, one may observe that the anthropological argument that individuals do not exist in solitary confinement (unless as a perverted existence) does apply to international life as well. States do not function in an encapsulated habitat, they are embedded in myriad external and internal structures, networks and relationships. The two features of international life – externalisation and sociality – explain why states construct the international world in its socio-cultural and psychological constitution. According to Peter L. Berger, man is not merely *homo socius* but also *homo faber/homo pictor*, or both 'world and culture maker'. The same could be said about states. In order to give meaning to their international environment, states produce, reify, internalise, externalise, alter political cultures. Foreign polices, like human actions, could hence be characterised as a 'world-making activity'.

It is only logical that a country such as the United States, with its communicative capabilities transmitted by international universities, a powerful state, think tanks and a worldwide media network 'externalises' culture on a global scale, reproducing itself and producing images of the world according to the country's internalised perceptions. After all, I would assert, that the communicative outreach of the United States is an important factor producing the labelling of the country as 'super-power', 'global power' or 'hyper power'. Taken one step further, the outlined sociological-anthropological notion about externalisation and sociality would suggest that the United States, like any actor in the international system, needs international society (or parts of it) as reference object in order to direct the country's externalisation *to* something (the transmitter of this externalisation being foreign policy). Until the end of the Cold War, that outflow was directed towards communism which constituted the point of ideological fixation. During this period, the US state used labels such as 'leader of the free world' to present, externalise, reproduce, communicate its self-perception to international society, delineating both its own role (leader) and its orbit of identification ('the free world'). By implication, the self-attribution of the leader-ship role and the definition of an ideological boundary around the free world (essen-tially the liberal-democracies, market economies of the Western hemisphere), fortified the 'in-group' against the 'out-group'. From the US perception then, the country and its allies were everything the communist block was not: market economies as opposed to planned economies, democracies as opposed to totalitarian systems, religious as opposed to atheist, producing 'a simple, dichotomous view that seemed to many if not most Americans to explain the often frustrating and infinitely more complex developments of the postwar world'.[329]

For over four decades, the binary cognitive structure of world politics reproduced the cultural formation labelled Cold War. This was the most fundamental structure of the bipolar system – a collective representation between the 'Western selves' and the 'Eastern others'. Once it was terminated, new cognitive guidelines had to be invented, suitable to provide policy meta-narratives for international life after the Cold War. Ultimately, the feeling in some academic and political circles that post-bipolarity was more disorderly, dysfunctional, dangerous, unstable and unruly than the Cold War *order* can be attributed to the fact that no new cognitive system had yet been put in place to restructure international politics. As was observed in a *National Journal* article about the ascendancy to prominence of neo-conservative thinking 'who or what was to be considered a threat to U.S. interests and values' was unclear.[330] In other words, nobody knew who the post-communist 'other' would be. Debates about an 'End of history' or 'Clash of Civilisation' epitomised the disparities of intellectual paradigms on the future of world politics and the role attributions designated to the United States.[331] Caught between the 'eclectic cacophony' of emotions of euphoria and the stymieing prospect of purpose-lessness in a pacified world, US decision-makers soon realised that 'externalising

America' would need alterations in the country's role identity – by definition a process that required new referential objects:

> Following the demise of the Soviet Union, and the strategic proclamation that uncertainty and unpredictability are the new enemies, U.S. foreign policy discourse [was] casting around for a new set of principles to guide action and aid judgement about the place of the United States in the world. Yet, for all the novelty of the situation, the debate associated with these developments is structured along traditional lines, as a battle between the advocates of 'isolationism' and the proponents of 'intervention'.... In the absence of few actual champions of isolationism, the argument countering intervention is largely a mythical construction of an impossible position on the part of those who intend to disparage it.... [T]here is little contention among those putatively at odds with one another that the United States must retain an internationalist policy.[332]

This was the ideological background out of which the 'new world order' norm emerged. Saddam Hussein's abomination in Iraq was taken as the opportunity by American elites to refashion the country's role in world politics. In hindsight, the internationalists won out – the United States was 'externalising' again, and the situation in Kuwait provided the first scenario to do so. In line with its self-perception as the 'force for good' in international affairs, the rhetoric about a new world order hence served the function to reconstitute the claim of the United States to international prominence, by positioning its post-Cold War mission in the tradition of the country's achievements in the past:

> The promise [of a new world order] was easily made because new orders are familiar terrain for an American people whose national experience began in the Enlightenment ambition to establish a 'novus ordo seclorum'. Mr. Bush's proposal is in the direct line of American reformist internationalism, begun with Woodrow Wilson's invention in 1917 of the principle of universal national self-determination, and then of the League of Nations. After that came Franklin Roosevelt's Atlantic Charter in 1941, promising 'Four Freedoms' to the people of the world, and after that the United Nations, an American idea.[333]

The effort to reconstitute and reproduce a new variant of what it meant to be 'American' was central to the Second Gulf War and the US policies in its aftermath. It concurrently satisfied the 'Americanist quest for a moral identity through virtuous conquest of evil, the sense of a people pursuing its self-interest while collectively embodying some transcendent ideal'[334] whilst serving the function to transcend the country's 'Vietnam complex'. The war was pasted into a larger effort to construct the image of a post-Cold War world that was more dangerous and unpredictable than the familiar symmetries of bipolarity had been.[335] As liberal analysts were caught in the euphoria of a new era of global peace and prosperity, neo-conservatives warned stridently of new risks and challenges, criticising the decline in US military spending and the neglect of President Reagan's missile defence system. Hence, by attacking Kuwait, Saddam Hussein unconsciously provided for the opportunity to invent new 'others', 'we' have to combat: rogue states, Islamic fundamentalists, Arab fanatics and so on. At least in American politics, 'clash of civilisation' not 'end of history' appeared to win out, with the United States pushing the country into the tendentious role of a militaristic, internationalist leviathan.[336]

The military success of the Second Persian Gulf War and the international legitimation of the US war role re-invoked the euphoria of American predominance in the absence of serious competition. From the perspective of the 'neo-conservative' political and academic elite, the war confirmed the country's self-perception as the unchallenged superpower in international politics.[337] At the heart of the ideological disposition of this cast in US politics is a firm belief in the superiority of American values, norms and principles, sometimes accompanied by insidiously racist undertones. The victory against Iraq then became not only a military success, it was presented as the inevitable triumph of superior values, norms and people, reinvigorating the 'America first syndrome' in some political (or politicised) circles in Washington:

> America's superior people were empowered by better ideas. This war was not just a clash of wills, nor was it only a conflict of national interests. The Persian Gulf war brought into battle a fundamental conflict of values, strategies, and operational concepts. In the end, the allies prevailed as much because they were fighting with the right ideas as because they had great people.[338]

Comparable to the intrinsically exclusionary and prejudiced tenor of Iranian notions of 'Aryanism', and (Iraqi) Arab nationalist discourse about the Jewish, Iranian or 'Western' threat to the Arab *umma*, post-Cold War American nationalism appeared to be anxious to propound the historically bestowed primacy of the 'American civilisation', in the face of a mediocre, barbaric 'other' whose abomination in Kuwait was threatening the cultural tenets of the 'civilised world'. What was creeping into the mainstream of American public and political culture was an insidiously ideologised world-view, abstracting in its international perception and polarising in its political formulas. In *The Politics of Dispossession*, the late Edward Said expressed his frustration about the emergence of such a culture in vivid terms:

> Nearly every recent movie about American commandos pits a hulking Rambo or a whizlike Delta Force against Arab-Muslim terrorist desperadoes. Now it is as if an almost metaphysical need to defeat Iraq has come into being, not because Iraq's offence, though great, is cataclysmic, but because a small non-white country has rankled a suddenly energised supernation imbued with a fervour that can only be satisfied with subservience from shaikhs, dictators, and camel jockeys. The truly acceptable Arabs are those like Sadat who can be made to seem almost completely purified of their national selfhood – folksy talk show guests.[339]

In strategic terms, 'neo-conservative *Weltanschauung*' assumes that unipolarity had eliminated the determinations of Cold War balance of power calculations, allowing

for the redefinition of world- and Persian Gulf politics along US interests. The end
of bipolarity and the systemically legitimated penetration of the region by US forces
were seen as reason enough to take a rather more offensive posture towards regional
challengers, a view that was shared by strategists in Washington. Hence, the dual
containment policy instead of the rather more passive balance of power rationale
which had dominated US policy towards the region for the last four decades. With
the modified structure of the international system, the United States felt reassured
that marginalising the two principal powers in the region, Iran and Iraq, would
secure long-term US interests in the Persian Gulf, without the threat of any serious
international backlash. As former National Security Advisor Anthony Lake put it:

> We no longer have to fear Soviet efforts to gain a foothold in the Persian Gulf
> by taking advantage of our support for one of these states to build relations with
> the other. The strategic importance of both Iraq and Iran has therefore been
> reduced dramatically, and their ability to play the superpowers off each other has
> been eliminated.[304]

My focus on the predominance of neo-conservatism does not suggest that there were
no rival narratives. It would be, of course, a gross oversimplification to reduce the post-
Cold War state identity of the United States to one abstract category. The ideational
plots floating around in contemporary America cannot be subsumed under one meta-
narrative without danger of oversimplification. Political elites in the country had, and
continue to have, fierce debates about the preferred identity, role, self-portrayal of the
US state in international affairs. In relation to the Persian Gulf, neo-conservatives are
pitted against rather more moderate voices coming from former high-ranking officials
such as Zbigniew Brzezinsky, Richard Murphy, Brent Scowcroft, Graham Fuller or
Gary Sick, who criticise the 'totalitarian' tendencies in neo-conservative thinking.
Exemplifying that position, a *Foreign Affairs* article authored by Brzezinsky, Scowcroft
and Murphy called for a 'nuanced' approach towards the Persian Gulf and détente with
the post-revolutionary government of Iran. In the same article, however, the authors
conceded that the 'desire to head off a challenge on Iran policy mounted by an increasingly bellicose Republican Congress' pushed the Clinton administration towards
announcing that it will institute 'a complete economic embargo against Iran'.[341] Under
pressure from hard-line Republicans and lobbying efforts by pro-Israeli groupings –
most notably the American-Israeli Public Affairs Committee (AIPAC) – the escalation
of US policies towards potential adversaries in the Gulf was pervasive and strategic,
subordinating the demands for moderation from rather more realistic circles of the
political establishment in Washington.[342] In terms of policy outcomes *vis-à-vis*
the Persian Gulf area, then, the neo-conservatives appeared to have greater leverage on
the decision-making process. The following section is dedicated to this development,
proposing that we may observe a constant (not-linear, not proportionate and by no
means non-eclectic) escalation of US policies in the Persian Gulf. Bringing the
argument of this chapter to its logical conclusion, we propose that this escalation
can be linked to the increasing prominence of a unilateral identity as the preferred
self-perception of the post-Cold War US state.

4.3.1.1   *Ideologising the state: neo-conservative strategy, US foreign policy and the Gulf*

Inherent in the notion of American superiority is an element of transnational motivation. Comparable to the internationalist ambitions of Iranian-Islamic revolutionaries and Iraqi pan-Arabists, the motivational drives to externalise values, norms, institutions, to 'others' by implication pushes the actors to transcend nation-state boundaries, and in so doing to transgress international law: Iranian revolutionaries saw their movement in romantic terms, as a transnational idea for the liberation of the oppressed masses; Iraqi-Arab nationalism subscribed to the utopian idea for the reunification of the Arab homeland under the guidance of a strong 'Bismarckian' leader. With a comparable hubristic self-understanding, American neo-conservatives present the United States as the vanguard for universal democracy and liberty. From this perspective exporting the 'idea of America' is an obligation of the state, not merely an instrument of legitimation. As Michael Ledeen of the American Enterprise Institute put it after the events on 11 September 2001:

> Now we know better, and our enemies will soon see the evidence in their own streets, deserts, and mountain redoubts. We have rediscovered the roots of our national character, which are an unshakeable confidence in the rightness of our mission, deep religious conviction, and a unique ability to come together to prevail against frightening obstacles. Once we have defeated the latest incarnation of servitude – this time wrapped in a religious mantle – we must remind ourselves of what we are, and the magnitude of our task. Next time, we must not listen to leaders who delight us with fables of peace and who tell us we are not worthy of our high calling. Next time, we must dismiss those who tell us that all people are the same, all cultures are of equal worth, all values are relative, and all judgments are to be avoided. Silvio Berlusconi was right: We've accomplished more than our enemies, and the overwhelming majority of mankind knows it.[343]

The first strategic document to promote a rather more aggressive US security and foreign policy after the end of the Cold War was already put forward in early 1992. In a classified but quickly leaked draft entitled 'Defense Planning Guidance for the Fiscal Years 1994–1999' devised under the supervision of Paul Wolfowitz, then Undersecretary for Policy at the US Defense Department and today Deputy Defense Secretary at the same institution, it was suggested that the United States should strive for the creation of a *Pax Americana*. Characteristic of neo-conservative ideology, the document was devoid of multilateral strategies, leaving out the United Nations as a forum for conflict prevention or resolution. Instead, the 'Defense Planning Guidance' proposed that

> while the U.S. cannot become the world's 'policemen' by assuming responsibility for righting every wrong, we will retain the pre-eminent responsibility for addressing selectively those wrongs which threaten not only our interests, but those of our allies or friends, or which could seriously unsettle international relations.

Hence, 'the United States should be postured to act independently when collective action cannot be orchestrated'.[344]

That the 'Defense Planning Guidance' was revised in order to divest the sections about the US role of their crusading tone does not change the fact that the proposal to pre-empt potential threats to US interests – if necessary without multilateral consent – was gaining prominence. 'Deprived of the disciplining restraint once imposed by the Cold War', critics of the internationalist vogue during the Clinton Presidency typically argued, 'a great expansion took place in the objectives it seemed plausible for the United States to pursue in the world'.[345] It was only logical that with the formalised security transactions after the Second Gulf War, the campaign towards internationalising the US role on the basis of universal 'American' values had an immediate effect on the country's policies in the Persian Gulf. The first example of the willingness of the United States to transgress existing rules and norms of international society under the pressure of its self-designated role was the Iran-Libya Sanctions Act (ILSA), lobbied for by AIPAC, put forward by Republican Senator Alfonso D'amato and signed by President Clinton in 1996.[346] Before the introduction of ILSA, US oil companies – only banned from importing crude oil from Iran to refineries in the United States but not from buying it or shipping it to other refineries – had become the most important lifters of Iranian crude oil.[347] In 1995, facing a Republican-controlled House of Representatives and Congress, President Clinton opposed a US$1 billion contract between Conoco and the National Iranian Oil Company (NIOC) for the development of the offshore oil fields Sirri A and E. This decision was followed by the Presidential Executive Order 12957, banning all US commercial contacts with the Islamic Republic and the introduction of ILSA in 1996. The important aspect for our argument is that in the spirit of the 'Helms-Burton-Act', ILSA had an extra-territorial connotation to it, providing for sanctions to be executed against any person or corporation investing US$40 million or more in the Iranian petroleum sector. In legal terms then, ILSA extended the jurisdiction of domestic US law to the international environment. The President was empowered to punish *any* foreign unit engaged in significant investment in Iran's oil sector.

The second, rather more serious deterioration of US policy in the Persian Gulf developed out of the unresolved situation in Iraq. Continued obstruction of the weapons inspections by the Iraqi leadership provided the pretext for two additional acts which were disputable from the perspective of international society. First, intensified bombardment of Iraqi targets, beginning in September 1996 and continuing through 1997 and 1998, escalated into a seventy-hour bombing campaign between 17 and 20 December 1998 by US American and UK air forces codenamed 'Desert Fox'.[348] Second, introduction of the 'Iraq Liberation Act (ILA)' by a bipartisan group of eight US Senators on 29 September 1998 overtly advocated 'regime change' in Iraq, by enhancing the position of the exiled Iraqi opposition (mainly the London based Iraqi National Congress), providing military assistance to the Iraqi opposition in the amount of up to US$97 million and organising funding by the United States Information Agency (USIA) in order to publicise the Iraqi opposition efforts.[349]

Whether or not these US policies were *subjectively legitimate* is a matter of the quality of the argument and is not necessarily pertinent to our concern here.

From Saddam Hussein's viewpoint, invading Kuwait was a legitimate act in his quest for Arab unification. Likewise, the Iranian students found it legitimate to take the diplomatic personnel of the US embassy hostage, because of previous interference in the internal affairs of Iran. An individual might deem him- or herself legitimated to act as a professor. Without the social recognition of this subjectively conceived self-attribution however, he or she will neither be able to effectively act out this role, nor turn self-perception into a socially legitimated role identity. Social legitimacy requires external recognition by society, and international legitimacy requires approval by international society. By adopting a unilateral posture, manifesting itself in extra-territorial laws, detachment from multilateral agreements and institutions, and military engagements without UN Security Council mandates, the US state self-consciously negated the importance of *international* legitimation, instead attempting to universalise its self-designated principles. Hence, whereas in the build-up to the Second Gulf War, the careful construction of an international alliance legitimated the war against Iraq, the internalised prospect of a 'new American century' pushed the US state increasingly towards circumventing the basic tenets of international society. The repeated insistence of the Clinton administration that it was containing Iraq on behalf of the 'free world' and for the good of world peace, gradually lost its (international) legitimating appeal, and appeared to be more and more for domestic consumption rather than external consensus building.

The irony for US decision-makers was that by positioning the country in contradiction to international political culture, the United States was increasingly isolated in the Persian Gulf. Hence, when the decision was made to bombard Iraqi targets in September 1996, France, Russia, regional states including Kuwait and NATO ally Turkey (which denied access to its air bases) overtly denounced the military action. Equally, the United States did not manage to secure support from the UN Security Council for the sustained bombardments in December 1998, being forced to circumvent the UN in their search for legal justification instead.[350] The decision to pursue active regime change in Iraq provoked even more opposition, with Russia, China and France seeing the Security Council as 'being held hostage to particular American interests, and the American position increasingly out of touch with international opinion'.[351] The same was observable in regard to the sanctions regime against Iran. Pointing towards the 'illegality' of extra-territorial sanctions under international law, the European Union (EU) adopted 'blocking legislation' on 22 November 1996, preventing companies in the EU from complying with ILSA. Not only that, the EU encouraged member states to impose their own sanctions on companies that were considering to comply with ILSA, and decided to file a complaint against the United States at the World Trade Organisation (WTO).[352]

Thus, prisoner of its self-consciously adopted identity as global leviathan, the United States did not only miss the opportunity to build a viable regional security architecture through multilateral action during a period when it had the international mandate to do so, but it also increasingly drove itself out of the political and diplomatic context of Persian Gulf politics. From the perspective of international society, the failure of US policies in the political-diplomatic sphere superseded its role as a deterrent and guardian of the embargo against Iraq. In terms of policy outcomes, the immediate consequence was the erosion of consensus in the UN Security Council and the demise of the UNSCOM and IAEA inspection regime – the legitimating principle of the postwar US engagement in Iraq in the first place. 'Desert Fox' and ILA hence failed to substantiate US policies in Iraq and manoeuvred the protagonists, including the UN, into a stalemate: the sanctions regime remained implemented without any monitoring of Iraqi WMD facilities, Saddam Hussein remained in power until the Third Persian Gulf War, and the December 1999 decision to replace UNSCOM with the UN Monitoring, Verification and Inspection Commission (UNMOVIC) did not yield any inspections until the eve of the UK/US invasion of Iraq in March 2003. As Rolf Ekeus, head of UNSCOM in an interview in March 2000 put it: 'The unity of the Security Council was the political fact that sustained the UNSCOM operation and the failure to maintain that unity undermined it.'[353]

Not only was the US policy destabilising in political terms, through sanctions against Iraq it also caused unprecedented human sufferings. When then UN human-itarian co-ordinator for Iraq Denis Haliday, noted that 6,000–7,000 children per month were dying of causes directly related to the sanctions, and argued that the US policy 'amounted to genocide', he echoed a widespread view that the sanctions regime had created a humanitarian crisis.[354] In terms of public opinion in the Persian Gulf at least, the pictures of dying Iraqi children, disseminated by burgeoning transnational media in the region, had a serious effect on how US policies were evaluated, strengthening pre-existent anti-American sentiments in the region and beyond.

4.3.1.2   *Dictating the grammar of war: the political culture of neo-conservatism*

Contemporary neo-conservatism reveals itself as a form of nativism, buttressed by a moral righteous and infallible American nationalism with an universal agenda. Charles Krauthammer, a Pulitzer Price winner and syndicated columnist for the *Washington Post*, is amongst the most prolific writers, advocating neo-conservative ideas with passionate zeal. Extending his argument about the US role in world politics beyond the 'unipolarity' hypothesis introduced after the demise of the Soviet Union, Krauthammer proposed in the aftermath of 11 September that the United States should follow a new, 'unilateralist' global strategy. 'The new unilateralism argues explicitly and unashamedly for maintaining unipolarity, for sustaining America's unrivaled [*sic*] dominance for the foreseeable future.'[355] According to Krauthammer, 'it could be a long future, assuming we successfully manage the sin-gle greatest threat, namely, weapons of mass destruction in the hands of rogue states'. This requires 'aggressive and confident application of unipolar power rather than falling back, as [the United States] did in the 1990s, on paralysing multilateralism'. Before concluding with the note that 'History has given you an empire, if you will keep it', Krauthammer cautioned that the only way to retain global US pre-eminence is to prevent 'gradually transferring power to multilateral institutions as heirs to American hegemony'.[356]

During the Clinton years the infrastructure supporting neo-conservative activism was only beginning to emerge and influence on the Washington establishment was still limited. The later 1990s and the beginning of the twenty-first century provided a more suitable atmosphere to extend the programme beyond the confines of institutionalised lobbying. Already before 11 September attacks on US interests at home and abroad were taken as opportunities to influence public discourse in the country. A plethora of theories, commentaries and policy manuals were produced, warning against the global threat by 'fundamentalist Koran-waving zealots', destined to destroy everything the United States stands for. September 11 was taken as proof that the prophecies about the 'global Islamic threat' were true. In a controversy with essayist and writer Susan Sontag, Charles Krauthammer countered the critique that such views were too abstract, too sanctimonious and 'unworthy of a mature democracy'.[357] 'Oversimplifying?' Krauthammer argued, '[h]as there ever been a time when the distinction between good and evil was more clear?'[358] For Ann Coulter, another prolific writer on the Washington scene the answer was quite clear:

> They hate us? We hate them. Americans don't want to make Islamic fanatics love us. We want to make them die. There's nothing like horrendous physical pain to quell angry fanatics. So sorry they're angry – wait until they see American anger. Japanese kamikaze pilots hated us once too. A couple of well-aimed nuclear weapons, and now they are gentle little lambs. That got their attention.[359]

We may detect the neo-conservative current in US politics on at least four interdependent levels: 'populist-academic', institutional, political and ideological. The last citation is to be positioned on the far-right wing of the latter category, where it is joined by comparably radical ideas expressed by current and former decision-makers and leaders of Christian fundamentalist organisations, namely: Fred Ikle, Undersecretary of Defense during the Reagan administration, who alluded to a nuclear war that 'might end up displacing Mecca and Medina with two large radioactive craters';[360] Louisiana Republican John Cooksey, who suggested that any airline passenger wearing a 'diaper on his head' should be 'pulled over'; or prominent Baptist preacher Jerry Falwell who asserted on the *CBS* news show '*60 minutes*' that 'Muhammad was a terrorist' and that he was 'a violent man, a man of war', a statement for which he later apologised after protests from the governments of the United States, United Kingdom and Iran.[361]

Less fundamentalist voices, who cover their ideological elucidation with an erudite smoke screen, are institutionally embedded in think tanks and pressure groups such as the American Enterprise Institute, Heritage Foundation, Committee for the Free World, Committee on Present Danger, Freedom Research Foundation, the Foundation for the Preservation of American Values and the Project for the New American Century. Established in 1997 as a non-profit educational organisation 'whose goal is to promote American global leadership', the role of the Project for the New American Century is especially significant in terms of immediate policy involvement.[362] Already in January 1998, the organisation sent a letter to the then President Clinton, supporting a 'strategy for removing Saddam's regime from power', demanding a 'full complement of diplomatic, political and military efforts' to that end. This appeal was followed by a letter to Newt Gingrich, Speaker of the House of Representatives and Trent Lott, Majority Leader in the US Senate, in May 1998, urging that 'U.S. policy should have as its explicit goal removing Saddam Hussein's regime from power and establishing a peaceful and democratic Iraq in its place'. Out of the 17 signatories to the two letters, 11 held posts in the Bush administration since the invasion of Iraq was launched in March 2003. Elliot Abrams, who had orchestrated the Iran-Contra scandal when the Reagan administration used the proceeds of arms sales to Iran (despite its own embargo) to circumvent a congressional prohibition on funding Nicaraguan rebels, was recruited as Senior Director for Near East, Southwest Asian and North African Affairs on the National Security Council; Richard Armitage was named Deputy Secretary of State; John Bolton, Under Secretary, Arms Control and International Security; Paula Dobriansky, Under Secretary of State for Global Affairs; Zalmay Khalilzad, Special Presidential envoy to Afghanistan and Ambassador-at-large for Free Iraqis; Richard Perle, chairman of the Pentagon's Defense Policy Board; Peter W. Rodman, Assistant Secretary of Defense for International Security Affairs; Donald Rumsfeld, Secretary of Defense; William Schneider, Jr, chairman of the Pentagon's Defense Science Board; Paul Wolfowitz, Deputy Secretary of Defense; and Robert B. Zoellick, the US Trade Representative. The institutionalisation of the neo-conservative idea in a myriad of inter-linked, not-for-profit 'think-tanks' and lobbying organisations, catered for the structural platform to position suitable candidates in high-ranking political, business and academic positions after the election success of George W. Bush. The systemic cohesiveness may be characterised as a 'neo-conservative *asabiyya*', where group loyalty is preserved by family ties, institutional/media power and inroads into the most lucrative sectors of the US industry, most notably the oil sector.[363]

Apart from the ideological, institutional and political tenets of neo-conservative political culture, there is also an academic translation of the idea of global US hegemony and belligerence towards the referential object of this mission – 'they' – after 11 September almost exclusively taken to be the peoples of the Islamic worlds. Apart from the 'clash of civilisation' theory and Bernard Lewis's writings which are repeatedly referred to in neo-conservative publications, the 'disconnectedness defines danger' theory put forward by Thomas P.M. Barnett, a professor of warfare analysis at the US Naval War College and Pentagon advisor, is perhaps less known. Writing in the holist tradition of US international relations theory and with striking similarities to the dichotomous 'west against the rest' notion underlying Huntington's clash of civilisations, Barnett separates the world into two camps: the 'functioning core', where 'globalisation is thick with network connectivity, financial transactions, liberal media flows, and collective security' and the 'non-integrating gap', where 'globalisation is thinning or just plain absent'.[364] The former regions of the world, comprising 'North America, much of South America, the European Union, Putin's Russia, Japan and Asia's emerging economies (most notably China and India), Australia and New Zealand, and South Africa,' benefit from 'stable governments, rising standards of living, and more deaths by suicide than murder'.[365] The disconnected rest is plagued with economic backwardness and political totalitarianism. From this dichotomous view of world politics, Barnett jumps to the mono-causal conclusion that the 'disconnectedness' of the 'gap states' causes their hostility towards the United States and its allies, epitomised by the attacks on the leader of the 'core' states on 11 September. This predicament requires therapeutic cure, and the United States is presented as the suitable master to provide the medicine. How? 'By getting them where they live', which requires immediate, long-term permeation of the Persian Gulf area:

> The only thing that will change that nasty environment and open the floodgates for change is if some external power steps in and plays Leviathan full-time. Taking down Saddam, the region's bully-in-chief, will force the U.S. into playing that role far more fully than it has over the past several decades, primarily because Iraq is the Yugoslavia of the Middle East – a crossroads of civilisations that has historically required a dictatorship to keep the peace. As baby-sitting jobs go, this one will be a doozy, making our lengthy efforts in postwar Germany and Japan look simple in retrospect.[366]

Barnett's theory may be positioned within a neo-conservative political culture that is structural, pervasive and in constant evolution. That his article was published in the *Esquire* shows that neo-conservative ideas are aggressively sold to a wider public. After 11 September, the ideological, media, academic and institutional impasses into the Washington establishment merged into a modified grand strategic posture, devised to define the foreign relations of the US state for years to come. Given this suggestion about an existing neo-conservative nexus, the similarities between publications by neo-conservative think tanks and official government manuals should not be surprising. So, for instance, a position paper published by the 'Project for the new American Century' in September 2000 and the 'National Security Strategy' published by the Pentagon two years later commence with strikingly similar designations of the US American position in world politics. The former asserts on the first page that

> The United States is the world's only superpower, combining pre-eminent military power, global technological leadership, and the world's largest economy. Moreover, America stands at the head of a system of alliances which includes the world's other leading democratic powers.[367]

The Pentagon paper commences with an almost identical disposition:

> The United States possesses unprecedented – and unequalled – strength and influence in the world. Sustained by faith in the principles of liberty, and the value of a free society, this position comes with unparalleled responsibilities, obligations, and opportunity. The great strength of this nation must be used to promote a balance of power that favours freedom.[368]

Both the Pentagon paper and the Project manual identify the United States as the only remaining superpower, democratic, free, prosperous and hence destined to promote its values abroad. The similarities in the designation of the US role in both documents is complemented by the threat perception and the strategies recommended. In that vein, the Project paper demands

> America must defend its homeland. During the Cold War, nuclear deterrence was the key element in homeland defence; it remains essential. But the new century has brought with it new challenges. While reconfiguring its nuclear force, the United States also must counteract the effects of the proliferation of ballistic missiles and weapons of mass destruction that may soon allow lesser states to deter U.S. military action by threatening U.S. allies and the American homeland itself. Of all the new and current missions for U.S. armed forces, this must have priority.[369]

The preface to the Pentagon's design for the US National Security Strategy, written by President Bush, concurs in tone and strategy:

> The gravest danger our Nation faces lies at the crossroads of radicalism and technology. Our enemies have openly declared that they are seeking weapons of mass destruction, and evidence indicates that they are doing so with determination. The United States will not allow these efforts to succeed. We will build defences against ballistic missiles and other means of delivery.[370]

The affinities in the designation of grand strategic designs and the similar threat scenario building are complemented with concurring identifications of the enemy 'other'. Revealingly, the 'axis of evil' named in the State of the Union Address by President Bush on 29 January 2002, was already identified (without employing the phrase) in the aforementioned think-tank document. The authors urged: 'We cannot allow North Korea, Iran, Iraq or similar states to undermine American leadership, intimidate American allies or threaten the American homeland itself.'[371] The same document also highlighted the extended version of the list of US enemies, adding Syria and Libya to the states that could threaten US predominance. More consequentially for future world politics, the five countries identified by the think tank as adversaries were also singled out in the Pentagon's 'Nuclear Posture Review' two years later, setting out new US guidelines for pre-emptive nuclear strikes, declaring that 'North Korea, Iraq, Iran, Syria and Libya are among the countries that could be involved in immediate, potential or unexpected contingencies'.[372] The 11 December 2002 issue of the *Washington Post* disclosed a classified version of the pre-emptive strike doctrine adopted by the Bush administration, explicitly naming Iran, Syria, North Korea and Libya as 'central' to the new approach.[373] Amidst these conversions in thinking and strategy, it should not surprise that the Project endorsed the gradual escalation of the foreign and security strategy of the Bush administration with three letters:[374] nine days after 11 September, supporting the call for 'a broad and sustained campaign against the terrorist organisations and those who harbour and support them'; in response to the State of the Union speech acclaiming 'the strong stance in support of the Israeli government' and asserting that '[n]o one should doubt that the United States and Israel share a common enemy'; and the latest letter at the time of our writing, confirming 'the bold new course...chartered for American national security strategy'.

In terms of US security policy, the threat scenario building served the purpose to push an increase in military spending through Congress (the overall defence spending now being higher than the aggregate amount of the following 191 countries); to legitimate the resumption of the Missile Defense System formerly pursued by Ronald Reagan and abandoned by President Clinton; to disrupt the six-year effort to find a consensus on the banning of germ warfare and to pull out from the Anti Ballistic Missile treaty. In terms of domestic politics, the Bush administration capitalised on the post-September 11 'opportunity'[375] in order to extend the power of the state *vis-à-vis* society, consciously pushing the 'war on terrorism' to the local level. Just six weeks after the attacks, Congress overwhelmingly approved the Uniting and Strengthening America by Providing Appropriate Tools Required to Intercept and Obstruct Terrorism Act (USA PATRIOT Act). On 26 October 2001, President Bush signed the act into law, instituting legal procedures that give individuals only limited recourse either to a proper defence or a fair trial, allowing secret searches, eavesdropping and detention without limit. The campaigns of the Bush administration have led to international criticism, including opposition to the treatment of the prisoners at Guantanamo Bay and the detention of approximately 1,100–2,000 people, the majority of Muslim descent.[376] Here and elsewhere, state policy concurs with neo-conservative thinking and institutional structure. Daniel Pipes, director of the Middle East Forum and columnist for the *New York Post* and *The Jerusalem Post* wrote in January 2003:

> There is no escaping the unfortunate fact that Muslim government employees in law enforcement, the military and the diplomatic corps need to be watched for connections to terrorism, as do Muslim chaplains in prisons and the armed forces. Muslim visitors and immigrants must undergo additional background checks. Mosques require a scrutiny beyond that applied to churches and temples.[377]

Danies Pipes is also behind an online portal named 'Campus Watch', where 'dossiers' on professors and academic institutions in the United States and information from students regarding their teachers' political opinions are comprised and maintained. In a similar spirit, another institution, the American Council of Trustees and Alumni (ACTA), founded among others by the wife of Vice President Cheney, Lynne V. Cheney, produced a document entitled 'Defense of Civilisation' in which it published the names, colleges and statements of about 100 academics who were accused of being critical to US policy. Naming professors as 'the weak link in America's response to the attack', the report castigated faculty members for invoking 'tolerance and diversity as antidotes to evil' and pointing 'accusatory fingers, not at the terrorists, but at America itself'.[378]

Yet, the partially successful campaign to monopolise public discourse on political Islam and the Muslim world has been criticised in the past and present by prominent voices opposed to neo-conservative totalitarianism. Graham Fuller, a former vice-chairman of the National Intelligence Council for long-range forecasting at the CIA, for instance, criticised that 'efforts to portray Iran with some analytical balance have grown more difficult, crowded out by inflamed rhetoric and intense pro-Israeli lobbying against Tehran in Congress', recommending that '[i]mproved U.S. ties with Iran should bring about a more balanced reckoning of just what Iran is and is not'.[379] Stanley Hoffmann, on the other side has expressed his criticism of neo-conservative ideology from a 'classical realist' angle, asking 'how long would the American public support a strategy of frequent preemptive uses of force – and concomitant "wartime" restrictions on liberties at home', concluding that '[e]mpire, or the dream of empire, has invariably gone to the heads of the imperialists'.[380] International criticisms are even stronger in their condemnation of US policies. A letter signed by 99 German intellectuals in response to a declaration by 60 American intellectuals that was published in all the major newspapers in Europe and West Asia stated:

> Many of us feel that the growing influence of fundamentalist forces in the United States on the political elite of your country, which clearly extends all the way to the White House, is cause for concern. The division of the world into 'good' and 'evil', the stigmatisation of entire countries and their populations, will tend to incite racist, nationalistic, and religious fanaticism, and to deprive people of their ability to perceive living reality in a differentiated way, and of the insight that differences and cultural variety are not a misfortune, but a blessing for all, and that even the most powerful persons on earth will only prosper in the long run if the world is seen as a whole, whose richness and beauty consists in the differences. Fundamentalism begins with declaring one's own culture to be the only true, good, and beautiful one. Fundamentalist reactions to the real conflicts in our world close our eyes to civilian and nonviolent solutions for these conflicts, and only speed up the mutual escalation of terrorism and war.[381]

The grammar of violence dictated by neo-conservative political culture is institutionalised and pervasive. By linking its ideological precepts and political idioms to deeply embedded signs and symbols of US American culture, the neo-conservative idea is presented as an indispensable patriotic narrative. That there appears to be a mainstream consensus about what it means to 'defend American values' and conduct 'just war' is evidenced by the institutional diversity, political cloud and intellectual backing that these ideas receive.[382] However, here and elsewhere there is no suggestion that culture presents itself as an unalterable continuum or monolithic entity. Neo-conservative political culture is contested on many levels and even within the Bush administration there are divisions between so-called 'doves' organised at Foggy Bottom and 'hawks' at the Pentagon (hence the phrase 'Potomac war'). Likewise, intellectuals and activists living in the United States do not identify with one political narrative, exemplified in a letter signed by 139 academics (as of 10 April 2002) opposed to the Bush administrations 'mad rush to war', pointing towards the 'moral desperation and hatred that are certain to be felt by millions of people who can only watch helplessly as their world is devastated by a country, the United States, which assumes that its moral authority is as absolute and unchangeable as its military power'.[383]

Notwithstanding domestic and international criticisms however, the ideological precepts of neo-conservatism remain dominant exactly because they are designed to appeal to US American culture. In that vein, employing categorical normative symbols such as *the* 'American way of life', embody 'a nativist or anti-foreign component to manufacture an imagined sense of community',[384] feeding into the process of polarisation, friction and structural enmity. When the definition of the self is totalitarian, creating a perennial sense of siege becomes the necessary determinant to assert the power of the state in times of crisis domestically and to claim legitimacy to extend that power externally. This is an essential factor in the rationale underlying the 'Fourth World War', to employ neo-conservative imagery. According to the former director of the CIA, James Woolsey, that war will 'sporadically involve the use of force' against 'fascist Middle East governments and totalitarian Islamists' outside of the United States and 'conflict between liberty and security' within.[385] Forced upon the US American political mind by nearly six decades of structural bipolarity, the *Denkmuster* of the current Bush administration and its neo-conservative nexus, remains committed to dichotic, black-and-white thinking. On the white side of the fortified boundary, stands the United States (and presumably Tony Blair), identified with righteousness, purity and good (hence the naming of the Iraq campaign as 'Operation Enduring Freedom'). On the other – black side – 'they', paralleled with equally absolute evil and barbarism. Invoking this duality serves the function to invent an almost metaphysical, sanctimonious and divine mission to convert the world, where America becomes a 'religion' and the US state the vanguard of 'armed evangelism'.[386] In that way, interconnectedness between 'us' and 'them' is denied, enabling the parties involved to crowd the masses behind 'our' common cause. That culture of thought constitutes the dominant narrative of contemporary elite politics in the United States, transforming the post-Cold War state identity of the country along the lines of the outlined neo-conservative precepts.

4.3.2 Circular interdependence: 11 September 2001 and the Third Persian Gulf War

The security transaction between the Persian Gulf area and the United States took place during a period when the country was undergoing a transformation in its ideational properties. The post-Cold war US state was pushed into the role of global leviathan, and 'American ideals' were presented as universally binding. In turn, this modified posture and its implications for US policies obstructed consensus building in the Persian Gulf, changing the perception of the country's role from systematically legitimated guardian of the status quo to regional hegemon. Interdependence (and by extension globalisation) is not a 'one way street' or unidirectional, however.[387] The increased security transaction between the United States and the Persian Gulf area after the Second Gulf War, did not only raise the vulnerability and sensitivity of regional actors to shifts in the identity of the US state, but made the US itself more receptive to events in the Gulf and beyond. The devastation caused in the heart of Manhattan by extremists associated with al-Qaeda ('the base') on 11 September 2001 made that vulnerability evident. The repeated request of Osama bin-Laden, leader and financier of the transnational terrorist network, to 'rise and defend the holy lands' and to 'remove evil from the Peninsula of Mohammad'[388] (i.e. Saudi Arabia) after the attacks on the United States and during the ensuing war against the 'Taliban' movement in Afghanistan, were indicative of the political violence that the US military presence provoked. As Ray Hinnebusch argued:

> While some interpreted the attacks as a symptom of a 'clash of civilisations', in fact, Osama bin Laden and his following of 'Arab Afghans' were partly a US creation, fostered against the Soviets in Afghanistan. They were turned against the US, not by religious or cultural differences, but by its continued presence in Saudi Arabia, 'home of the two mosques', its perceived control over Arab oil, its siege of Iraq, and its support for Israeli oppression of the Palestinians.[389]

Hinnebusch rightly asserts that the attacks on 11 September were not motivated by cultural rancour in the sense employed by Huntington, that is as a manifestation of conflict between seemingly homogenous cultural entities or civilisations. The causes were cultural in a different sense. They may be regarded as the culmination of violent opposition to the presence of US troops in the Persian Gulf (most notably in Saudi Arabia), which was in contradiction to the international political culture shared amongst agents in the region. In other words, although *state* actors (i.e. the governments of the GCC) accommodated the massive deployment of US troops on their soil, other culture bearing units – intellectuals, media conglomerates, transnational terrorist networks – projected norms, roles and institutions that were in opposition to the presence of US troops and the dependencies it generated. Having outlined the ideational shift of the post-Cold War US state, the following sections are designed to explore the emergence of 'neo-fundamentalism' amongst the elites in some Arab countries and its influence on regional politics. In order to avoid ad hoc statements and mono-causalities, the investigation is linked to the emergence of Islamic anti-imperialist thought from the turn of the twentieth century onwards, developing the discussion of the intellectual invention and reproduction of identities by elites in the Persian Gulf offered in Chapter 2. In a final development of the argument it is asserted that it was not power politics which determined the events leading to the invasion of Iraq in March 2003. Rather, the war was the outcome of the clash of two versions of absolutist, political-ideational systems – neo-fundamentalism and neo-conservatism. Both systems of thought did not accommodate diplomatic engagement and both legitimated their struggle on the basis of their exclusionary ideological precepts.

4.3.2.1 *Clash within civilisation? Contextualising the contemporary political culture of Islam*

The theories, ideologies and ideational agents constituting the international political culture of the Persian Gulf, as discussed thus far, converge in their strong emphasis on independence and fulminate rejection of (perceived or real) imperialism. In conflict with each other but united in their immanent revulsion against foreign dominance, Arab nationalism (and Ba'thism), Iranian nationalism and Islamic revolutionism and 'Wahhabism' share the view that struggling against hegemony is constitutive to salvage the self from the undue influence of the other (which is equally true for communist movements that I have not discussed here). Moreover, the identity, symbols, ideas and semantics of both Arab nationalism (in its Iraqi Ba'thist, Syrian Ba'thist and Nassirist versions) and political Islam – the two most influential ideational currents in modern West Asia – and their different national variations were deeply embedded in the struggle against imperialism in the first half of the twentieth century. For post-Ottoman Arab polities, both nationalist theory and political Islam provided the intellectual impetus to organise viable protest movements against the perils of foreign domination. Revived and constantly reinvigorated by the wars against Israel and the occupation of Palestine, post-colonial Arab elites turned towards religious and nationalist ideology to attain and legitimate political power domestically and secure the political entities from undue influence from without. In short, both nationalist and religious discourse were conducive to mobilisation of the populace against Western imperialism and the occupation of Palestine.[390]

Likewise, both Iranian-Islamic nationalism in its popular version put forward by Mohammad Mossadegh and Mehdi Bazargan, organised in the *nahdat-e azad-ye Iran* (Iran Freedom Movement) and Iranian-Islamic revolutionary theory as presented by Ali Shariati, Jalal al-e Ahmad and Ayatollahs Muttahari, Khomeini, Shariatmadari and Taleqani amongst others, discoursed on the imperative of resisting cultural penetration from – and political dependency on – the 'West'. As discussed in Chapter 2, Khomeini employed a modernised version of the Quaranic *mostazafan-mostakbaran* dichotomy in order to depict the contemporary struggle between the 'ones who are weak, disinherited, wretched' and 'the arrogant powers'. In his revolutionary semantics, Ayatollah Khomeini borrowed from two prominent intellectuals whose influence transcended the context of pre-revolutionary Iran and for whom struggling against 'Western' imperialism was central, namely Ali Shariati and Jalal al-e Ahmad.[391]

In one of the most influential anti-dependency theories in Iran, disseminated beyond the pre-revolutionary intellectual context in the country, Jalal al-e Ahmad equated penetration and dependency on the 'West' with a state of cultural and economic mediocrity he termed *gharbzadegi* ('westtoxification', 'occidentosis' or westitis). He defined *gharbzadegi* as:

a complex of circumstances which comes about in the life, culture, civilisation, and way of thinking of a people in one spot on the globe without any kind of supporting cultural context or historical continuity, or any evolving method of integration, coming about only as a result of the charity of machines.[392]

Employing a medical analogy, al-e Ahmad deprecated the decadent, mediocre and inauthentic status of Pahlavi Iran. If left untreated, he argued, the spread of the disease-like status would lead to the demise of the country's cultural, political and economic independence, because society was made susceptible to 'Western' penetration. Moving beyond the Iranian context, al-e Ahmad saw the struggle against *gharbzadegi* in terms of a conflict between the 'Occidental West' and the 'Oriental East'. Employing the metaphor of 'the machine', he argued that whilst the 'West' had learned to master the 'technology of modernity', the mediocre 'East' is kept in a state of political and economic dependency. The definition of this milieu of subjugation and power was dramatised as a means to alert the 'Eastern mind' about the creeping intrusion of 'westtoxification' and its corrupting symptoms on societies programmed to be subservient to their imperialist masters:

> Our sense of competition has been lost and a sense of powerlessness has taken its place, a sense of subservience.... One would think that all of our own standards are extinct. It has reached such a state that we are even proud to be their vermiform appendix. Today the fate of those two old rivals is, as you see, this: one has become a lowly groundskeeper and the other the owner of the ballpark. And what a ball game it is! Nine innings of genitals and thighs, charges of stupidity, mutual flattery, and bluster.[393]

Ali Shariati developed an equally critical position towards imperialism and cultural, political and socio-economic dependencies on the 'West'. During his education at the Sorbonne in Paris, Shariati was in contact with figures of the French left whose political outlook and intellectual paradigms were influential in his later writings. Those included Catholic Islamologist Louis Massignon to whom he was a research assistant during 1960 and 1962, the Jewish-Russian émigré George Gurvitch who was his professor in sociology, Islamologist Jacques Berque whose class on the 'Sociology of Islam' Shariati audited in 1963–1964, Frantz Fanon whose seminal *The Wretched of the Earth* he translated (in collaboration with others) into Persian, and Jean-Paul Sartre whose attempt to reconcile existentialism with Marxism and humanism had an important influence on Shariati's own attempt to synthesise social scientific concepts with Shia-Islamic political thought.[394] Ironically, he employed aspects of these ('foreign') ideas in one of his main publications entitled 'return to oneself (*bazgasht be-khish*), which appeared as serialised articles in the Iranian daily *Kayhan* between 22 April 1976 and 22 June 1976. Shariati argued that discovering the 'true identity' of Iran as a nation requires rejecting 'Western' cultural influences and foreign ideologies and reverting to the 'authentic' Iranian-Islamic self instead. Pointing towards the corrupting influences of 'Western' culture, he demurred the subordination of indigenous ideas, values and morals of the people in favour of an uncritical imitation of alien world-views.[395] Comparable to the views of al-e Ahmad then, Shariati developed his ideas in close relation to the 'imperialist' other which made the invention of the necessary journey back to the 'Iranian-Islamic self' possible in the first place.

Islamic anti-imperialist theory, that is intellectual paradigms opposed to the political, economic and cultural dependency of Muslim societies on imported

('Western') concepts, and favouring instead reinvigoration of Islamic tenets of the kind which gained prominence in different national contexts and versions in the 1960s and 1970s, was affiliated with modernist Islamic discourse developed in the nineteenth and early to mid-twentieth century by Muslim thinkers such as Jamal al-Din al-Afghani, Mohammad Abduh, Rashid Rida, Hassan al-Banna, Abu-l-Ala Mawdudi and Sayyid Qutb. It would go beyond the confines of this study to review the political thought of these theoreticians and activists and explore its manifestations in the Islamic world which has been pursued elsewhere.[396] What we are interested in are the nuances of anti-imperialism in the Islamic world, adopted in the manifestos of political elites, codified in political culture and institutionalised as fundamentals of the modern nation-states. This serves our interest to contrast the emergence of the neo-fundamentalist current propagated by bin-Laden and his followers with other movements reverting to the symbols and imageries of political Islam. Converging in their opposition to foreign dominance and in their reference to Islamic precepts, the intellectual paradigms differ considerably in their political and socio-economic outlook and in the sanctioning of the methods of opposition. In order to appreciate these variations, we differentiate between 'neo-critical Islam', embracing the ideas and paradigms of both 'progressive' *ulema* (Islamic clergy) and lay intellectuals who believe that democracy, pluralism, civil society or other manifestations of political modernity are principally compatible with Islamic precepts, condoning both discursive epistemology and dialectical methodology to bring Islam and modernity into dialogue with the 'West'; and 'neo-fundamentalist Islam', advocating passive adherence to literal reading of the Quran and the *hadith*, favouring orthodox implementation of the *sharia* (Islamic law) and isolation from the cultural, economic and political determinations of modernity. In other words, whilst the former accommodated 'Western' tenets, the latter promoted violent struggle against everything associated with the 'West'. The clash of that protest movement with neo-conservative ideology, it is suggested, constituted the context that led to the US led invasion of Iraq in March 2003.

4.3.2.2 'Neo-critical Islam': the social construction of Islamic intégrisme

One of the intellectual forefathers of 'Islamic anti-imperialism' is Jamal al-Din al-Afghani (also Asadabadi) who was born into a Shia community in Asadabad, Iran around 1838.[397] Experiencing Britain as a colonial power during his travels through India and Afghanistan, al-Afghani employed Islamic political philosophy to devise an anti-colonialist programme suitable to mobilise political action against European imperialists. Through his writings and political activism 'Al-Afghani vigorously opposed the racist notions then current in Europe which claimed that only Europe could produce a culture and civilisation and ignored all highly developed non-European cultures including Islam'.[398] Comparable to (Arab) nationalist theory (see the discussion of al-Husri in Chapter 2), the intellectual paradigm was developed in response to Ernest Renan's assertions about the inherent superiority of European civilisation, and emerged hence in dialogue with, rather than in isolation from, ideas produced in Western Europe.[399]

The anti-imperialist discourse inspired by Afghani and his pupil Mohammad Abduh (1849–1905) presented Islamic tenets within a modernist interpretation, adopting and refining European concepts in an attempt to reconcile the past with the present. Opening up the traditional monopoly of the *ulema* on the interpretation of Islamic law (the textual interpretation or *tafsir*) and jurisprudence (*feqh*) was central to this task. Demanding the resumption of individual interpretation or *ijtihad* of both the Quran and the *hadith* (compilation of the Prophets words and deeds), hence also rejecting uncritical imitation (*taqlid*) of religious verdicts (*fatwa*) central to Shia religious practice, the critical Islam of Afghani and Abduh was in an innovative dialogue with concepts developed in Europe, rather than in opposition to them. Incorporating nationalist ideas into an Islamic framework, Afghani's political Islam was primarily conceived as 'a communal identity – a basis for solidarity that distinguished the conquered from the conqueror and gave the conquered the cohesion and confidence necessary for rebellion and triumph'.[400] In order to resist European imperialism, he urged allegiance to the Ottoman state, whose leader Abdul-Hamid II co-opted Afghani's ideas as a means to legitimate his domestic rule and mobilise the populace against 'Western' forces.[401] In his political deliberations and intellectual writings, Afghani was hence indeed 'responding to imperialism' as Nikki Keddie observed, glorifying the Islamic past and the city state of Medina under the leadership of Prophet Mohammad (*madinat al-nubi*) as a means to transcend the overbearing present under imperial subordination.

Afghani's interpretation of Islamic political theory and philosophy, was adopted and developed by his pupil Mohammad Abduh with whom he founded the journal *Al-Urwa al-wuthqa* (The Indissoluble Link) in Paris in 1884. Educated at al-Azhar, Abduh became a judge in the Egyptian courts and was appointed 'Grand Mufti' of the country in 1899. His institutionalised authority allowed him to emphasise the compatibility between Islam and 'Western' science, advocating the reformation of the curriculum of the al-Azhar accordingly. By returning to the 'original' Islam of the pre-Umayyad period and a purified understanding of the Quran and the *hadith*, Abduh argued, a synthesis between Islam and manifestations of 'Western' modernity (especially the sciences) was achievable. Modernity as such was not seen as inherently threatening and in opposition to Islam. Rather, it is through reforming Islam (*islihat*) that Muslim societies would be empowered

> to liberate thought from the shackles of imitation [*taqlid*] and understand religion as it was understood by the community before dissension appeared; to return, in the acquisition of religious knowledge, to its first sources, and to weigh them in the scale of human reason, which God has created in order to prevent excess or adulteration in religion, so that God's wisdom may be fulfilled and the order of the human world preserved; and to prove that, seen in this light, religion must be accounted a friend to science, pushing man to investigate the secrets of existence, summoning him to respect established truths and to depend on them in his moral life and conduct.[402]

The ideas and constructs of Afghani and Abduh inspired scholars – explicitly or implicitly – to devise Islamic theories in at least two directions. Prominent Muslim intellectuals such as, Hamid Enayat, Muhammad Iqbal (1877–1938) and Ali Shariati (differences notwithstanding) developed innovative theoretical constructs as a means to advocate a critical understanding of the plurality of meanings in Islam, rejecting the monopolisation of religious thought by the *ulema*.[403] Backwardness (*ta'akhur*) and inertia (*jumud*) were juxtaposed with progress (*taraqqi*) and evolution (*tatawwur*). In dialectic cross-fertilisation with European thought, the idea of an Islamic awakening (*sahwa Islamiyya*) contributed to a strong 'anti-imperialist' culture. 'Western' *modernity* on the other side was not rejected *in toto*. Rather more to the contrary, scientific achievement and technological modernisation were seen as necessary prerequisites for the progress of Muslim countries. As Afghani noted in his reply to Renan

> If it is true that the Muslim religion is an obstacle to the development of sciences, can one affirm that this obstacle will not disappear someday? How does the Muslim religion differ on this point from other religions? All religions are intolerant, each one in its way. . . . I cannot keep from hoping that Muhammadan society will succeed someday in breaking its bonds and marching resolutely in the path of civilisation after the manner of Western society, for which the Christian faith, despite its rigours and intolerance, was not at all an invincible obstacle. No, I cannot admit that this hope be denied to Islam. I plead here with M. Renan not the cause of the Muslim religion, but that of several hundreds of millions of men, who would thus be condemned to live in barbarism and ignorance.[404]

The themes of *islahat* (reform), *tarraqi* (progress) and *tattawur* (evolution) continue to position prominently in the paradigms of contemporary Muslim thinkers such as Abdol-Karim Soroush, Ali Mazrui, Muhammad Arkoun and Rashid Ghannouchi. The *political* translation of neo-critical Islam and its contemporary engagement with the 'West' on the other side is exemplified in the *Weltanschauung* of reformist decision-makers such as Malaysian Prime Minister Mohammad Mahatir or Iranian President Mohammad Khatami who both advocate institutionalised dialogue with the West. The former authored the 'Dialogue Amongst Civilisations' theme which was adopted by the UN as the motto for the year 2001 and the latter convenes a yearly international conference on Islam and Democracy which has evolved into an international venue, focusing on improving relations between the 'Western' and Muslim worlds.

4.3.2.3 *Inventing 'neo-fundamentalism': anti-imperialism turned anti-Western*

Historically, 'neo-critical Islam' has benefited from the philosophical spiritualism practised by Islamic mystics (*sufis*) and is affiliated with the writings of Ibn-Sina (Avicenna, 980–1037) and Abu Hamid Muhammad al-Ghazali and the proponents of dialectical theology (*ilm al-kalam*), developed in the tenth and eleventh century AD.[405] Analytically, this tradition is distinguishable from the Hanbali school and its interpretation by Ibn Taymiyya in the thirteenth century AD. In agreement in their methodology to return to the precedent of the Prophet and his companions (*al-salaf al-salih*, hence the occasional designation as 'salafists'), modern interpretations of those classical writings differed considerably in their tolerance of internal dissent and external co-operation. Whilst adherents to the former tradition demanded deconstruction of traditional Islamic tenets in accordance with the determinations of modernity, the group of Islamic thinkers relating their ideas to the latter tradition reverted to a rather more fundamentalist reading of the Quran and the *hadith*. In contrast to the dialectical reasoning (*kalam*) and the philosophical tradition of Islamic thought presented by Ibn-Sina, Ibn Rushd Averroes (1126–1198) and Fakr al-Din al-Razi (1149–1209) amongst others, the school of thought deriving its ideas from the teachings of Ibn Hanbal 'was strongly opposed to all attempts at reducing the principles of Islam to a construction of the human intelligence, but showed great flexibility in applying them to the problems of social life'.[406] The Hanbali school has repeatedly functioned as a point of reference for neo-fundamentalist movements such as al-Qaeda. Hence, having outlined the signs and symbols of the philosophical tradition, we proceed with an examination of the neo-fundamentalist system of thought, exploring how the 'Hanbali' tradition was developed and politicised (some would say perverted) as a transnational protest movement against 'Western' modernity in general and the United States in particular.

In the thirteenth–fourteenth century, the Hanbali tradition was revived by Ibn Taymiyya (1263–1328), who preferred a literal and traditional reading of the revealed texts over the interpretative approach followed by the philosophical schools. In modern discourse, the works of Ibn Taymiyya (most notably the political treatise, *al-Siyasa al-shariyya* and the multi-volume *Fatawa*, religious verdicts and legal opinions) functioned as a point of reference for a host of thinkers and activists who were opposed to philosophical interpretations of Islamic thought and mystical practice within the *umma*, and reconciliation with 'Western' ideas outside of the community. The writings of Rashid Rida (1865–1935) emerged as the most prominent reinterpretation of Ibn Taymiyya and the Hanbali school of thought. Inspired by the politicisation of Islam by his mentor Abduh and al-Afghani, but not engaged in a comparable reconciliation with 'Western' modernity, Rida advocated a rather more fundamentalist reading of the Quran and *hadith*, without, however, refuting the principle of *ijtihad*. Perhaps the most consequential political move was his alliance with the Wahhabi movement in central Arabia and the policies of its leader Abdal Aziz ibn Sa'ud. Defending the new movement against allegations of unorthodoxy, Rida turned into an advocate of Wahhabism, condoning the Wahhabi conquest of the Hejaz and the holy cities which led to the foundation of the Saudi Arabian nation-state.[407]

The interpretation of the Sunni Hanbali tradition by Rida was developed into political-organisational programmes by Hassan al-Banna, Sayyid Qutb and Abu-l-Ala Mawdudi, each setting their agendas according to the historical contexts they were embedded in. Hassan al-Banna, who founded the Muslim Brotherhood (*Al-Ihkwan al-Muslimun*) in Egypt in 1928 and was assassinated in the same country in 1949 advocated political activism and socio-economic reform according to Islamic principles. During his leadership of the Brotherhood – which evolved into a transnational movement with branches in Syria, Sudan, Kuwait, North Africa, Jordan and elsewhere in the Arab world – al-Banna called for reform rather than revolution, preferring social engagement, spiritual development and moral achievement over political propagation against the state:

> You are not a benevolent society, nor a political party, nor a local organisation having limited purposes. Rather, you are a new soul in the heart of this nation to give it life by means of the Qur'an.... When asked what it is for which you call, reply that it is Islam, the message of Muhammad, the religion that contains within it government, and has as one of its obligations freedom. If you are told that you are political, answer that Islam admits no such distinction. If you are accused of being revolutionaries, say, 'We are voices for right and for peace in which we dearly believe, and of which we are proud. If you rise against us or stand in the path of our message, then we are permitted by God to defend ourselves against your injustice.'[408]

Despite al-Banna's apparent conservatism in relation to the political conduct of the *Ikhwan*, the Brotherhood played a pivotal role in mobilising volunteers to fence off Zionist aspirations of statehood in Palestine. Moreover, the organisation's institutional structure, encompassing schools, hospitals, companies and factories, empowered the Brotherhood to conduct a violent campaign against the Egyptian monarchy and Jewish and British interests in the country. As a consequence, Prime Minister Nuqrashi Pasha ordered the disbanding of the Brotherhood on 8 December 1948, less than three weeks before his assassination by the Ikhwan. Two months later, on 12 February 1949, al-Banna himself was assassinated by government agents.[409]

The second earlier Sunni movement that was created within the context of a struggle for political empowerment, the *Jama'at-e Islami* established in 1941, was created by the Indian/Pakistani theoretician Abu-l-Ala Mawdudi (1903–1979). Most of Mawdudi's theoretical ideas and political activism were developed in British ruled India between 1937 and 1941. Translated into Arabic by Ali Nedvi, Mawdudi's most prominent works – *Jihad in Islam, Islam and Jahiliyya* and *The Principles of Islamic Government* – reached a considerable audience in politicised Muslim circles. The central argument of Mawdudi's theory was that the Muslim *umma* had regressed into a state of *jahiliyya* (pre-Islamic ignorance). To overcome this all-encompassing crisis, Mawdudi argued, a return to the 'true' tenets of Islam and the creation of an Islamic state was imperative. A Muslim in exile in a colonised country, Mawdudi advocated a total *jihad* against the manifestations of non-religious (*la dini*) ideas in the Islamic world, opposing the encroachment of Islam by Western modernity *in toto*.[410] Consequently, Mawdudi argued that struggling against colonialism and imperialism is the central prerequisite for the creation of a purified, supreme society under the aegis of a fundamentalist, pan-Islamic 'kingdom of god'.[411]

The concept of *jahiliyya* anchored in the writings of Ibn Taymiyya and adopted by Maudoodi was popularised by Sayyid Qutb (1906–1966) in his publications *Hadha al-din* (This Religion), *Al-Mustaqbal li hadha al-din* (The Future is For This Religion) and *Ma'alim fi al-tariq* (Signposts along the Way). Confronted with the loss of Palestine and disillusioned with the conduct of military-authoritarian regimes, Qutb and his disciples dramatised the *jahiliyya* idea, transforming it into a revolutionary ideology, suitable to provide an intellectual underpinning of his leadership of the *Ihkwan*. After a short period of being so close to the movement of Abd-al Nassir's Free Officers that Qutb was appointed Secretary General of the regime's Liberation Rally in 1953, relations deteriorated to the degree that members of the *Ihkwan* were jailed and executed. Eventually, the conflict led to the arrest of Qutb himself (after an unsuccessful assassination attempt by one Brotherhood member on the life of Nassir in 1954) and his execution by the regime in 1966. Embittered about the political situation in Nassirist Egypt and rejecting the socialist, Arab nationalist populism of the state, Qutb used his prison years to advocate total opposition to the status quo both in Egypt and throughout the Islamic world:

> We are today in a jahiliyya similar to that contemporaneous to Islam or worse. Every thing around us is a jahiliyya: people's perceptions and beliefs, habits and customs, the sources of their culture, arts and literature, and their laws and legislations. Even much of what we think of as being Islamic culture, Islamic sources or Islamic philosophy and thought is in fact the making of this jahiliyya.[412]

Common to the ideas of Sayyid Qutb is a dichotomous and polarised world-view, permeated by seemingly inconceivable duality: *jahiliyya* vs. *the* Islamic order, the righteous *umma* vs. the infidels, *din* (true religion) vs. *kufr* (impiety) or the rightly guided prophets (*salaf*) vs. the polytheist (*mushriukkun*) or pagans (*wataniyyun*). Confronted with authoritarian regimes and engaged in an escalating power struggle with the post-colonial state, these variants of political Islamic theories laid down some of the nuances observable in the writings of Abdu and al-Afghani in favour of radical activism. In the political and cultural sphere at least, critical deconstruction of Islamic tenets in dialogue with the 'West' gave away to holist rejection of manifestations of modernity encapsulated in the 'Western' sciences and democratic-secular principles. According to Qutb:

> The leadership of western man in the human world is coming to an end, not because western civilisation is materially bankrupt or has lost its economic or military strength, but because the western order has played its part, and no longer possesses that stock of 'values' which gave it its predominance.... The scientific revolution has finished its role, as have 'nationalism' and the territorially limited communities which grew up in its age.... The turn of Islam has come.[413]

One would conflate goal-orientation with method, however if one would interpret the theories of al-Banna, Mawdudi and Qutb as anachronistic. Whilst the ultimate political goal was the establishment of a fundamentalist Islamic state and a 'morally pure society', method and methodology to achieve this goal accommodated modern strategies. The adoption of revolutionary theory, most notably in the writings of Qutb (leading to the preposterous charge by the Nassirist state that he was plotting to establish a Marxist regime in the country) indicates that advocating religious fundamentalism did not proscribe propagating modern methods to combat the state. Rather more to the contrary, revolutionary strategy was considered to be the prerequisite to seizing political power. In the following decades after the death of Qutb, the synthesis between utopian goal orientation and modern strategy continued to influence the campaigns of neo-fundamentalist groups who advocated armed struggle and political violence against either state or society or both.[414] In its contemporary, 'post-modern' manifestation, al-Qaeda's employment of the Internet for propagation purposes and its mode of attack on 11 September 2001 exemplify that advocating fundamentalist ideology is not synonymous with employing archaic strategies. Rather, 'Al-Qaeda's use of the internet and videotapes demonstrate that "perception management" is central to the conduct of its war with the West. In fact, it is possible to view all of Al-Qaeda's operations – including acts of violence – as one vast perception management operation.'[415]

Notwithstanding various differences between contemporary neo-fundamentalist groups, there are at least three issues on which they converge: in order to lead a pious life according to the 'true' principles of the Quran and hadith – purified from the 'distortions' brought about by neo-platonic philosophy and logic, Iranian (Persian) mythology and metaphorism, Jewish scripture and Christian theology – Muslims should organise themselves in the 'ultimate' Islamic state. Second, because every thing surrounding the umma is *jahiliyya*, Muslims should withdraw from modern society and engage in 'self-purification' (in the Islamic state). Third, the urgent need to establish *the* Islamic state legitimates total, offensive *jihad*, against both 'the hyp-ocrites' within the community – 'apostate' rulers who stand in the way of creating God's laws – and the infidels harassing Islam from *dar al-harb* (the abode of war or the forces of evil). These themes occupy neo-fundamentalist ideologies presented by Muhammad 'Abd al-Salam Faraj (see his *Al-Farida al- gha'iba*, The Absent Commandment), Abd al-Salam Yassin, Ayman al-Zawahiri (former leader of the Egyptian *Jihad* which in 1998 merged with bin-Laden's organisation to establish the 'International Front for Fighting Jews and Crusaders') and Osama bin-Laden himself. Partly because of political expediency, partly because of marginalisation in the various domestic political contexts, neo-fundamentalist groups do not limit themselves to confined opposition anymore. They are engaged in 'vertical jihad' – total war against Muslim states and societies which are perceived to have deviated from the true path of Mohammadian Islam – and 'horizontal jihad' – total war against the United States which is perceived as morally corrupt, hegemonic and the chief culprit in a Zionist-Imperialist conspiracy to destroy Islam. In Yassin's words:

> At the head of the Islamist caravan advancing with assurance on the road towards power and autarchy, you will find no Westernised fellowtravellers given over to the enemy both intellectually and culturally. You will find no friendships or alliances with the enemy. Neither will you find anyone of neat appearance and 'position of responsibility', who is in fact a dreary spy and whose life is spent in

a succession of 'apparatchniks' conferences and parties where information about the potential of the country is hawked about in exchange for hard currency. You will find no clients of Hilton hotels, dance halls and other dens of vice or habitués of seminars airing views akin to those of free-masons, Zionism, capitalism or intelligence agencies. You will find only soldiers of God mobilised to serve the material and economic cause of the community and considering this as an act of worship rewarded by God.[416]

That is the self-other delineation transnational neo-fundamentalist groups, including al-Qaeda identify with. The most radical adherents of the 'jihadist' paradigm emerged out of marginalised circles of the Wahhabi establishment in Saudi Arabia.[417] They gained 'radical maturity' within two political contexts: the war of independence against the Soviet Union in Afghanistan and the Second Gulf War against Iraq and here especially the ensuing alliance between Saudi Arabia and the United States. Whereas rather more 'moderate' Saudi organisations such as the 'Committee for the Defence of Legitimate Rights (CDLR)' led by Muhammad al-Mas'ari and the 'Movement for Islamic Reform in Arabia (MIRA)' under the leadership of Sa'd al-Faqih largely limited themselves to opposing the policies of the al-Saud leadership domestically, the Advice and Reform Committee (ARC) led by Osama bin-Laden, subscribed to a more ambitious programme.[418] The ARC defined itself as 'an all-encompassing organisation that aims at applying the teachings of God to all aspects of life', which requires 'a comprehensive understanding of Islam, the holy book and the Prophet's tradition as it was interpreted by our Sunni predecessors'.[419] In a communiqué entitled 'An Open Letter to King Fahd', bin-Laden outlined his grievances against the foreign policy of the Saudi government:

> In its foreign policy, your government ties its destiny to that of the crusader Western governments, It is shameful that a government that claims the protection of the Two Holy Mosques pays $4 billion in 1991 to help the Soviet Union before the Soviets washed their blood from killing Muslims in Afghanistan. In 1982, your government also aided the infidel regime in Syria with billions of dollars as a reward for killing tens of thousands of Islamists in the city of Hama. Your government also aided with millions a tyrannical regime in Algeria that kills Muslims. And finally your government aided the Christian rebels in southern Sudan.[420]

Apart from radicalising the agenda of Osama bin-Laden, the war experience in Afghanistan and the dependencies of the Saudi state on the United States in the aftermath of the Second Gulf War also constituted his organisation as a *transnational* force. Fighting Soviet occupation for over a decade – fuelled with Saudi money, political alignment and institutional backing and armed and trained by the CIA – the former context led to the internalisation of the ethics of war and the emergence of a transnational mercenary force of 'Arab-Afghans', indoctrinated to sacrifice their lives for the millenary cause of the organisation. When the occupation of Afghanistan terminated in 1989, Osama bin-laden and the Taliban appeared to follow the Qutbian notion that escaping the *jahiliyya* of modern society and establishing the ultimate Islamic state requires complete withdrawal from society and the formation of a nucleus of dedicated fighters willing to engage in political violence and martyrdom. This was what the Taliban-al-Qaeda alliance attempted to achieve in Afghanistan. A recent speech attributed to bin-Laden seems to demonstrate that goal:

> In order to establish the Islamic state and spread the religion, there must be [five conditions], a group, hearing, obedience, a *Hijra* and a *Jihad*. . . . We are in a situation of no longer having a country to which to make *Hijra*. There was an opportunity [to create such a country] – a rare opportunity. Since the fall of the Caliphate, the Crusaders made sure not to enable the true Islam to establish a state. . . . The Crusaders relinquished their resolve [to prevent the establishment of an Islamic state] because of their fear of the U.S.S.R. [They] had no choice but to repel the U.S.S.R. by any and all means, even by means of the *Mujahideen*, the fundamentalists, and the young *Jihad* warriors of Islam.
>
> Thus the gate opened. But unfortunately, a decade later, the [Islamic] nation – particularly the clerics, preachers, and sermonisers, and Islamic universities – did not meet the obligation. Those who came to the land of *Jihad* in order to support the Muslims and the *Mujahideen* were a small handful of the youth of the [Islamic] nation, in addition to the funds donated by some merchants; these were not sufficient to establish a strong country detached from geographical and tribal loyalties. Our Afghan brothers found themselves in a unique situation; an Islamic state could easily have been established according to Islamic, not national or geographic, standards.[421]

In contrast to movements such as the Palestinian Hesbollah, HAMAS or the Front Islamique du Salut (FIS) in Algeria which act within contextual boundaries and do not propagate a wholesale combat against the United States, Osama bin-Laden's network self-consciously divorced itself from any regulatory framework. Before the war in Afghanistan ousted the Taliban movement, the Taliban-al-Qaeda coalition had reduced the country to the status of an Emirate, rather than a nation-state, without an official capital, avoiding the definition of Afghan nationhood and adherence to secular law. Accordingly, the leader of the Taliban, Mullah Omar, did not take up the position of 'head of state', but declared himself 'leader of the faithful', preferring to staying in Kandahar rather than in the Afghan capital Kabul.[422] This explains why bin-Laden continues to propagate that 'it is a compulsive obligation upon the Ummah today to lend assistance to the Jihad in Afghanistan'.[423] From his perspective, Afghanistan could still be turned into *the* (pan) Islamic state from where he could organise his war against the United States and spread his political message throughout the Islamic world.

The second political context that gave impetus to the transnational appearance and appeal of neo-fundamentalism was the Second Gulf War and its aftermath. The reinvention of the secular, Ba'thist state by Saddam Hussein who had personally ordered the execution of religious leaders, as the vanguard of Islamic resistance against imperialism affected public opinion both in the Muslim world and in developing countries.[424] Whilst invoking anti-Israeli, anti-Saudi and anti-imperialist imageries did not secure the support of the *majority* of Islamic and developing states and their populace, alluding to 'emotionally charged, interconnected symbols in the Muslim political imagination',[425] rekindled organised, political opposition to US policies.[426] Pre-existing grievances grew stronger in the aftermath of the war, fuelled by pictures of starving Iraqi children transmitted by burgeoning Arabic satellite TV stations. The human suffering in Iraq hence became one of the points of fixations of the Muslim world and was perceived as yet another injustice brought about by 'Western' neo-imperialism.

From the neo-fundamentalist point of view, the situation in Iraq, together with the Russian war in Chechnya, and since 11 September the wars in Afghanistan and Iraq legitimated and continue to legitimate targeting US interests. Those political struggles are central to the propaganda of neo-fundamentalist groupings such as al-Qaeda al-Jihad, Hizb at-Tahrir or Jama'at al-Muslimin. Intellectually mediocre, their political activism is framed by a radical paradigm which legitimates political violence not only against Christian, Jews and US economic interests but also against Muslim minorities, evidenced by the killings of Shia in Pakistan and the Shia Hazara in Taliban Afghanistan. 'Jihadism' is self-consciously invented by selectively taking the combative passages from the Quran and the *hadith* out of context and combining them with the most puritanical writings in classical Islamic thought. That very perversion of the scriptures and writings, constitutive to the imagery and phraseology of the 'jihadist' paradigm, together with the indiscriminate violence employed against civilians, disqualified al-Qaeda as an organisation with structural support even amongst rather more militant organisations in the Islamic worlds. Revealingly, forty-six leaders, including those of the Egyptian Muslim Brotherhood, the Jama'at-e-Islami in Pakistan and Ahmad Yassin the founder of HAMAS, condemned the attacks of 11 September, stating that the

> undersigned, leaders of Islamic movements, are horrified by the events of Tuesday 11 September 2001 in the United States, which resulted in massive killing, destruction and attack on innocent lives. We express our deepest sympathies and sorrow. We condemn, in the strongest terms, the incidents, which are against all human and Islamic norms. This is grounded in the Noble Laws of Islam, which forbid all forms of attacks on innocents. God Almighty says in the Holy Quran: 'No bearer of burdens can bear the burden of another'.
>
> (Surah al-Isra 17:15)[427]

The effort to homogenise contemporary discourse on political Islam along the lines of the 'jihadist' denominator failed not least because there is no consensus on the ontology of political Islam. Here, contemporary debates reflect the idiosyncrasies in the writings of 'classical' advocates of political Islamic activism. Revealingly, in his earlier writings (hence before he was radicalised by the prison experience in Nassirist Egypt) the very Sayyid Qutb, whose 'signpost' has often been cited as the manual for contemporary radical movements,[428] praised the love and mercy in Islam, contrasting it to the antagonistic nature of communist ideology:

> [I]n the Islamic view, life consists of mercy, love, help, and a mutual responsibility between Muslims in particular, and between all human beings in general.

Whereas in the Communist view, life is a continual strife and struggle between the classes, a struggle which must end in one class overcoming the other; at which point the Communist dream is realised. Hence, it is patent that Islam is the undying goodness of humanity, embodied on a living faith, working in the world; while communism is the evil of human nature, limited to a single nation.[429]

4.3.2.4 The psychology of violence: mapping the neo-conservative and neo-fundamentalist mind

The argument of this section has been guided by the proposal that the interdependence between the United States and the Persian Gulf after the Second Gulf War exacerbated the vulnerability and sensitivity towards ideational shifts in the constituencies of respective agents in a manner powerful enough to influence the relationship between the two units of analysis. Exploring the conflictual side of interdependence further, we may discern linkage of a rather more psychological kind – an inter-subjectively shared, and alas increasingly hegemonic *Denkmuster*, rooted in a shared disregard of complex realities in favour of abstract and totalitarian solutions. The signposts of escalation – the Second Gulf War, the bombing of the World Trade Centre in 1993, the attacks on American military personnel in Riyadh in November 1995 and Dharan in June 1996, the US embassy bombings in Nairobi and Dar es Salaam in 1998, 11 September 2001, the war in Afghanistan and the invasion of Iraq in March 2003 – invested discourse in the United States and some Islamic countries with the idea that seemingly a-historical dichotomies set the two worlds apart. That this idea was implanted into the public imagery by two well-organised, well-funded ideological conglomerates with political leverage, makes the influence even more pervasive. On the one side, the dominance of neo-conservative thinking in the United States gave credence to the mendacity of *the* Islamic threat, typically asserting that

> we are facing a mood and a movement far transcending the level of issues and policies and the governments that pursue them. This is no less than a clash of civilisations – a perhaps irrational but surely historic reaction of an ancient rival against our Judaeo-Christian heritage, our secular present, and the worldwide expansion of both.[430]

On the other side, neo-fundamentalist stereotypes are anchored in a comparable reductionist world-view, abstracting from both the self and the other in order to propagate an inescapable stand-off between two diametrically opposed, seemingly monolithic entities:

> The Arabian Peninsula has never . . . been stormed by any forces like the crusader armies spreading in it like locusts, eating its riches and wiping out its plantations. All this is happening at a time in which nations are attacking Muslims like people fighting over a plate of food. In the light of the grave situation and

the lack of support, we and you are obliged to discuss current events, and we should all agree on how to settle the matter.[431]

The grammatical similarities in both citations, reflected in the employment of the pronouns 'our' 'we' and 'you', hint towards affinities in the mode of persuasion. For Prof. Lewis, the 'irrational, fanatic, Muslim other' is essential to delineate the 'secular, civilised, Jewish-Christian self'. Conversely, for bin-Laden and those who sympathise with him, that very Judaeo-Christian 'other' constitutes the 'infidel, overbearing, crusading force', threatening to destroy the 'humble, oppressed Muslim self'. Discourse analysis would inform us that using the pronouns we, you or our, instead of a noun substantive to designate an object without specifying it, serves the purpose of abstraction. Political psychology would add that reducing the 'other' to unspecified labels is constitutive to organising collective passions against the object which has already been rendered 'lifeless' by language. In turn, organising passions of belligerence is the prerequisite to 'crowd' collective violence, which is at base what both neo-conservatives and neo-fundamentalists want their addressees to be drawn to. Metaphorically, we may characterise the inter-subjective relationship as 'Janus faced' – two faces positioned on a body of absolutist thought looking away from each other by necessity of their immanent constitution. Attached to the same mindset, both *need* each other because the 'other' has become the referent for determining the self. In other words, the invention of an imagined community on which to base the communal identity of the in-group is integral with a perception of an inimical out-group reduced to an undifferentiated abstraction imprisoned in the term 'they'. Having discussed the consequences of that mindset in the Islamic worlds, we will propose in the following paragraphs that at least since 11 September, US neo-conservatism converged primitive passions and sophisticated strategies in ways that give credence to the mendacity of an a-historic clash between *dar-al Islam* and *dar-harb* or the 'West against the Rest' in Samuel P. Huntington's phraseology. Relating the argument back to our discussion about the transformations in the identity of the US state after the Cold War, it is argued that the internalisation of neo-conservative ideas by the current Bush administration – by implication of its ideological precepts – may be isolated as the primary cause for the decision to launch the invasion of Iraq in March 2003.

4.3.2.5   *The second neo-conservative war*

On 17 March 2003, President Bush spoke on US television (transmitted by a translated radio broadcast to Iraq), announcing the end of diplomatic efforts to secure a second UN resolution and giving Saddam Hussein 48 hours to leave Iraq or face war. Two days later, the US army, acting on intelligence that Iraq's leadership including Saddam Hussein and his two sons had gathered in one place, bombed the Iraqi capital. On 21 March, the unsuccessful attempt to assassinate the Iraqi leadership was followed by the highly publicised 'shock and awe' campaign, raining an estimated 1,500 cruise missiles and precision-guiding bombs down on strategic targets in Baghdad and other major cities in Iraq in 24 hours alone.[432] Concurrently, coalition soldiers launched the ground invasion of the country from the south.

The invasion of Iraq may be viewed as the second 'neo-conservative war' not only because it was the second inter-state war after 11 September, but specifically because it represented the second major conflict caused by neo-conservative ideology and strategic dogma. A review of the key pre-war policy speeches shows that the Bush administration gradually built up a 'portfolio' of strategic enemies, suitable to legitimate the introduction of the doctrine of pre-emption. Immediately after crisis struck the US mainland, President Bush introduced the new polarities of world politics in his 'address to the nation' on the evening of 11 September, declaring that the United States will 'make no distinction between the terrorists who committed these acts and those who harbour them',[433] introducing two abstract enemy categories ('terrorists' and 'harbouring states') which were further specified as the administration's move towards war became more determined. In his address to a joint session of Congress nine days later, President Bush remained committed to the dichotomous world-view intrinsic to neo-conservative ideology, declaring that '[e]very nation, in every region, now has a decision to make. Either you are with us, or you are with the terrorists. From this day forward,' Bush added 'any nation that continues to harbour or support terrorism will be regarded by the United States as a hostile regime'.[434]

Up until the address to the nation on 20 September, the list of adversaries was still evolving and there had been only behind the curtain deliberations about widening 'the war on terrorism' to include Iraq. Apart from naming the Taliban in Afghanistan (the 'harbouring state' category), and al-Qaeda, the Egyptian Islamic Jihad and the Islamic Movement of Usbekistan (the terrorist category), no other organisations or states were added to the enemy list. At this stage, the US administration, under the influence of the State Department, was still in the process of carefully building a coalition to attack the Taliban movement in Afghanistan, securing international legitimacy to that end on both the societal and inter-state levels. On 4 October 2001, the British government released a study, showing the close ties between al-Qaeda and the Taliban. Three days later 'Operation Enduring Freedom' was launched. Having secured a broad alliance, both the United States and the British government notified the United Nations Security Council that the attack was an exercise of individual and collective self-defence in compliance with the UN Charter Article 51, which allows for the use of force against an armed attack.[435]

Whilst the attack against the Taliban in Afghanistan was legitimated internationally, the invasion of Iraq was not. Six months before the attack on Iraq, the 'Task Force on Terrorism' of the 'American Society of International Law', issued a paper warning that '[p]reemptive self-defence...is clearly unlawful under international law'.[436] The paper concluded that the 'United States has no right...to invade another state because of speculative concerns about that state's possible future actions' and that the 'current international order does not support a special status for the United States or a singular right to exempt itself from the law'.[437] Despite such warnings, however, the institutional power of neo-conservatives, especially exerted by the 'Defense Policy Board' headed by Richard Perle which had been established at the Pentagon soon after 11 September, ensured that the administration remained committed to neo-conservative grand strategy.[438] After alluding to potential military action against Iraq at a press conference on 11 October 2001, President Bush used his 'State of the Union Address' on 29 January 2002, to build up the case against the regime of Saddam Hussein and allocate more states and organisations to the two categories invented immediately after 11 September. Hence, Hamas, Hesbollah, Islamic Jihad and Jaish-i Mohammad were added to the 'terrorist' category, whilst the 'harbouring state' category was embedded into the imagery of an 'axis of evil', comprising the governments of Iraq, Iran and North Korea. 'By seeking weapons of mass destruction' Bush declared 'these regimes pose a grave and growing danger'.[439] Reasserting the government's new pre-emption doctrine Bush announced further:

> We'll be deliberate, yet time is not on our side. I will not wait on events, while dangers gather. I will not stand by, as peril draws closer and closer. The United States of America will not permit the world's most dangerous regimes to threaten us with the world's most destructive weapons.
>
> Our war on terror is well begun, but it is only begun. This campaign may not be finished on our watch – yet it must be and it will be waged on our watch.[440]

Even after the State of the Union Address, the internal debate, or 'Potomac War', between the State Department under the leadership of Colin Powell who pointed out that a war against Iraq may not have the backing of US allies, and the Pentagon led by Donald Rumsfeld, who did not feel that this support was necessary in the first place, appeared to be still undecided. The former position was supported amongst others by former national security advisor Brent Scowcroft, who warned that a war without conclusive international support may cause 'an explosion of outrage', arguing that the United States would 'be seen as ignoring a key interest of the Muslim world in order to satisfy what is seen to be a narrow American interest'.[441] Despite voices of internal dissent however, the decision to pre-empt a future threat emanating from Iraq was strategic, inextricably linked to neo-conservative political culture and hence by implication pervasive, long term and decisive. Indeed, bringing the regime in Iraq down by force was presented as a strategic effort to 'reform' the whole 'Middle-East', indiscriminately enmeshing disparate contexts – Iraq, pre-emption, 'Middle East politics', weapons of mass destruction and al-Qaeda – into one eclectic narrative. Here, administrative officials went to great lengths to 'intellectualise' their case. In a speech to war veterans in Nashville, for instance, Vice-President Cheney quoted Fouad Ajami to support the government's case for war:

> Regime change in Iraq would bring about a number of benefits to the region. When the gravest of threats are eliminated, the freedom-loving peoples of the region will have a chance to promote the values that can bring lasting peace. As for the reaction of the Arab 'street', the Middle East expert Professor Fouad Ajami predicts that after liberation, the streets in Basra and Baghdad are 'sure

to erupt in joy in the same way the throngs in Kabul greeted the Americans'. Extremists in the region would have to rethink their strategy of Jihad. Moderates throughout the region would take heart.[442]

The official, international case for war was presented by President Bush to the United Nations General Assembly in his speech on 12 September 2002. Calling for a new resolution on Iraq, Bush concomitantly stressed that '[t]he purposes of the United States should not be doubted. The Security Council resolutions will be enforced – the just demands of peace and security will be met – or action will be unavoidable. And a regime that has lost its legitimacy will also lose its power.' On 8 November 2002, the UN Security Council passed Resolution 1441 unanimously, warning of 'serious consequences' if the Iraqi government would not offer unrestricted access to UN weapons inspectors. On 13 November, the Foreign Minister of Iraq, Naji Sabri, sent a letter to Kofi Annan readmitting UN weapons inspectors to Iraq, declaring that 'Iraq has not developed weapons of mass destruction, whether nuclear, chemical, or biological . . .'.[443] After four years, the UN resumed weapons inspections in Iraq on 27 November, kicking off a diplomatic row about the eligibility and legality of the use of force if compliance is not guaranteed. Opposed by France, Germany, Russia, China and Syria in the UN Security Council and hence unable to secure a second resolution authorising military intervention, the US and UK governments decided to launch an invasion of Iraq without further diplomatic deliberations. On 17 March 2003, President Bush spoke on television from the White House, declaring the end of efforts to secure a second UN resolution. Addressing the Iraqi people he announced:

> We will tear down the apparatus of terror. And we will help you to build a new Iraq that is prosperous and free. In a free Iraq there will be no more wars of aggression against your neighbours, no more poison factories, no more executions of dissidents, no more torture chambers and rape rooms. The tyrant will soon be gone. The day of your liberation is near.[444]

According to US National Security Advisor Condoleezza Rice the US decision to go to war was backed by a so-called 'coalition of the willing' comprising more than fifty countries.[445] Only Australia and Britain, however, agreed to send troops. On 19 March 2003, the US Army ordered the bombing of Baghdad followed by the full-scale invasion of Iraq one day later. After forty-three days of combat, on 1 May 2003, President Bush announced that 'major combat operations' were over, instituting a provisional administration of Iraq under US leadership. Since then, 'coalition forces' continue to face three of the most pervasive ideational narratives permeating contemporary Persian Gulf societies: religious- and secular-nationalism and transnational-fundamentalism. The former two versions of nationalism fuel the resistance against the US-led occupation of Iraq, engaging UK and US forces in a guerrilla war, with killings on both sides almost on a daily basis. The appeal of the latter continues to be exploited by groups such as al-Qaeda, leading to a significant and immediate upsurge in global terrorism since the war in Iraq was officially ended. On 12 May 2003, four co-ordinated attacks on housing compounds in Riyadh used primarily by US Americans and a residential compound used by the US Vinnel Corporation killed thirty-four people; on 18 May, at least forty-one people were killed in an organised attack in Casablanca; and on 7 June, four German peacekeepers were killed in the apparently 'pacified' Afghan capital Kabul.[446] Hence, despite of the termination of Taliban rule in Afghanistan and the demise of Saddam Hussein in Iraq, the ideological legacies permeating the two societies concerned continue to exercise their influence. Whilst the state or quasi-state structures have been dismantled, the political cultures continue to resist subordination.

It is not too far fetched to suggest that comparable to the invasion of Kuwait by Saddam Hussein, the US/UK invasion of Iraq may be identified as the second 'illegitimate' war in the Persian Gulf. The social construction of legitimacy has been a constant theme in this study and it has been repeatedly argued that role legitimation is dependent upon external approval. In contrast to the Iraqi invasion of Iran and 'Operation Desert Storm' which were represented as legitimate wars by international society (at least at that time), both the Iraqi invasion of Kuwait and the US led invasion of Iraq in March 2003 were opposed by the majority of international society – states and people – before, during and after the conflicts. Despite the deliberate efforts by the UK and US governments to present the war as 'just' and to secure a sufficient degree of international acquiescence to that end, the very fact that both states failed to secure UN compliance was an indicator for the structural opposition to the war. After all, even one week before the launch of the invasion, a US-UK draft resolution was still on the table, followed by an amendment giving Iraq until 17 March to disarm, the publication by the US government of a so-called 'road map' for the Palestinian-Israeli conflict, and another proposal by the British government, suggesting specific conditions that Saddam Hussein would have to meet swiftly in order to avoid war: going on Iraqi television to admit his possession of weapons of mass destruction (the official reason to go to war in the first place), allowing thirty scientists to be interviewed outside the country, with their families, within ten days, and surrendering the country's stocks of and product facilities for biological and chemical weapons.[447] In a last symbolic effort, the British and US governments hoped to get at least ninety votes to pass their draft resolution and to secure a diplomatic victory against the French government which had previously declared that it will veto any resolution authorising war. All of these efforts would not have failed, if there would have been sufficient international legitimisation comparable to the first war against Iraq in 1991 and the war against the Taliban in Afghanistan.

4.4   Parameters of co-operation and conflict

This chapter began by presenting the argument that international politics in the Persian Gulf after the Kuwait war revealed both processes of contestation of the regional culture of anarchy and reification of its underlying ideational structure. Anarchy was contested due to the strengthening of communitarian norms after the election success of Mohammad Khatami in 1997, and the ensuing reconstruction of the Iranian state identity. Reciprocated by the GCC states, the call for dialogue by the Khatami administration contributed to the stabilisation of regional order. Benefiting from the diplomatic engagements, Iran and the GCC states demonstrated the desire to promote face-to-face negotiations, to co-ordinate their policies and to foster cultural exchange. In contrast to the period between 1979 and 1991, the emergence of 'realism' in the conduct of external relations and reforms domestically reconstituted relatively stable relations between regional states. With the 'passion' for ideological experiments contained and the adoption of expedient foreign policies instead, the outbreak of war within the GCC and between one of the member states and Iran was rendered highly unlikely.

The second part of this chapter dealt with the reification of the regional culture of anarchy. Exploring shifts in the US state identity after the demise of communism, it was asserted that the dominance of neo-conservative political culture in the United States and the adoption of a unilateral posture by the state were the primary factors determining the country's policies towards the Gulf. After the events of 11 September and the strategic outline of the doctrine of pre-emption by the Bush administration, neo-conservative ideology had created its own self-fulfilling prophecies, determining the drive towards the invasion of Iraq in March 2003.

The second major source of conflict affecting the international political culture of the Persian Gulf was the emergence of a neo-fundamentalist current in political Islam. In contrast to the anti-imperialism promoted by neo-critical Muslim thinkers and activists at the turn of the twentieth century, neo-fundamentalist groups propagated total war against the West. Rejecting any form of accommodation and threatening the stability of conservative regimes in power (especially Saudi Arabia), transnational terrorist networks such as al-Qaeda rationalised their vertical and horizontal jihad on two grounds: the de-legitimisation of Arab states due to their dependencies on 'Western' security guarantees and the continued 'war against the *umma*' in Palestine, Iraq and Chechnya. Taken together, the clash of neo-fundamentalism and neo-conservatism, reified and 'facticised' from the one side as a 'global war against terrorism' and from the other as a 'global war against the crusaders', constituted the main sources of conflict in the post-romantic Persian Gulf. Both ideational currents, albeit to a different degree and in dissimilar proportions, transgressed rules, norms and institutions of international society, exacerbating regional conflict and disorder.

The empirical evidence marshalled in this chapter suggests that at no time was the post-Second Gulf War interdependence between the Persian Gulf area and the United States without crisis. Rather the contrary. By stationing large numbers of military personnel in the region and by formalising its security relationships with the Gulf monarchies, the United States de-legitimised the governments in power (especially Saudi Arabia) and turned itself into a target of violent political rancour. Why then did interdependence not bring about co-operation? One aspect pertaining to the conflictual outcomes of the interdependence was the nature of the relationship itself. At no stage was there a genuine dialogue between US decision-makers and allied governments in the Gulf about the future of the region – no joint 'US-Persian

Gulf task force', no formal and institutionalised venues for dialogue and debate, no organised intellectual exchange, tackling the political, economic, cultural and social issues pertaining to the peoples of the Gulf and the United States. The interdependence between the GCC states and the United States was hegemonic, artificial and not grounded in institution building, inter-cultural dialogue or other trust-building measures. From the perspective of opposition groups who were against the 'mono-dependency' of the Gulf monarchies, the interdependence must have appeared as a master and servant relationship, with some Gulf monarchies playing the role of 'Uncle Tom' in order to have partial access to the citadels of power in the United States and to lessen their security dilemmas at home. 'To a very considerable extent' Hinnebusch wrote before the Third Persian Gulf War

> the regional status quo, lacking indigenous popular legitimacy, is erected on hegemonic external force and on economic and security relations which benefit a relative few. The continued application of American force in the region is thus essential to maintain the status quo but, paradoxically, further undermines its legitimacy.[448]

After the second war against Iraq, the United States appears to be even more isolated, depending almost solely on military might to secure its position in Iraq.

The realisation of co-operative interdependence would have required the minimal normative identification between the US and the Gulf monarchies beyond narrow self-interests. From the perspective of the GCC states, the relationship with the United States and the 'West' in general was purely utilitarian: the typical realist phenomenon of bandwagoning with a hegemonic power against external threats. There was no incentive to rationalise the relationship beyond these confines because it was solely based on elite consensus, excluding engagement at the societal level, which remained marginalised, oppressed and if necessary outlawed. Influential segments of the US elite on the other side remained committed to the caricature of the Persian Gulf as an abstract, geo-strategic object with oil, the strategic prize vital to US national interests, dangerously ignorant about the inherent complexity and fluidity of national and international politics in the region itself. As a retired US Foreign Service officer and ambassador to the UAE observed:

> [T]o many people in the Gulf, the American presence seems to be solely military. Although high-level political leaders from European and other countries, including prime ministers, frequently visit Gulf rulers to seek their advice and support, senior American officials rarely do so. When they visit the Gulf, American officials are often more interested in asking for money than in consultation.[449]

The mutual ignorance to follow up security and economic relationships with inter-cultural and inter-societal dialogue caused conflict, because culture bearing units beyond the state level – intellectuals, institutions, 'terrorist' networks – projected norms and ideas that fostered opposition to the security dependencies created after the Second Gulf War. The influence of this political culture did not diminish with the demise of the Taliban or Saddam Hussein. The resistance against the occupation in Iraq, which is rationalised as a legitimate combat against an occupying force both in the region and beyond, exemplifies that one of the most dominant parameters constituting the contemporary international political culture in the Persian Gulf continues to be anti-imperialism – an institution that is rooted in the very intellectual and ideational fabric of contemporary 'post-colonial' Islamic societies.

Let me conclude with a theoretical note. From an analytical perspective (neo) realists would argue that the continued occurrences of inter and intra-state violence can be attributed to one or two independent variables put forward by (neo)realist theory. Our point was not necessarily to dismiss the 'realist' character of these policies, but to demonstrate that even the core components of (neo)realist theory and their policy manifestations have a social dimension to them. Security dilemmas can only be felt in relation to another actor, balancing (and 'bandwagoning' for that matter) makes only sense against something (or somebody) and self-interest requires delineating what the self (and hence the other) 'is' in the first place. Utilising experimentally proven cases in social psychology known as 'social identity theory',[450] we find that the cognitive differentiation needed for such processes requires having an alternate reference group. It has been a constant argument of this study that one of the primary factors causing conflict in the Persian Gulf was the adoption of exclusionary identities by regional actors. Alas, whilst the inclination towards 'othering' by regional states receded after the Second Gulf War, the US state and transnational terrorist networks such as al-Qaeda invented new enemy categories that were inherently conflictual. Again, the 'out-group' was discriminated in favour of the 'in-group' in order to create 'positive distinction', because the 'triumph of identity by one culture or state almost always is implicated directly or indirectly in the denial, or suppression of equal identity for *other* groups, states or cultures'.[451] It is our proposal that this 'ethnosuicidal' tendency was (and continues to be) the dominant source of conflict in the post-romantic Persian Gulf. The inability to transcend the process of 'othering' prevents institutionalisation of amicable relations amongst regional states, impeding movement of the Gulf society towards what IR theorists associate with 'Kantian' systems – an identification of the self which includes the other.[452]

5 Towards a cultural genealogy of anarchy in the Persian Gulf

Concluding reflections and ideas for future research

The subject of this study was the cultural genealogy of international politics in the Persian Gulf. I have started from the epistemological contention that anarchy cannot be subsumed under one narrative and has a cultural genealogy which requires investigation. In order to frame the empirical analysis, an epistemological discussion was presented. That discussion offered three principal methodological questions for studying conflict in the Persian Gulf: (1) What are the dominant political norms, institutions, values, identities and other cultural artefacts at a given period of time? (2) How are they invented, changed, reified and transcended by dominant political actors, most notably the state? (3) How do cultural artefacts condition the appearance of power and interest and how do they manifest themselves in strategic preferences?

In relation to the first question, empirical evidence was marshalled which demonstrated that the Persian Gulf did not constitute a 'Hobbesian' self-help system, determined by unending antagonism, perpetual security dilemmas and absolute realpolitik. Despite short periods of confined violence in the conduct of regional affairs, interaction between regional states did not justify realist pessimism. The empirical evidence showed that the death rate among states was nil, that crisis was contained and that in the end even small Persian Gulf states such as the United Arab Emirates, Bahrain, Kuwait, Qatar and Oman survived. After the atypical period of confined violence between 1979 and 1991, territorial boundaries have 'hardened' and since the latter half of the 1990s, inter-state war between littoral states has become highly unlikely. In short, in the contemporary Persian Gulf the weak are relatively secure because of the restraint of the strong and are not threatened in their very existence.

The Persian Gulf society did not constitute a 'security community' either. Despite forms of security and economic integration, most notably among the GCC member states but since the latter part of the 1990s also between the GCC and Iran, Persian Gulf states did not integrate to the extent that a sense of community emerged. Chances to institutionalise a viable security architecture were lost: in the pre-revolutionary period due to exclusionary identity politics projected most notably by Pahlavi Iran and Ba'thist Iraq; and after the Second Gulf War by the unwillingness of the victorious alliance to pursue inclusive security arrangements. Hence, although there was a relatively stable order, there was no stable peace. Despite trust-building measures among the littoral states, the continued pressures of transnational loyalties and exclusionary identity politics prevented movement of the cultural system towards rather more amicable relations, hence preventing the emergence of an inclusive, pluralistic 'West Asian community'.

How then can the Persian Gulf system be characterised? The central argument is that, since the modern emergence of the area, regional states have acted on the premise of a 'culture of rivalry', constituting an international society varying between mutual enmity and amity, the 'Other' represented as unambiguously neither enemy nor friend. Regional politics continued to have occasional 'shoot outs', without bringing about the annihilation of an actor, evidenced by the fact that the territorial composition of the contemporary Gulf has not changed in the last three decades. The most fundamental institution binding the culture of rivalry together was sovereignty. Sovereignty was not only an intrinsic property of the state, it was accepted as a right, mutually recognised by the majority of regional states and reinforced by the wider international society. That socially accepted right to existence provided a relative respite from life-threatening conflicts, allowing for the taming of anti-systemic movements, if necessary by collective force.

In relation to the second question – how are the cultural artefacts invented, changed, reified and transcended by dominant political actors, most notably the state – it was discussed how change towards self-help anarchy was prevented and the regional culture of rivalry was reiterated. Building the post-colonial state in search of institutional structure and ideational orientation, political elites reverted to exclusionary identity politics. That process of 'world production' was anathema to multilevelled dialogue between regional states that would have transcended the fortified boundaries between the peoples of the Persian Gulf. Not only were nation-state identities insulated as imagined communities, but 'othering' was institutionalised against the significant, immediate Other next door. Hence, Arab nationalists in their idioms and from within their own compromised locality attacked the 'untrustworthy Persians'. Whilst Iranian nationalists, on the other side of the cognitive divide, slowly perfected the metaphysical mendacity of naturally given superiority, equally devoid from empathy, critical attention to detail and historical consciousness. These categorisations were expressions of essentialisation – a pattern of doctrinaire, linear and seemingly unchallengeable self-aggrandisement that infested discourse in the Persian Gulf in the period of state-building in the twentieth century. From the regional perspective, the role of the United States was equally destabilising. Perhaps the most dangerous legacy of the American engagement in the Persian Gulf was the precedence set by invading Iraq without an international mandate. That must be taken seriously because it constituted an assault on the legal underpinning of sovereignty as a structural property of the international system and normative prerequisite for the functioning of order in international society.[453]

Finally, it was asked how cultural artefacts conditioned the appearance of power and interest and how they manifested themselves in strategic preferences. The empirical analysis demonstrated that rivalry in the Persian Gulf meant that the majority of regional states tended to act in a 'status quo fashion' towards each other. Since the institution of sovereignty made security more available, the anarchical society was not in a state of constant *Angst*. This did not mean that security was absolute, however. Although the 'fear from death' had been removed, the use of force remained an important foreign-policy choice. Hence, inter-state violence and war were simultaneously accepted and contained. If war erupted, regional states rallied round to punish whichever state was perceived to be the primary anti-systemic force – most notably Iran during the First Gulf War and Iraq during the second. If sovereignty had not been a structural property shared among the majority of regional states and reinforced by international society, then the culture of rivalry would have degenerated into a self-help culture, closer to what realists describe as 'Hobbesian' anarchy.

Legitimacy was central to the challenge to – and defence of – sovereignty. Sovereignty was challenged when actors did not accept the legitimacy of states, exemplified by the posture of revolutionary Iran in the decade after 1979, Saddam Hussein's Iraq after the war against Iran, transnational terrorist networks such as al-Qaeda in the late 1990s until the present day and the United States after 11 September. From the perspective of the Iranian revolutionaries, the regional order was essentially an 'American' order sustained and nurtured by weak proxy states on the Arabian peninsula. The challenge by the Ba'thist regime in Iraq was directed towards the same states, based on the claim that after the Iran war, the oil monarchies were blocking the development of Iraq, hence threatening the country's leadership role in the Arab world. Agents of an emergent 'jihadist' paradigm within political and socio-economic elites in 'Wahhabi' circles, transnational terrorist networks questioned the legitimacy of key states such as Saudi Arabia on political and politicised religious grounds, waging a war on two fronts: within these countries and against the United States as the most prominent ally of the conservative regimes. The policies of the Bush administration were equally conflictual. By advocating regime change in Iran and realising that goal in Iraq without a decisive international mandate to legitimate these actions, the Bush administration negated one of the principal foundations of international political culture – that legitimacy requires international recognition or multilateral consent and that inter-state rivalry in the Persian Gulf is constrained by international law.

The empirical analysis demonstrated that the revolutionary mandate of Iran, the territorial ambitions of Iraq, the transnational programme of terrorist organisations and the pre-emptive doctrine of the United States were contradictory to the norms and institutions of regional (and global) political culture. In the case of the former two, sovereignty was defended *explicitly* because Islamic Iran's revolutionary mandate and Iraqi pan-Arabism were perceived to threaten the regional status quo in its entirety. Consequently, both were balanced out by a combination of diplomatic brinkmanship, gunboat diplomacy and military force. In the case of the latter two, the situation is still evolving. Central to my argument is that in all four cases the challenges to legitimacy caused conflict, which in turn highlighted the importance of the institution of sovereignty to the affected states. Despite sympathetic allegiance to the ideas of Iranian-Islamic revolutionism, Iraqi Ba'thist Arab nationalism, Osama bin-Laden's 'jihadism' and nervous acquiescence in US claims to hegemony, the self-bestowed roles of the respective actors were neither decisively legitimated in the region, nor by global forces. In all four cases – to highly dissimilar degrees – international society found its ways to isolate or condemn what it considered to be the offending actor.

Taken to its logical conclusion, this argument about the centrality of sovereignty as a *structural* phenomenon suggests pressures towards conformity exercised by the cultural parameters of the contemporary international society. By interacting with the international system, nation-state units automatically claim the attributes enshrined in international culture. No government willingly forfeits its right to the artefacts of that culture, such as sovereignty, the domestic monopoly of violence, territorial integrity and so on. Without the formal, external affirmation of these rights, however, governments would not be able adequately to act them out (the fate of Saddam Hussein's Iraq). By claiming external affirmation the nation-states subordinate their 'desires' (transnational loyalties for instance) to the rules of the international game. There is hence a socially constructed layer of shared formal rules and established norms of international society that exercise pressures on the nation-state units to conform. Socialisation in these global structures constitute the states as 'rationalised' actors. In other words, the dependency of governments on the minimal external recognition about their legitimacy as nation-states pushes the states towards confirming with the parameters of international culture. By trial and error, nation-states experience how far they can stretch that culture (as Iran and Iraq did and the United States continues to do). Eventually, however, the push towards isomorphism exercised by the international system appears to be stronger than the pull towards transnational loyalties (pan-Arabism in the case of Iraq and revolutionary internationalism in the case of Iran) and perhaps unilateral pre-emption (the United States?). According to 'world cultural theorists' this mechanism organises nation-states into 'functionally undifferentiated', unitary actors. 'As creatures of exogenous world culture' it is argued 'states are ritualised actors marked by intensive decoupling and a good deal more structuration than would occur if they were responsive only to local, cultural, functional, or power processes'.[454] In turn this would mean that the more Persian Gulf states claimed the key features of rational state actors, the more structurally similar or 'isomorphic' they became. By implication, this contributed to a systemically constituted de-coupling from the pressures of transnational loyalties such as pan-Arabism or Islamic internationalism. Even the most strident transnational agents of these two ideational systems, Iraq and Iran respectively, were affected by global political culture, shaping the two states into entities which digested the formal rules and established norms of international society. Taken together with the de-legitimisation of the pan-Arab cause due to the Second Gulf War, the pressures of international political culture can hence be isolated as the second structural cause for the primacy of state sovereignty *vis-à-vis* transnational loyalties in the post-romantic Persian Gulf.

With an eye on future developments it is well worth it to develop ideas about what 'thinking' might yield movement towards the communitarian end of international life in the Persian Gulf, that is *change* of the anarchic culture of rivalry towards amicable relations. In their seminal work Karl Deutsch and his associates defined a security community as a group of people that had gone down the path of integration to the degree that there is 'real assurance that the members of that community will not fight each other physically, but will settle their disputes in some other way'.[455] They differentiated between two variants: 'amalgamated security community' (the United States is given as an example), defined as the 'formal merger of two or more previously units into a single larger unit, with some type of common government after amalgamation';[456] and 'pluralistic security community' which preserves the formal independence of autonomous governments. Communication processes and transaction flows between peoples is central to the emergence of pluralistic security community. With migration, tourism, cultural and educational exchanges, a reflexive social fabric is created which appreciates process on both elite and societal level. The transaction and communication processes, Deutsch argued, instils the sense of community, which turns into a 'matter of mutual sympathy and loyalties; of 'we feeling', trust, and mutual consideration; of partial identification in terms of self-images and interests; of mutually successful predictions of behaviour'.[457]

Central to thinking in communitarian terms is an understanding of interdependence that is prior to empirical phenomena such as communication and transaction processes. We borrow from post-modern notions here, highlighting that the origin of an agent – individual or state – is inextricably linked to the differentiation between Self and Other. Self–Other delineation has been a central theme in this study, whether in my emphasis on notions of Iranian superiority inherent in Iranian nationalist discourse, the equally invented myth of the 'Persian' threat to the Arab *umma* in some Arab nationalist writings or the issues surrounding US neo-conservatism. 'If we proceed from the basis of recognising that the very being of a state . . . derives from its relationship with the Other', David Campbell argues, 'that state is thus always already engaged with the Other and can feign neither ignorance about nor lack of interest in the Other's fate'.[458] That states can not afford to insulate themselves from the world, is not at least a by-product of globalisation, in its perverse form evidenced by the events on 11 September. There is hence an in-built 'common fate' in the relation between states which demands 'self-restraint' because any act of violence is likely to have repercussions for both the Other *and* the Self. Realists would emphasise that the inability to foresee benign intentions and willingness towards self-restraint in the absence of a central arbitrating authority, may have fatal consequences for the very survival of the actor. 'Yet despite our limited telepathic abilities' Wendt rightly points out 'human beings do manage to make correct inferences about each other's – even strangers – intentions, much, even most, of the time'.[459] If that would not be the case, we would engage with society in a state of constant *Angst* for our physical survival. Culture, in this case shared knowledge that most people around us do not intend to threaten our life, helps us to live in relative security. We have argued the same in relation to international society, even if there is no central body enforcing international political culture. Small states do not interact with international society with the constant fear that they will be annihilated by more powerful actors. If this *relative* security would not be there, small states would not constitute a considerable part of the international system. Indeed, the contemporary international system is not only inhibited by a large number of small states, but states such as Kuwait, the UAE, Singapore are among the richest and most prosperous members of international society.

If our knowledge about the Other is central to our understanding of each others intentions, dialogue, transactions and communication become the necessary tools to create trust. Here, instituting communicative action and institutionalising regional forums for dialogue ensure that diplomacy evolves as the only permissible 'language' of inter-state interaction in the Persian Gulf. The region cannot afford to be treated as an area for ideological experiments, whether intra-regional or extra-regional. Recent efforts between the GCC states and Iran have demonstrated that a 'communitarian Gulf' does not have to remain a remote utopia. Even the states of Saudi Arabia and Iran, from an orientalist perspective condemned to eternal antagonism because of their apparently diametrically opposed religious-ideological orientations (i.e. Wahhabi-conservatism vs. Shia-revolutionism), found ways to transcend their insecurities, extending their dialogue into the contested realm of religion.[460] As a Saudi Arabian daily pointed out: 'The facts that favour an existential partnership between the Kingdom and Iran are many. They go beyond such things as common border and they [include the common] Islamic faith'.[461]

The emergence of a sense of community in the Persian Gulf commands restraint, sanctions non-violence, requires a degree of solidarity and prohibits the use of war in the conduct of inter-state affairs. The current positive trends are not irreversible and it remains to be seen how an independent Iraq will fit into the security equation, but at the time of our writing, decision-makers on both sides of the Gulf appear to feel relatively reassured that they will not fight each other in the near future. Structural change, by definition of the meaning of the term 'structure', is difficult to bring about. But, there is no a priori, god given, natural reason why a region that is embedded in a 'thick' social structure, which has emerged out of several millennia common history and intensive interaction, evidenced relatively few major wars, which is economically linked by a powerful cartel and which is inhibited by shared religious bonds and cultural idioms, should be condemned to follow a specific narrative that guides it towards conflict and enmity. Cultures of anarchy do not imply ontologically predetermined and eternally valid uniqueness, unalterable character or any privileged status as something complete, closed and total in and of themselves. If Persian Gulf states treat each other as enemies, than international life will be determined by conflict, self-help, insecurity. If they treat each other as friends, than 'our' interest becomes 'theirs', self-interest is broadened to include the collective interest, tribal *asabiyya* turns into 'Gulf *asabiyya*', the Self and Other emerge as a single 'cognitive region'.[462]

Communitarian thinking has figured prominently in classical Islamic thought and, reformulated to the realities of the contemporary state system, may provide points of reference for future research. To a certain extent 'de-reification' of existent cultural systems, both as an intellectual effort and political praxis, requires the disintegration of 'taken-for-granted' structures in international society – both in the Persian Gulf and beyond. This is not an ideological plea for revolutionary upheaval, but an 'emphatic' case for an equitable international order. History provides for many examples of how crisis led to the questioning – indeed abolishment of 'complex reifying systems' that have previously been taken for granted as facts of nature. Such transformative times of crisis have revealed that structure and culture are man-made, empowering society to assert itself *vis-à-vis* overbearing systems. If it is accepted that the post-11 September disorder is produced as proof for the perennial state of war in international relations, the 'fact' of anarchy would be no longer recognisable as product – but taken for granted as the standard for objective reality. Once self-help anarchy constitutes the dominant narrative of international society, its culture exercises structural pressures on the state to conform. Living in such an *alien* reality would mean that the state *has* to adopt an aggressive role identity in order to survive. The danger of pre-emption lies in this gloomy prospect for world politics, because it precipitates moments of international 'a-sociality'. States adopting that strategy do not reduce themselves to 'rhetorical deterrence'. Once accommodated as an acceptable norm, the whole military-industrial apparatus is made to believe in pre-emptive strikes – the officers, army, functionaries and other segments of society are made to mean 'to do it'. In such a context, even hypocrites become captive to declared intentions, yielding to the psychological pressures to achieve a level of consistency with the institutionalised norm. This study has demonstrated how countries were pushed towards acting out what was constantly reified and reproduced as the primary source of identity of the state, breaking the borderline between political idiom and political action. In terms of behavioural prescription, pre-emption and unilateralism are not very different from pan-Arabism and Iranian revolutionism. All three ideas command transnational – indeed expansionist and hegemonic foreign policies from their agents.

Finally, allow me to return to the disciplines that this study referred to: International Relations and Area Studies. The comprehensive approach that we alluded to in the preface demands the appreciation of international political cultures, and discussion of the ideational belief systems against the background of social-scientific IR theory. This is not an eclectic perspective, but follows with necessity from the self-declared deficiencies of contemporary 'Middle East' studies and International Relations. Whilst on epistemological grounds both disciplines may be positioned on two different ends of a duality – 'parsimonious/theoretical-holism' vs. 'atomistic, empiricist-particularism' – the inclinations towards positivism and essentialism(s) is shared. On the one hand side, orthodox IR scholars abstract from 'the periphery' in favour of global-systemic politics. On the other, area specialists tend to abstract from global-systemic politics in favour of regionalist mono-causalities. In both cases, analysis is characterised by an either-or-contraposition (global systemic vs. regional sub-system), too often a result of lacking inter-disciplinary perspective and integrative methodologies and in its empirical and theoretical elucidation hence unappreciative of shifting determinations between the two interacting contexts of international society.

This study has demonstrated that cultural analysis does not presuppose the superiority of one mode of enquiry over the other a priori. The same relativistic perspective that permits visualisation of the constructedness of international 'reality', forces critical evaluation of the nature of scientific evidence.[463] Instead of taking scientific 'proof' for granted, critical cultural analysis deals with the 'symbolic-expressive' constitution of international society, identifying empirical regularities and patterns that specify the meaning of a particular political act, by exploring patterns of interaction between dominant actors of society. Critical analysis of political cultures hence determines what is specifically social in international life, reconstituting the importance of the avowed object of the study of world politics, namely international political *action*. In the current period of crisis, we can no longer afford conceptions of world politics that stress linear development; any more that we should yield to the temptations of confining world politics to one iron-clad master narrative with universal applicability. There needs to be room to contest teleological theory and for intellectual exchange that partakes neither of orthodoxy, nor of the partisan affirmation about the supremacy of one world-view. Unless there is no systematic effort to resist what is too often presented as authoritative discourse, both enquiry into international life and 'practising' world politics threatens to remain devoid of one of the central features of intellectual and political freedom – *choice*.

Notes

Introduction

1 Friedrich Nietzsche, *The Birth of Tragedy; and The Genealogy of Morals*, translated by Francis Golffing, Garden City: Anchor Books, 1956, p. 157.

2 Andrew Linklater, *Beyond Realism and Marxism: Critical Theory and International Relations*, London: Macmillan, 1990, p. 27. See further Andrew Linklater (ed.), *International Relations: Critical Concepts in Political Science*, London: Routledge, 2000, especially volumes IV and V.

3 For a critical review see Stephanie G. Neuman (ed.), *International Relations Theory and the Third World*, London: Macmillan, 1998 and Arlene Tickner, 'Seeing IR Differently: Notes from the Third World', *Millennium: Journal of International Studies*, Vol. 32, No. 2, 2003, pp. 295–324.

4 The lack of theoretical bridge building in 'Middle Eastern' Studies has been noted in L. Carl Brown (ed.), *Diplomacy in the Middle East. The International Relations of Regional and Outside Powers*, London: I.B. Tauris, 2001, p. 304.

1 Studying conflict in the Persian Gulf: an epistemological introduction

5 The necessarily imperfect term is intended to supplement the equally undefined phrase 'Middle East', denoting the Western area of the Asian continent excluding the Maghrib (North Africa) and encompassing Israel, Turkey, Syria, Lebanon, Jordan, Iraq, Iran and the other Persian Gulf littoral states. On the invented delineation of the Middle East see Pinar Bilgin, 'Inventing Middle Easts: The Making of Regions Through Security Discourses', in Bjørn Olav Utvik and Knut S. Vikør (eds), *The Middle East in a Globalised World. Papers from the Fourth Nordic Conference on Middle Eastern Studies, Oslo 1998*, London: C. Hurst & Co., 2000, pp. 10–37; Roderic H. Davison, 'Where is the Middle East?', in Richard Nolte (ed.), *The Modern Middle East*, New York: Columbia UP, 1963, pp. 13–29; Ghassan Salamé, 'The Middle East: Elusive Security, Indefinable Region', *Security Dialogue*, Vol. 25, No.1, 1994, pp. 17–35; Bassam Tibi, *Conflict and War in the Middle East. From Interstate War to New Security*, second edition, London: Macmillan, 1998, pp. 43–60.

6 For a review of the core components of realist theory see among others Joseph M. Grieco, 'Realist International Theory and the Study of World Politics', in Michael W. Doyle and G. John Ikenberry (eds), *New Thinking in International Relations Theory*, Oxford: Westview, 1997, pp. 163–201 and Robert O. Keohane (ed.), *Neorealism and its Critics*, New York: Columbia UP, 1986.

7 See on this point Richard Wyn Jones (ed.), *Critical Theory and World Politics*, London: Lynne Rienner, 2001.

8 See Emanuel Adler, 'Seizing the Middle Ground: Constructivism in World Politics', *European Journal of International Relations*, Vol. 3, No. 3, 1997, pp. 319–363; John Gerard Ruggie, 'What Makes the World Hang Together? Neo-utilitarianism and the Social Constructivist Challenge', *International Organization*, Vol. 52, No. 4, 1998, pp. 855–885; Ronald L. Jepperson, Alexander Wendt and Peter J. Katzenstein, 'Norms, Identity, and Culture in National Security', in Peter J. Katzenstein (ed.), *The Culture of National Security. Norms and Identity in World Politics*, New York: Columbia UP, 1996, pp. 33–75; Yosef Lapid and Friedrich Kratochwil (eds), *The Return of Culture and Identity in IR theory*, London: Lynne Rienner, 1996; Alexander Wendt, *Social Theory of International Politics*, Cambridge: Cambridge UP, 1999, chapters 1 and 2.

9 See amongst others Peter Wilson, 'The English School of International Relations: A Reply to Sheila Grader', *Review of International Studies*, Vol. 15, No.1, 1989, pp. 49–58; R.J. Barry Jones, 'The English School and the Political Construction of International Society', in B.A. Roberson (ed.), *International Society and the Development of International Relations Theory*, London: Pinter, 1998. For a critical view see Roy Jones, 'The English School of International Relations: A Case for Closure', *Review of International Studies*, Vol. 7, No. 1, 1981, pp. 1–13.

10 See John W. Meyer, 'The World Polity and the Authority of the Nation-State', in Albert Bergesen (ed.), *Studies of the Modern World System*, New York: Academic Press, 1980, pp. 109–137; John W. Meyer, John Boli, George M. Thomas, and Francisco O. Ramirez, 'World Society and the Nation-State', *American Journal of Sociology*, Vol. 103, No. 1, 1997, pp. 144–181; John W. Meyer and Ronald L. Jepperson, 'The "Actors" of Modern Society: The Cultural Construction of Social Agency', *Sociological Theory*, Vol. 18, No. 1, 2000, pp. 100–120.

11 See Richard K. Ashley, 'The Poverty of Neorealism', *International Organization*, Vol. 38, No. 2, 1984, pp. 225–286; Richard Ashley, 'Untying the Sovereign State: A Double Reading of the Anarchy Problematique', *Millennium*, Vol. 17, No. 2, 1988, pp. 227–262; James Der Derian and Michael J. Shapiro (eds), *International/Intertextual Relations. Post-modern Readings in World Politics*, Lexington: Lexington Books, 1989; James Der Derian, *Antidiplomacy. Spies, Terror, Speed, and War*, Oxford: Blackwell, 1992. For further post-modernist readings and discussion see Pauline Marie Rosenau, *Postmodernism and the Social Sciences: Insights, Inroads and Intrusions*, Princeton, NJ: Princeton UP, 1992; D.S.L. Jarvis, *International Relations and the Challenge of Postmodernism: Defending the Discipline*, Columbia, MO: University of South-Carolina Press, 1999.

12 See Rebecca Grant and Kathleen Newland (eds), *Gender and International Relations*, Bloomington, IN: Indiana UP, 1991; J. Ann Tickner, *Gender in International Relations: Feminist Perspectives on Achieving Global Security*, New York: Columbia UP, 1992.

13 See especially Raymond Hinnebusch, *The International Politics of the Middle East*, Manchester: Manchester UP, 2003; Shibley Telhami and Michael Barnett (eds), *Identity and Foreign Policy in the Middle East*, London: Cornell UP, 2002; Michael Barnett, *Dialogues in Arab Politics: Negotiations in Regional Order*, New York: Columbia UP, 1998; Michael Barnett and F. Gregory Gause III, 'Caravans in Opposite Directions: Society, State and the Development of a Community in the Gulf Cooperation Council', in Emanuel Adler and Michael Barnett (eds), *Security Communities*, Cambridge: Cambridge UP, 1998, pp. 161–197.

14 See Kenneth N. Waltz, *Theory of International Politics*, New York: McGraw-Hill, 1979.

15 See Barry Buzan and Ole Waever, *Regions and Powers: The Structure of International Security*, Cambridge: Cambridge UP, 2003; Shibley Telhami, *Power and Leadership in International Bargaining: the Path to the Camp David Accords*, New York: Columbia UP, 1990; Stephen Walt, *The Origins of Alliances*, Ithaca, NY: Cornell UP, 1987. More recently, realist theory has been adopted by regional experts. See Raymond Hinnebusch and Anoushiravan Ehteshami (eds), *The Foreign Policies of Middle East States*, London: Lynne Rienner, 2002. For a (global) systemic account of regional politics in the Waltzian neo-realist tradition see Birthe Hansen, *Unipolarity and the Middle East*, Richmond, Surrey: Curzon, 2000.

16 See among others Samir Amin, *The Arab Nation: Nationalism and Class Struggles*, London: Zed, 1978; Abbas Alnasrawi, *Arab Nationalism, Oil and the Political Economy of Dependency*, London: Greenwood, 1991; Simon Bromley, *American Hegemony and World Oil: The Industry, the State System and the World Economy*, Cambridge: Polity Press, 1990 and *Rethinking Middle East Politics. State Formation and Development*, Cambridge: Polity Press, 1994; Jaqueline Ismael, *Kuwait: Dependency and Class in a Rentier State*, Gainesville, FL: University Press of Florida, 1993; Paul Salem, *Bitter Legacy. Ideology and Politics in the Arab World*, Syracuse, NY: Syracuse UP, 1994.

17 See Michael Barnett and Jack S. Levy, 'Domestic Sources of Alliances and Alignments: the Case of Egypt, 1962–73', *International Organization*, Vol. 45, No. 3, 1991, pp. 369–395; Also Bahgat Korany, Paul Noble and Rex Brynen (eds), *The Many Faces of National Security in the Middle East*, London: Macmillan, 1993.

18 See Buzan, Barry and Ole Waever, *Regions and Powers: The Structure of International Security*, Cambridge: Cambridge UP, 2003, part 3.

19 Margaret Mead, 'Warfare is Only an Invention – Not a Biological Necessity', in Leon Bramson and George W. Goethals (eds), *War. Studies from Psychology, Sociology, Anthropology*, London: Basic Books, 1964, pp. 269–274.

20 See Alexander Wendt, 'Anarchy is What States Make of It: the Social Construction of Power Politics', *International Organization*, Vol. 46, No. 2, 1992, pp. 391–425.

21 Gordon W. Allport, 'The Role of Expectancy', in Bramson and Goethals (eds), *War*, p. 179, emphasis in original.

22 Robert W. Cox, 'Social Forces, States and World Orders: Beyond International Relations Theory', in Keohane (ed.), *Neorealism*, p. 207.

23 Michel Foucault, 'Nietzsche, Genealogy, History', in Paul Rabinow (ed.), *The Foucault Reader*, London: Penguin Books, 1984, p. 78. For an IR perspective on Foucault's genealogical analysis see Richard K. Ashley, 'The Geopolitics of Geopolitical Space: Toward a Critical Social Theory of International Politics', *Alternatives*, Vol. 12, No. 4, 1987, pp. 403–434.

24 Foucault, in Rabinow, *The Foucault Reader*, p. 81.

25 I have moved beyond the confines of the IR literature here. See Alan Nelson, 'How "Could" Scientific Facts be Socially Constructed?', *Studies in History and Philosophy of Science*, Vol. 25, No. 4, 1994, pp. 535–547. See also André Kukla, *Social Constructivism and the Philosophy of Science*, London: Routledge, 2000.

26 Edward Hallett Carr, *The Twenty Years' Crisis, 1919–1939. An Introduction to the Study of International Relations*, London: Macmillan, 1961, p. 10.

27 See also Robert Cox's distinction between problem-solving theories (such as realism) and critical theories. Cox, Robert W., 'Social Forces, States and World Orders: Beyond International Relations Theory', in Robert O. Keohane (ed.), *Neorealism and its Critics*, New York: Columbia UP, 1986, p. 208.

28 See Clifford Geertz, *The Interpretation of Cultures*, New York: Basic Books, 1973, p. 14.

29 See Arshin Adib-Moghaddam, 'Islamic Utopian Romanticism and the Foreign Policy Clture of Iran', *Critique: Critical Middle Eastern Studies*, Vol. 14, No. 3, pp. 265–292.

30 Eric Hobsbawm, *Nations and Nationalism Since 1780. Programme, Myth, Reality*, second edition, Cambridge: Cambridge UP, 2004, p. 10.

31 In the tradition of Waltz, *Theory*, and recently invigorated by Wendt, *Social Theory*.

32 For a formalised model of the complementary-contradictory dualism see Margaret S. Archer, *Culture and Agency: The Place of Culture in Social Theory*, revised edition, Cambridge: Cambridge UP, 1996, especially chapter 6 and Mlada Bukovansky, *Legitimacy and Power Politics. The American and French Revolutions in International Political Culture*, Princeton, NJ: Princeton UP, 2002.

33 See Hedley Bull, *The Anarchical Society. A Study of Order in World Politics*, second Edition, London: Macmillan, 1995.

34 On sovereignty as a 'right' see among others John Ruggie, 'Continuity and Transformation in the World Polity: Toward a Neorealist Synthesis', *World Politics*, Vol. 35, No. 2, 1983, pp. 261–285; Wendt, *Social Theory*, p. 280 ff.

2 The Persian Gulf between independence and revolution: ideational shifts and regional repercussions

35 Unfortunately there are no officially published Iraqi records available, yet.

36 *Islamic Republic News Agency* (*IRNA*) September 2000 and *Iran Times*, 10 November 2000, p. 4.

37 Cited by Robert Fisk, *The Independent*, 25 June 1995.

38 In an off the record interview with the author (November 2002), an Iranian Foreign Ministry official gave following numbers: 60,000 dead, 124,000 with over 25% exposure, 200,000 under 25%, 120,000 minimal contamination and 600 with 80% and higher who are close to death. According to Iranian health officials, about 60,000 Iranians were exposed to Iraqi chemical weapon attacks during the war (*Agence France Press [AFP]*, 13 March 2000). Over 15,000 war veterans suffering from chemical weapons syndrome reportedly died in the 12 years after the end of Iran–Iraq war, according to Abbas Khani, the head of the Legal Office for War Veterans (*IRNA*, 13 November 2000).

39 Sick puts the casualty figures at approximately as 370,000 people killed and nearly twice as many maimed and injured, which is close to Farhang Rajaee's estimate of 367,000 killed and over 700,000 maimed and injured. See Lawrence G. Potter and Gary G. Sick (eds), *The Persian Gulf at the Millennium. Essays in Politics, Economy, Security, and Religion*, London: St Martin's, 1997, p. 1 and Farhang Rajaee (ed.), *Iranian Perspectives on the Iran–Iraq War*, Gainesville, FL: University Press of Florida, 1997, p. 2. More recently the Persian-speaking Shargh newspaper published the following numbers: Iranian soldiers killed in battle: 172,056; civilians killed in cities by bombardments, missiles and canon shells: 15,959; civilians and soldiers died later because of injuries: 30,852; the whole number of those killed due to the war: 218,867; total number of injured people: 386,653 (including 48,420 who continue to suffer from exposure to chemical weapons). See http://www.sharghnewspaper. com/830630/societ.htm#s112668 (accessed 29 August 2005).

40 *The Final Report of the Assessment of the Economic Damages of the War Imposed by Iraq on the I.R. of Iran (1980–1988)*, Tehran: Plan and Budget Minsitry, 1991.

41 Dilip Hiro, 'The Iran–Iraq War', in Hooshang Amirahmadi and Nader Entessar (eds), *Iran and the Arab World*, London: Macmillan, 1993, p. 65, also cited in Rajaee, Farhang (ed.), *Iranian Perspectives on the Iran–Iraq War*, Gainesville, FL: University Press of Florida, 1997, p. 2.

42 For an overall analysis of the economic consequence of the Iran–Iraq war see among others Kamran Mofid, *The Economic Consequences of the Gulf War*, London: Routledge, 1990.

43 See Barry Buzan and Ole Waever, *Regions and Powers: The Structure of International Security*, Cambridge: Cambridge UP, 2003, part 3.

44 On Foucault and Iran in English, see amongst others Didier Eribon, *Michel Foucault*, translated by Betsy Wing, London: Faber and Faber, 1991, p. 281 ff.; James Miller, *The Passion of Michel Foucault*, London: HarperCollins, 1993, p. 306 ff. See also Foucault's essays 'Open Letter to Mehdi Bazargan' and 'Useless to Revolt?', in Michel Foucault, *Power: Essential Works of Foucault, 1954–1984 Vol. 3*, translated by Robert Hurley and others, London: Penguin, 1997.

45 J.E. Peterson, 'The Historical Pattern of Gulf Security', in Lawrence G. Potter and Gary G. Sick (eds), *Security in the Persian Gulf. Origins, Obstacles, and the Search for Consensus*, Houndmills: Palgrave, 2002, p. 23.

46 See Richard Haass, 'Saudi Arabia and Iran: The Twin Pillars in Revolutionary Times', in Hossein Amirsadeghi (ed.), *The Security of the Persian Gulf*, London: Croom Helm, 1981, pp. 160–161.

47 See Pirouz Mojtahed-Zadeh, 'Regional Alliances in the Persian Gulf: Past Trends and Future Prospects', *The Iranian Journal of International Affairs*, Vol. X, Nos 1 & 2, 1998, pp. 14–15.

48 Henry Kissinger lamented that the Shah was an accomplice in the decision, asserting that '[n]ever before in history has a group of such relatively weak nations been able to impose

with so little protest such a dramatic change in the way of life of the overwhelming majority of the rest of mankind.' Henry Kissinger, *Years of Upheaval*, London: Weidenfeld and Nicolson, 1982, p. 887.

49 See the conventional definition of 'regulative norms' in Peter J. Katzenstein (ed.), *The Culture of National Security. Norms and Identity in World Politics*, New York: Columbia UP, 1996, p. 5 or Martha Finnemore and Kathryn Sikkink, 'International Norm Dynamics and Political Change', *International Organization*, Vol. 52, No. 4, 1998, p. 891.

50 See Bahgat Korany, 'Defending the Faith: The Foreign Policy of Saudi Arabia', in Bahgat Korany and Ali E. Hillal Dessouki (eds), *The Foreign Policies of Arab States*, Boulder, CO: Westview, 1984, p. 248.

51 Mojtahed-Zadeh, 'Regional Alliances in the Persian Gulf: Past Trends and Future Prospects', p. 15.

52 According to the Qur'an (17:1) Masjid al-Aqsa is the site in Jerusalem where the Prophet ascended to heaven in the eleventh year of his mission. The fire of 1969 destroyed a large part of the complex of mosques and seminary buildings.

53 For an analysis of King Faisal's attitude towards pan-Islamism see A.M. Sindi, 'King Faisal and Pan-Islamism', in Willard A. Beling (ed.), *King Faisal and the Modernisation of Saudi Arabia*, London: Croom Helm, 1986, pp. 184–201.

54 Haass, 'Saudi Arabia and Iran', p. 163.

55 John Duke Anthony, 'The Persian Gulf in Regional and International Politics: the Arab side of the Gulf', in Amirsadeghi (ed.), *The Security*, 1981, p. 176.

56 Ibid., p. 177.

57 Eric Hobsbawm, *Nations and Nationalism since 1780. Programme, Myth, Reality*, second edition, Cambridge: Cambridge UP, 2004, p. 10.

58 For the emergence of the smaller Gulf sheikhdoms as nation-states see Rosemary Said Zahlan, *The Making of the Modern Gulf States: Kuwait, Bahrain, Qatar, the United Arab Emirates and Oman*, Reading, PA: Ithaca Press, 1998. For an introduction into the development of the wider Middle Eastern state system see Roger Owen, *State, Power and Politics in the Making of the Modern Middle East*, second edition, London: Routledge, 2000 or Simon Bromley, *Rethinking Middle East Politics. State Formation and Development*, Cambridge: Polity Press, 1994.

59 Wajih Kawtharani, 'Mutual Awareness between Arabs and Iranians', in Khair el-Din Haseeb (ed.), *Arab–Iranian Relations*, Beirut: Centre for Arab Unity Studies, 1998, p. 75.

60 Indeed, one of the many titles of Mohammad Reza Shah included *Aryamehr*, which means 'light of Aryans' in Persian. His father, Reza Khan, who established the Pahlavi dynasty, renamed the country 'Iran' (Land of Aryans) from Persia (in its international usage) and supported the elimination of Arabic terms from the Persian language.

61 Shahrokh Meskoob, *Iranian Nationality and the Persian Language 900–1900. The Roles of Court, Religion, and Sufism in Persian Prose Writing*, translated by Michael C. Hillmann, edited by John R. Perry, Washington, DC: Mage Publishers, 1992, p. 31.

62 For a critical deconstruction of Ernest Renan's study of 'semitic' and 'orientalist' discourse see Edward W. Said, *Orientalism*, London: Penguin, 1995, especially pp. 140–150.

63 For an overview about the variants of Iranian nationalism(s) see Firoozeh Kashani-Sabet, 'Cultures of Iranianness: The Evolving Polemic of Iranian Nationalism', in Nikki R. Keddie and Rudi Matthee (eds), *Iran and the Surrounding World. Interactions in Culture and Cultural Politics*, Seattle, WA: University of Washington Press, 2002, pp. 162–181.

64 For a comparison of the representation of 'self' and 'other' in textbooks before and after the revolution see Golnar Mehran, 'The Presentation of the "Self" and the "Other" in Postrevolutionary Iranian School Textbooks', in Keddie and Mathee (eds), *Iran and the Surrounding World*, pp. 232–253.

65 See Mohammad Reza Shah Pahlavi, *Answer to History*, New York: Stein and Day, 1980, p. 156.

66 Rouhollah K. Ramazani, *The Persian Gulf: Iran's Role*, Charlottesville, VA: University of Virginia Press, 1972, p. 26.

67 The term *Ajam*, often used in a pejorative sense, was used to identify the non-Arabs (particularly the Iranians) peoples of the Islamic Empire in medieval Arabic literature. During later periods the term became an ethnic and geographic designation to separate Arabs from Iranians.

68 See Kashani-Sabet, 'Cultures of Iranianness', in Keddie and Mathee (eds), *Iran and the Surrounding World*, pp. 165–166.

69 See Basssam Tibi, *Arab Nationalism. Between Islam and the Nation-State*, third edition, Macmillan: London 1997, pp. 127–138.

70 Sati al-Husri, *Ara' wa ahadith fil-qawmiyya al-'arabiyya* (Speeches and Reflections on Arab Nationalism), Egypt: Al-I'timad, 1951, p. 45. Quoted in Paul Salem, *Bitter Legacy. Ideology and Politics in the Arab World*, Syracuse, NY: Syracuse UP, 1994, p. 57.

71 See Tibi, *Arab Nationalism*, p. 204.

72 'The Constitution of the Ba'ath Party, 1947, Article I (Unity and Freedom of the Arab Nation), reprinted in Tareq Ismael, *The Arab Left*, Syracuse, NY: Syracuse UP, 1976, p. 126.

73 Michel Aflaq, *Fi Sabil al Ba'th*, Beirut: Dar al-Tali'ah, 1959, p. 49. Quoted in Kanan Makiya, *Republic of Fear. The Politics of Modern Iraq*, updated edition with a new introduction, Berkeley, CA: University of California Press, 1998, p. 198, emphasis added.

74 Talal Atrissi, 'The Image of the Iranians in Arab Schoolbooks', in Haseeb (ed.), *Arab-Iranian Relations*, Beirut: Centre for Arab Unity Studies, p. 155.

75 Abdullah K. Alshayji, 'Mutual Realities, Perceptions, and Impediments Between the GCC States and Iran', in Potter and Sick (eds), *Security*, p. 220.

76 See Bijan Khajehpour-Khoei, 'Mutual Perceptions in the Persian Gulf Region', in Potter and Sick (eds), *Security*, p. 240.

77 Joya Blondel Saad, *The Image of Arabs in Modern Persian Literature*, Lanham, MD: University Press of America, 1996, p. 134.

78 See Arshin Adib-Moghaddam, 'Islamic Utopian Romanticism and the Foreign Policy Culture of Iran', *Critique: Critical Middle Eastern Studies*, Vol. 14, No. 3, Fall 2005, pp. 265–292.

79 Mehrzad Boroujerdi, 'Iranian Islam and the Faustian Bargain of Western Modernity', *Journal of Peace Research*, Vol. 34, No.1, 1997, p. 1.

80 For a comprehensive compilation of the impact of the revolution see among others Rouhollah K. Ramazani, *Revolutionary Iran. Challenge and Response in the Middle-East*, Baltimore, MD: Johns Hopkins UP, 1986; John L. Esposito (ed.), *The Iranian Revolution. Its Global Impact*, Miami, FL: Florida International UP, 1990.

81 Karl Marx, 'The Eighteenth Brumaire of Louis Bonaparte', in David Fernbach (ed.), *Survey from Exile*, Harmondsworth: Penguin, 1973, p. 146.

82 For an analysis of the Iran–Iraq war see among others Shahram Chubin and Charles Tripp, *Iran and Iraq at War*, London: I.B. Tauris, 1988; Dilip Hiro, *The Longest War: The Iran–Iraq Military Conflict*, London: Grafton, 1990.

83 See Herbert Marcuse, *One-dimensional Man: Studies in the Ideology of Advanced Industrial Society*, second edition, London: Routledge, 1991, p. 10 ff.

84 See Adib-Moghaddam, 'Islamic Utopian Romanticism and the Poreign policy Culture of Iran', p. 270 ff.

85 *Constitution of the Islamic Republic of Iran*, translated from the Persian by Hamid Algar, Berkeley, CA: Mizan, 1980, p. 13 (Preamble).

86 Ibid., p. 14.

87 Opening announcement of *Radio Tehran* broadcasts in Arabic, *BBC Summary of World Broadcasts*, Part 4, The Middle East and North Africa, ME/7675/A2 21, June 1984.

88 See Roy P. Mottahedeh, 'Shi'ite Political Thought and the Destiny of the Iranian Revolution', in Jamal S. al-Suwaidi (ed.), *Iran and the Gulf: A Search for Stability*, Abu Dhabi: The Emirates Center for Strategic Studies and Research, 1996, pp. 70–80.

89 For Khomeini's perception of international affairs see Farhang Rajaee, *Islamic Values and World View: Khomeyni on Man, the State and International Politics, Volume XIII*, Lanham, MD: University Press of America, 1983.

90 See Ervand Abrahamian, *Khomeinism. Essays on the Islamic Republic*, London: I.B. Tauris, 1993.

91 *Constitution of the Islamic Republic of Iran*, p. 19.

92 For a comparative analysis see Fred Halliday, *Revolution and World Politics. The Rise and Fall of the Sixth Great Power*, Durham, NC: Duke UP, 1999.

93 Ayatollah Rouhollah Khomeini, *Sahifey-e Nur*, Vol. 18, Tehran: Vezarat-e Ershad, 1364/1985, p. 129.

94 See Rajaee, *Islamic Values*, pp. 83–84 and Ramazani, *Revolutionary Iran*, p. 26.

95 For further analysis see Farhang Rajaee, 'Iranian Ideology and Worldview: The Cultural Export of Revolution', in Esposito (ed.), *The Iranian Revolution. Its Global Impact*, Miami, FL: Florida International UP, 1990, pp. 63–80.

96 Halliday, *Revolution*, p. 96.

97 'First Communiqué of the Muslim Students Following the Line of Imam', in Massoumeh Ebtekar, *Takeover in Tehran. The Inside Story of the 1979 U.S. Embassy Capture*, as told to Fred A. Reed, Vancouver, WA: Talonbooks, 2000, p. 70.

98 The occupation occurred at the time when the Shah was permitted to the United States for medical treatment.

99 'First Communiqué', in Ebtekar, *Takeover*, p. 70.

100 Fred Halliday, 'Iranian Foreign Policy Since 1979: Internationalism and Nationalism in the Islamic Revolution', in Juan R.I. Cole and Nikki R. Keddie (eds), *Shi'ism and Social Protest*, New Haven, CT: Yale UP, 1986, p. 96.

101 See David George, 'Pax Islamica: An Alternative New World Order', in Abdel Salam Sidahmed and Anoushiravan Ehteshami (eds), *Islamic Fundamentalism*, Boulder, CO: Westview, 1996, p. 80 ff.

102 *BBC Survey of World Broadcasts*, Part IV (A), The Middle East, 24 November 1979, ME/6280/A/8.

103 See also Abrahamian, *Khomeinism*.

104 For literature in English see Ali Rahnema, *An Islamic Utopian. A Political Biography of Ali Shariati*, London: I.B. Tauris, 2000; Jalal Al-e-Ahmad, *Plagued by the West (Gharbzadegi)*, translated from the Persian by Paul Sprachman, New York: Caravan, 1982. For an excellent overview of modern Iranian intellectual thought see Mehrzad Boroujerdi, *Iranian Intellectuals and the West. The Tormented Triumph of Nativism*, Syracuse, NY: Syracuse UP, 1996.

105 Ayatollah Rouhollah Khomeini, Sermon delivered on 5 November 1982. *Kayhan*, Tehran, 6 November 1982. Quoted in Rajaee (1983), p. 75.

106 Boroujerdi, 'Iranian Islam and the Faustian Bargain of Western Modernity', p. 4.

107 Ramazani, Rouhollah K., 'Shi'ism in the Persian Gulf', in Juan R. I. Cole and Nikki R. Keddie (eds), *Shi'ism and Social Protest*, New Haven, CT: Yale UP, 1986, p. 33.

108 Shireen T. Hunter (eds), 'Iran and Syria: From Hostility to Limited Alliance', in Amirahmadi and Entessar (eds), *Iran and the Arab World*, p. 202. See also Mahmood Sariolghalam, 'Conceptual Sources of Post-Revolutionary Iranian Behaviour toward the Arab World', in Amirahmadi and Entessar (eds), *Iran and the Arab World*, pp. 19–27.

109 Morteza Muttahari, *Islam and Iran*, Beirut: Dar al-Ta'aruf, n.d., p. 22. Quoted in Kawtharani, 'Mutual Awareness between Arabs and Iranians', in Haseeb (eds), *Arab–Iranian Relations*, p. 74.

110 See Olivier Roy, *The Failure of Political Islam*, translated by Carol Volk, London: I.B. Tauris, 1999, p. 187 ff.

111 Rouhollah Khomeini, *Islam and Revolution. Writings and Declarations of Imam Khomeini*, translated and annotated by Hamid Algar, Berkeley, CA: Mizan, 1981, p. 204.

112 Ibid., pp. 204–205.

113 Ibid., p. 31.

114 Ibid., p. 60.

115 Jacob Goldberg, 'The Shi'i Minority in Saudi Arabia', in Cole and Keddie (eds), *Shi'ism*, p. 243.

116 Members of the Wahabbi call themselves *Al-Muwahhidins* (Unitarians) because of their emphasis on the absolute oneness of God (*tawhid*). They reject all acts of polytheism

(*shirk*), such as visiting tombs and venerating saints, and advocate a return to the original teachings of Islam as incorporated in the Quran and *hadith* (traditions of the Prophet Muhammad) with condemnation of all innovations (*bidah*). Wahabbi theology and jurisprudence based respectively, on the teaching of Ibn Taymiyyah and on the legal school of Ahmed ibn Hanbal stress literal belief in the Quran and *hadith*, and the establishment of a Muslim state based only on Islamic Law (*sharia*). In the following the necessarily imperfect terms Wahhabi and Wahhabism are used for matters of convenience to refer to the official school of thought in Saudi Arabia.

117 Ramazani, 'Shi'ism in the Persian Gulf', in Cole and Keddie (eds), *Shi'ism*, pp. 44–45.

118 Goldberg, 'The Shi'i Minority in Saudi Arabia', in Cole and Keddie (eds), *Shi'ism*, p. 232.

119 Khomeini, *Islam and Revolution*, p. 302.

120 See also Akbar Ahmed, *Discovering Islam. Making Sense of Muslim History and Society*, revised edition, London: Routledge, 2002, p. 30 ff.

121 See also Joseph A. Kechichian, 'The Role of the Ulama in the Politics of an Islamic State: The Case of Saudi Arabia', *International Journal of Middle East Studies*, Vol. 18, No. 1, 1986, pp. 53–71.

122 See Wilfried Buchta, 'The Failed Pan-Islamic Program of the Islamic Republic: Views of the Liberal Reformers of the Religious "Semi-Opposition"', in Keddie and Matthee (eds), *Iran and the Surrounding World*, Seattle, WA: University of Washington Press, 2002, p. 283.

123 Ibid., p. 284.

124 See Articles 12 and 115 of the Constitution respectively.

125 Quoted in Buchta, 'The Failed Pan-Islamic Program of the Islamic Republic: Views of the Liberal Reformers of the Religious "Semi-Opposition"', in Keddie and Matthee (eds), *Iran and the Surrounding World*, p. 293.

126 For a formalised definition of 'role' and 'role identities' see Alexander Wendt, *Social Theory of International Politics*, Cambridge: Cambridge UP, 1999, p. 259.

127 For more on the 'Shiite factor' in Iran's foreign policy see Roy, *The Failure*, chapter 11.

128 Established in 1982, SCIRI called for an Islamic Republic close to the Iranian model. After its leaders fled to Iran, the party continued its operations from its headquarters in Tehran. SCIRI's former leader, Ayatollah Muhammad Baqr al-Hakim, was among about 100 people killed in a massive car bombing in the Shia holy city of Najaf in August 2003. His brother Abdel Aziz and other party officials have played a major role in post-Saddam Iraq. SCIRI's armed wing – the 10,000 strong Badr Brigade – has been renamed the Badr Organisation after the ban of party militias in September 2003.

129 See Salem, *Bitter Legacy*, pp. 112–114. Also Charles Tripp, *A History of Iraq*, second edition, Cambridge: Cambridge UP, 2000, pp. 229–230.

130 Tripp, *A History of Iraq*, p. 230.

131 Dilip Hiro even argued: 'By supplying secret information, which exaggerated Iran's military weakness, to Saudi Arabia for onward transmission to Baghdad, Washington encouraged Iraq to attack Iran.' Hiro, *The Longest War*, p. 71.

132 This is elaborated as a legal case by Majid Khadduri, *The Gulf War. The Origins and Implications of the Iraq–Iran Conflict*, Oxford: Oxford UP, 1988. See especially chapter VIII.

133 Quoted in Khadduri, *The Gulf War*, p. 85.

134 See Trip, *A History of Iraq*, pp. 231–233.

135 Ofra Bengio, *Saddam's Word. Political Discourse in Iraq*, Oxford: Oxford UP, 1998, p. 137.

136 Ibid., p. 137.

137 Ibid., pp. 142–143.

138 Ibid., p. 142.

139 After the Second Persian Gulf War, Iraqi-Kurds operating in the semi-autonomous Northern no-fly zone forwarded thousands of documents from the Iraqi intelligence agencies and its four primary agencies, including the *al-Amn al-Khas* (Special Security), *al Amn al-'Amn* (General Security), *al-Mukhabarat al-Amma* (General Intelligence) and *al Istikhbarat al-'Askariyya* (Military Intelligence), to the US government. Many of them are available on the Internet at the Iraq Research and Documentation Program at the Centre

for Middle East Studies of Harvard University. Available at http://www.fas.harvard.edu/~irdp/ (accessed 21 September 2002).

140 Ibrahim al-Marashi, *The Mindset of Iraq's Security Apparatus*, unpublished paper presented at a workshop by the Cambridge Security Program in International Society (C-SIS), Cambridge, UK, 13 March 2003.

141 *The Modern and Contemporary History of the Arab Homeland*, for Third Year Intermediate, Ministry of Education, Baghdad 1994, p. 105. Quoted in Atrissi, 'The Image of the Iranians in Arab Schoolbooks', in Haseeb (ed.), *Arab–Iranian Relations*, p. 161.

142 Neguin Yavari, 'National, Ethnic and Sectarian Issues in the Iran–Iraq War', in Rajaee, *Iranian Perspectives*, pp. 75–76.

143 See Makiya, *Republic of Fear*, p. 265.

144 *Al-'Iraq*, 24 April 1980. Quoted in Bengio, *Saddam's Word*, p. 145.

145 Makiya, *Republic of Fear*, pp. 270–271.

146 Ibid., p. 286.

147 See especially Peter Berger and Thomas Luckmann, *The Social Construction of Reality*, New York: Anchor Books, 1966 and George Herbert Mead, *Mind, Self, and Society*, Chicago, IL: Chicago UP, 1934.

148 See also Lawrence A. Hirschfeld and Susan A. Gelman (eds), *Mapping the Mind: Domain Specificity in Cognition and Culture*, Cambridge: Cambridge UP, 1994.

149 See Wendt, *Social Theory*, p. 227.

150 Many arguments about the causes of the Iraq war merge on this point, without, however, making the link between Iraqi state identity (under Saddam Hussein), external confirmation and the decision to launch the invasion explicit. See among others Tripp, *A History of Iraq*, p. 231 and Anoushiravan Ehteshami and Gerd Nonneman, *War and Peace in the Gulf. Domestic Politics and Regional Relations into the 1990s*, Reading, PA: Ithaca, 1991, p. 39 ff.

151 See Hedley Bull, *The Anarchical Society. A Study of Order in World Politics*, second edition, London: Macmillan, 1995, pp. 181 ff.

152 Ehteshami, Anoushiravan and Gerd Nonneman, *War and Peace in the Gulf. Domestic Politics and Regional Relations into the 1990s*, Reading, PA: Ithaca, 1991, pp. 39–43.

153 Ibid., p. 43. For a similar view see Bahman Baktiari, 'Revolutionary Iran's Persian Gulf Policy: The Quest for Regional Supremacy', in Amirahmadi and Entessar (eds), *Iran and the Arab World*, 1993, p. 74 ff.

154 For details on that involvement see Gerd Nonneman, *Iraq, the Gulf states & the War: A Changing Relationship, 1980–1986 and Beyond*, London: Ithaca, 1986 and Ehteshami and Nonneman, *War and Peace in the Gulf*, chapter 3.

155 See Saideh Lotfian, 'Taking Sides: Regional Powers and the War', in Rajaee (ed.), *Iranian Perspectives*, p. 18.

156 See Chubin and Tripp, *Iran and Iraq at War*, p. 154.

157 See Lotfian, 'Taking Sides: Regional Powers and the War', in Rajaee (ed.), *Iranian Perspectives*, p. 19.

158 See Chubin and Tripp, *Iran and Iraq at War*, p. 172.

159 Quoted in Chubin and Tripp, *Iran and Iraq at War*, p. 153.

160 See Sir Anthony Parsons, 'Iran and the United Nations, with Particular Reference to the Iran–Iraq war', in Anoushiravan Ehteshami and Manshour Varasteh (eds), *Iran and the International Community*, London: Routledge, 1991, pp. 16, 18.

161 Julian Perry Robinson and Jozef Goldblat, 'Chemical Warfare in the Iraq–Iran War', Stockholm International Peace Research Institute, *SIPRI Fact Sheet*, Chemical Weapons I, May 1984.

162 Parsons, 'Iran and the United Nations, with particular reference to the Iran–Iraq war', in Ehteshami and Varasteh (eds), *Iran and the International Community*, p. 19.

163 Ibid., pp. 19–20.

164 Ibid., Appendix B: United Nations Security Council Resolution 598 adopted on 20 July 1987, p. 29.

165 Raymond Hinnebusch, *The International Politics of the Middle East*, Manchester: Manchester UP, 2003, p. 200.

166 Leader of the Patriotic Union of Kurdistan (PUK), referred to as *Ulama Iran* (Agents of Iran) by the Iraqis because of their collusion with Iran in the latter periods of the war.

167 Advisor or Consultant. Kurdish tribal leader of paramilitary units officially referred to as *Qiyadet Jahafel al-Difa' al-Watani* (National Defence Battalions) by the Iraqi regime and derided by other Kurds as *jahsh* or 'donkey foals' because of their alliance with the state.

168 The Ali Hassan al-Majid tapes obtained by Human Rights Watch after the Second Persian Gulf War have been published as Appendix A to HRW's Report entitled 'Genocide in Iraq. The Anfal Campaign Against the Kurds'. It is available at http://www.hrw.org/reports/1993/iraqanfal/ (accessed 14 June 2001).

169 For details see among others Adam Tarock, *The Superpowers Involvement in the Iran–Iraq War*, Commack: Nova Science, 1998 or Hiro, *The Longest War*, especially chapters 4, 7 and 9.

170 Tarock, *The Superpowers Involvement*, p. 69.

171 I am drawing on the set of documents obtained by the National Security Archive (NSA) at George Washington University under the US Freedom on Information Act. See National Security Archive Electronic Briefing Book No. 82, 25 February 2003, edited by Joyce Battle, 'Shaking Hands with Saddam Hussein. The U.S. Tilts toward Iraq, 1980–1984'. Available at http://www.gwu.edu/~nsarchiv/NSAEBB/NSAEBB82/index.htm (accessed 27 February 2003). Following quotations referring to 'National Security Archive' are taken from the declassified documents listed on that page.

172 I am using the term 'contravene' on purpose here. From a legal perspective the US support to Iraq can indeed be seen in violation with both US domestic law and international law. For a convincing case, arguing that the US support to Iraq was in violation of both US domestic law and international law see Francis A. Boyle, 'International Crisis and Neutrality. US Foreign Policy Toward the Iran/Iraq War', *Counterpunch*, 14 December 2002. Available at http://www.counterpunch.org/boyle1214.html (accessed 21 December 2002).

173 Tarock, *The Superpowers Involvement*, p. 61.

174 US House of Representatives, 27 July 1992. Speech by Henry B. Gonzalez, 'Bush Administration Had Acute Knowledge of Iraq's Military Industrialisation Plans'. Available at http://www.fas.org/spp/starwars/congress/1992/h920727g.htm (accessed 24 July 2002).

175 US Senate Committee on Banking, Housing, and Urban Affairs, 7 October 1994. Committee Staff Report No. 3: Chemical Warfare Agent Identification, Chemical Injuries, and Other Findings. Principal Investigator James J Tuite III, 'U.S. Chemical and Biological Exports to Iraq and their Possible Impact on the Health Consequences of the Persian Gulf War'. Available at http://www.chronicillnet.org/PGWS/tuite/chembio.html (accessed 24 July 2003).

176 See United States Senate, 103rd Congress, Second Session, 25 May 1994. A Report of Chairman Donald W. Riegle, Jr and Ranking Member Alfonse M. D'Amato of the Committee on Banking, Housing and Urban Affairs with Respect to Export Administration: 'The Riegle Report. US Chemical and Biological Warfare-Related Dual Use Exports to Iraq and their Possible Impact on the Health Consequences of the Gulf War'. Available at http://www.gulfweb.org/bigdoc/report/riegle1.html (accessed 23 June 2001).

177 This is a reference to a National Security Decision Directive signed by Ronald Reagan in June 1983 which was co-authored by Howard Teicher together with another NSC staff member, Geoffrey Kemp. The content of the NSDD and even its identification number remain classified.

178 United States District Court (Florida: Southern District) Affidavit. 'United States of America, Plaintiff, v. Carlos Cardoen [*et al.*].' [Charge that Teledyne Wah Chang Albany Illegally Provided a Proscribed Substance, Zirconium, to Cardoen Industries and to Iraq], 31 January 1995. Teicher also stated that the CIA encouraged Iraq to use cluster bombs

against the Iranian 'human wave' attacks. Available from the National Security Archive. The quotes are on pp. 3 and 4 respectively.

179 Department of State, Bureau of Near Eastern and South Asian Affairs Information Memorandum from Jonathan T. Howe to Lawrence S. Eagleburger. 'Iran–Iraq War: Analysis of Possible U.S. Shift from Position of Strict Neutrality', 7 October 1983. Available from the National Security Archive. The quote is on p. 7.

180 United States Embassy in Italy Cable from Maxwell M. Rabb to the Department of State. 'Rumsfeld's Larger Meeting with Iraqi Deputy PM [Prime Minister] and FM [Foreign Minister] Tariz [Tariq] Aziz, December 19', 20 December 1983. Available from the National Security Archive. The quote is on p. 3.

181 United States Embassy in United Kingdom Cable from Charles H. Price II to the Department of State. 'Rumsfeld Mission: December 20 Meeting with Iraqi President Saddam Hussein', 21 December 1983. Available from the National Security Archive. The quote is on page 8.

182 Department of State, Bureau of Politico-Military Affairs Information Memorandum from Jonathan T. Howe to George P. Shultz. 'Iraq Use of Chemical Weapons', 1 November 1983. Available from the National Security Archive. The quote is on page 1.

183 Department of State, Office of the Assistant Secretary for Near Eastern and South Asian Affairs Action Memorandum from Jonathan T. Howe to Lawrence S. Eagleburger. 'Iraqi Use of Chemical Weapons' [Includes Cables Entitled 'Deterring Iraqi Use of Chemical Weapons' and 'Background of Iraqi Use of Chemical Weapons'], 21 November 1983. Available from the National Security Archive. The quote is on p. 6, emphasis added.

184 Department of State, Bureau of Near Eastern and South Asian Affairs Memorandum from James A. Placke to James M. Ealum [*et al*.]. [U.S. Condemnation of Iraqi Chemical Weapons Use], 4 March 1984. Available from the National Security Archive. The quote is on p. 2.

185 Ibid., p. 3.

186 United States Interests Section in Iraq Cable from William L. Eagleton, Jr to the Department of State. 'Iraqi Warning re Iranian Offensive', 22 February 1984. Available from the National Security Archive. The quote is on p. 1.

187 Department of State Cable from George P. Shultz to the United States Embassy in Lebanon [*et al*.]. 'Department Press Briefing, March 30, 1984', 31 March 1984. Available from the National Security Archive. The quote is on p. 3.

188 Department of State, Bureau of Near Eastern and South Asian Affairs Cover Memorandum from Allen Overmyer to James A. Placke. [United Nations Security Council Response to Iranian Chemical Weapons Complaint; Includes Revised Working Paper], 30 March 1984. Available from the National Security Archive. The quote is on p. 1.

189 It was later established that the Iranian allegation that the US cruiser was in Iranian territorial waters was accurate. The captain of the *USS Vincennes* Will Rogers and even more surprisingly the Air Warfare Co-ordinator Scott Lustig would later receive medals for their engagements in the Persian Gulf. The latter even achieved the Navy Commendation Medal with Combat V authorisation for what was summarised as his 'heroic achievements'.

190 In a tragic irony, the *USS Stark* was hit by Exocet missiles acquired by Iraq in a deal with France that was backed up by the United States. In his speech to the US House of Representative, the late Texas Democrat Henry Gonzales touched on that point: 'I ask you how could we be supplying Iraq with everything from intelligence – because we had an intelligence-gathering agreement all during that war with Iraq – supplied them with everything else, even backed up foreign countries like France to make sure they supplied military things all the way from Mirages to Exocet missiles, one of which, incidentally, was the one that killed 37 of our sailors in the Persian Gulf', note 174.

191 In spite of congressional hearings and independent investigations the details of the Iran-Contra-Affair remain undisclosed. What is known is that the Reagan administration together with Israeli implications was engaged in a massive arms deal with the Islamic Republic. The profits of these arms deals were intended to finance the guerrilla war of the

'Contras' in Nicaragua. For the congressional hearings see Joel Brinkley (ed.), *Report of the Congressional Committee Investigating the Iran-Contra Affair*. New York: Times Book, 1988. For a discussion of the Iran-Contra-Affair and its impact on the Iran–Iraq war see Tarock, *The Superpowers Involvement*, pp. 91–122.

192 'The Glaspie Transcript: Saddam Meets the US Ambassador (25 July 1990)', in Micah L. Sifry and Christopher Cerf (eds), *The Gulf War Reader. History, Documents, Opinions*, New York: Times Books, 1991, p. 125.

193 Mlada Bukovansky, *Legitimacy and Power Politics. The American and French Revolutions in International Political Culture*, Princeton, NJ: Princeton UP, 2002, p. 39.

194 Indeed one might argue that the acceptance of resolution 598 by Iran came about at a stage when the Islamic Republic was threatened to be destabilised by the strains of the war from within. Mounting domestic opposition was a decisive factor in the decision of Imam Khomeini, reflected in his speech on 20 July 1988 where he accentuated that 'drinking the cup of poison' of ending the war was in the interest of the system and the revolution. For the domestic political and economic context of the decision see Hiro, *The Longest War*, p. 243 ff.

195 Edward Hallett Carr, *The Twenty Years' Crisis, 1919–1939. An Introduction to the Study of International Relations*, London: Macmillan, 1961, pp. 19–20.

3 Westphalia and the anarchic Gulf society: the second Persian Gulf War and its aftermath

196 For an account of US and Israeli collusion with the Shah see Henry Kissinger, *Years of Renewal*, London: Weidenfeld & Nicolson, 1999, p. 576 ff.

197 'The Glaspie Transcript: Saddam Meets the US Ambassador (25 July 1990)', in Micah L. Sifry and Christopher Cerf (eds), *The Gulf War Reader. History, Documents, Opinions*, New York: Times Books, 1991, p.127.

198 See Olivier Roy, *The Failure of Political Islam*, translated by Carol Volk, London: I.B. Tauris, 1999, chapter 11.

199 Alexander Wendt, *Social Theory of International Politics*, Cambridge: Cambridge UP, 1999, p. 176.

200 For a critical overview of the pros and cons of the Iraq–Kuwait war and the international reactions see Sifry and Cerf, *The Gulf War Reader*.

201 Quoted in Lawrence Freedman and Efraim Karsh, *The Gulf Conflict 1990–1991. Diplomacy and War in the New World Order*, London: Faber and Faber, 1993, p. 50.

202 See 'The Glaspie Transcript', in Sifry and Cerf, *The Gulf War Reader*, p. 133.

203 See Adeed Dawisha, 'Footprints in the Sand. The Definition and Redefinition of Identity in Iraq's Foreign Policy', in Shibley Telhami and Michael Barnett (eds), *Identity and Foreign Policy in the Middle East*, London: Cornell UP, 2002, p. 130. See also Ahmad Yousef Ahmad, 'The Dialectics of Domestic Environment and Role performance: The Foreign Policy of Iraq', in Bahgat Korany and Ali E. Hillal Dessouki (eds), *The Foreign Policies of Arab States*, Boulder, CO: Westview, 1984, p. 166.

204 Adeed Dawisha, 'Footprints in the Sand. The Definition and Redefinition of Identity in Iraq's Foreign Policy', in Telhami and Barnett (eds), *Identity and Foreign Policy*, p. 129. See also Adeed Dawisha, ' "Identity" and Political Survival in Saddam's Iraq', *The Middle East Journal*, Vol. 53, No. 4, 1999, pp. 553–567.

205 Kaveh L. Afrasiabi, *After Khomeini. New Directions in Iran's Foreign Policy*, Boulder, CO: Westview, 1994, p. 91.

206 Adeed Dawisha, 'Iraq: The West's opportunity', *Foreign Policy*, Vol. 41, 1980–1981, pp. 134–148.

207 PBS Frontline, 'Oral History of Gulf War II, Interview with Brent Scowcroft, US National Security Advisor'. Available at http://www.pbs.org/wgbh/pages/frontline/gulf/oral/scowcroft/1.html (accessed 10 June 2002).

208 'The Glaspie Transcript', in Sifry and Cerf (eds), *The Gulf War Reader*, p. 129.

209 'The Glaspie Transcript', in Sifry and Cerf (eds), *The Gulf War Reader*, p. 130.
210 'U.S. Senators Chat with Saddam (12 April 1990)', in Sifry and Cerf (eds), *The Gulf War Reader*, p. 121.
211 Speech by Henry B. Gonzalez, 'Bush Administration Had Acute Knowledge of Iraq's Military Industrialisation Plans'. Available at http://www.fas.org/spp/starwars/congress/1992/h920727g.htm (accessed 24 July 2002).
212 Robert Springborg, 'Selling War in the Gulf', in St John Kettle and Stephanie Dowrick (eds), *After the Gulf War*, Sydney: Pluto, 1991, p. 33.
213 Quoted in Elaine Sciolino, *The Outlaw State*, New York: John Wiley & Sons, 1991, p. 146.
214 See 'US Had Key Role in Iraq Buildup. Trade in Chemical Arms Allowed Despite Their Use on Iranians, Kurds'. *The Washington Post*, 30 December 2002, p. A01. The quote is attributed to Joe Wilson, April Glaspie's former deputy at the US Embassy in Baghdad and the last US Official to meet with Saddam Hussein.
215 'Genocide in Iraq. The Anfal Campaign Against the Kurds'. Available at http://www.hrw.org/reports/1993/iraqanfal/ (accessed 14 June 2001).
216 See Joost Hilterman, 'Elusive Justice. Trying to Try Saddam', *Middle East Report*, No. 215, Vol. 30, No. 2, 2000, p. 32 and Charles Tripp, *A History of Iraq*, second edition, Cambridge: Cambridge UP, 2000, p. 245.
217 Hilterman, 'Elusive Justice. Trying to Try Saddam', p. 32.
218 Voice of the Masses, Baghdad, 19 March 2003, in *Foreign Broadcast International Service*, FBIS-NES, 21 March 1988, pp. 22–23. Reprinted in HRW's Anfal Report, 'Genocide in Iraq. The Anfal Campaign Against the Kurds'.
219 *The Military Balance between 1987–1988*, London: International Institute for Strategic Studies (IISS), 1987, p. 100.
220 Saddam Hussein used the term in a derogatory way. See 'The Glaspie Transcript', in Sifry and Cerf (eds), *The Gulf War Reader*, p. 132.
221 Ibid., p. 125.
222 Fred Halliday, *Islam and the Myth of Confrontation. Religion and Politics in the Middle East*, London: I.B. Tauris, 1996, p. 84.
223 Ibid.
224 Ofra Bengio, *Saddam's Word. Political Discourse in Iraq*, Oxford: Oxford UP, 1998, p. 48.
225 Wendt, *Social Theory*, p. 186.
226 See Walid Khalidi, 'Iraq vs. Kuwait: Claims and Counterclaims', in Sifry and Cerf (eds), *The Gulf War Reader*, p. 60.
227 For the originals and English translations of the correspondence see *The Texts of Letters Exchanged between the Presidents of the Islamic Republic of Iran and the Republic of Iraq 1369 (1990)*, translated by Maryam Daftari, Tehran: Publishing House of the Ministry of Foreign Affairs, The Institute for Political and International Studies, 1374/1995.
228 Ibid., 'Text of the Iraqi President's Letter Dated 26 Ramadan 1410 H.Q. [2 Ordibehesht 1369 H.S., 21 April 1990], p. 3.
229 Fred Halliday, 'The Crisis of the Arab World', in Sifry and Cerf (eds), *The Gulf War Reader*, p. 397.
230 Robert Wuthnow, James Davison Hunter, Albert Bergesen and Edith Kurzweil, *Cultural Analysis. The Work of Peter L. Berger, Mary Douglas, Michel Foucault, and Jürgen Habermas*, London: Routledge & Kegan Paul, 1984, p. 45.
231 Note that the strategic goals of the Iraq state in its invasion of Iran were related to the pan-Arab project in that Saddam Hussein requested full Iraqi sovereignty over the Shatt al-Arab, the 'reintegration' of the partially Arabic-speaking Iranian border province of Khusestan ('Arabistan' in Iraqi maps) and the return of the three Persian Gulf islands ceded by the Shah.
232 *The New York Times*, 9 August 1990. Quoted in Nozar Alaolmolki, *Struggle for Dominance in the Persian Gulf. Past, Present, and Future Prospects*, New York: Peter Lang, 1991, p. 166.
233 Ibid.

234 Kanan Makiya, *Cruelty and Silence. War, Tyranny, Uprising, and the Arab World*, London: Jonathan Cape, 1993, p. 270.

235 Iraqi Revolutionary Command Council, 'Iraq is Ready to Deal (Radio Address of 15 February 1991)', in Sifry and Cerf (eds), *The Gulf War Reader*, p. 339.

236 Nazih N. Ayubi, *Over-stating the Arab State. Politics and Society in the Middle East*, London: I.B. Tauris, 1995, p. 141.

237 Quoted in Kanan Makiya, *Republic of Fear. The Politics of Modern Iraq*, updated edition with a new introduction, Berkeley, CA: University of California Press, 1998, p. 220.

238 Quoted in Bengio, *Saddam's Word*, p. 51.

239 Ibid., p. 52.

240 See Bassam Tibi, *Conflict and War in the Middle East. From Interstate War to New Security*, second edition, London: Macmillan, 1998, p. 169.

241 Quoted in Makiya, *Republic of Fear*, p. 223, emphasis added.

242 Quoted in Bengio, *Saddam's Word*, p. 71.

243 Ibid.

244 Tibi, *Conflict and War*, p. 166.

245 Ibid., p. 173.

246 George Bush, 'The Letter to Saddam (9 January 1991)', in Sifry and Cerf (eds), *The Gulf War Reader*, p. 179. The letter was read by Tariq Aziz during his meeting with Baker but not transferred to the Iraqi President, because he deemed the language 'improper' for the correspondence between heads of states.

247 'The Geneva Meeting (Remarks of 9 January, 1991)', in Sifry and Cerf (eds), *The Gulf War Reader*, p. 172.

248 'The Glaspie Transcript', in Sifry and Cerf (eds), *The Gulf War Reader*, p. 126.

249 Saddam Hussein quoted in Freedman and Karsh, *The Gulf Conflict 1990–1991*, p. 46.

250 Fouad Ajami, *The Arab Predicament. Arab Political Thought and Practice Since 1967*, updated edition, Cambridge: Cambridge UP, 1992, pp. 12–13, emphasis added.

251 Elizabeth Drew, 'Washington Prepares for War', in Sifry and Cerf (eds), *The Gulf War Reader*, p.187.

252 See John Gerard Ruggie, 'Territoriality and Beyond: Problematising Modernity in International Relations', *International Organization*, Vol. 47, No.1, 1993, pp. 162–163.

253 George Bush, 'The Liberation of Kuwait Has Begun', speech of 16 January 1991, in Sifry and Cerf (eds), *The Gulf War Reader*, p. 312.

254 See Kenneth N. Waltz, *Theory of International Politics*, New York: McGraw-Hill, 1979.

255 See C. Jochnick and R. Normand, 'The Legitimation of Violence: A Critical History of the Laws of War', *Harvard International Law Journal*, Vol. 35, No. 2, 1994, pp. 49–95.

256 See Scott Cooper and Brock Taylor, 'Power and Regionalism: Explaining Economic Cooperation in the Persian Gulf'. Paper prepared for the 97th annual meeting of the *American Political Science Association*, San Francisco, CA, 30 August–2 September 2001.

257 See Hedley Bull, *The Anarchical Society. A Study of Order in World Politics*, second edition, London: Macmillan, 1995, pp. 46–47.

258 Charles Tripp, 'The Future of Iraq and of Regional Security', in Geoffrey Kemp and Janice Gross Stein (eds), *Powder Keg in the Middle East: The Struggle for Gulf Security*, London: Rowman & Littlefield, 1995, p.154.

259 See Michael Barnett, 'Regional Security after the Gulf War', *Political Science Quarterly*, Vol. 111, No. 4, 1996/1997, p. 602.

260 See among others Ibrahim Karawan, 'Arab Dilemmas in the 1990s: Breaking Taboos and Searching for Signposts', *The Middle East Journal*, Vol. 48, No. 3, 1994, pp. 433–454; Muhammad Faour, *The Arab World After Desert Storm*, Washington, DC: United States Institute of Peace Process, 1993.

261 Bernard Lewis, 'The Decline of Pan-Arabism', in Sifry and Cerf (eds), *The Gulf War Reader*, 1991, p. 406.

262 Albert Hourani, *A History of the Arab People*s, London: Faber and Faber, 2002, p. 449.

263 Kenneth Katzman, 'The Gulf Co-operation Council: Prospects for Collective Security', in M.E. Ahrari and James H. Noyes (eds), *The Persian Gulf After the Cold War*, London: Praeger, 1993, p. 203.

264 *Al-Sharq al'-Awsat*, 7 March 1991, p. 1.

265 *Radio Cairo*, 27 June 1991. Quoted in Pirouz Mojtahed-Zadeh, 'Regional Alliances in the Persian Gulf: Past Trends and Future Prospects', *The Iranian Journal of International Affairs*, Vol. X, Nos 1 & 2, 1998, p. 20.

266 See also Anwar Gargash, 'Iran, the GCC states, and the UAE: Prospects and Challenges in the Coming Decade', in Jamal S. Al-Suwaidi (ed.), *Iran and the Gulf. A Search for Stability*, Abu Dhabi: The Emirates Center for Strategic Studies and Research, 1996, pp. 142–143.

267 F. Gregory Gause, III, 'Saudi Arabia: Desert Storm and After', in Robert O. Freedman (ed.), *The Middle East after Iraq's Invasion of Kuwait*, Gainesville, FL: University Press of Florida, 1993, pp. 213–214.

268 *Foreign Broadcast International* Service, FBIS-NES-92-034, 20 February 1992, p. 3.

269 See Afrasiabi, *After Khomeini*, p. 95; Gause, 'Saudi Arabia: Desert Storm and After', in Freedman (ed.), *The Middle East After Iraq's Invasion*, p. 214; and Bernard Burrows, John Moberly and Gerd Nonneman, 'Towards a Security Community in the Gulf', in Gerd Nonneman (ed.), *The Middle East and Europe. The Search for Stability and Integration*, London: Federal Trust for Education and Research, 1993, pp. 64–65.

270 Richard N. Schofield, 'Border Disputes in the Gulf: Past, Present and Future', in Lawrence G. Potter and Gary G. Sick (eds), *The Persian Gulf at the Millennium. Essays in Politics, Economy, Security, and Religion*, London: St Martin's, 1997, p. 142.

271 See Michael Barnett and F. Gregory Gause III, 'Caravans in Opposite Directions: Society, State and the Development of a Community in the Gulf Cooperation Council', in Emanuel Adler and Michael Barnett (eds), *Security Communities*, Cambridge: Cambridge UP, 1998, pp. 161–197.

272 Quoted in Tibi, *Conflict and War*, p. 173.

273 Burrows *et al.*, 'Towards a Security Community in the Gulf', in Nonneman (ed.), *The Middle East and Europe*, p. 64.

274 Nozar Alaolmolki, *The Persian Gulf Region in the Twenty First Century, Stability and Change*, London: UP of America, 1996, p. 40.

275 'Le Chef mythique de la révolte', *Corriere della sera*, 26 November 1978. Quoted in Didier Eribon, *Michel Foucault*, translated by Betsy Wing, London: Faber and Faber, 1991, p. 287, emphasis in original.

276 Suzanne Maloney, 'Identity and Change in Iran's Foreign Policy', in Telhami and Barnett (eds), *Identity and Foreign Policy*, London: Cornell UP, 2002, p. 110.

277 The phrase is Ehtesahmi's. See Anoushiravan Ehteshami, *After Khomeini. The Iranian Second Republic*, London: Routledge, 1995.

278 See Ibid.; Afrasiabi, *After Khomeini* and Maloney, 'Identity and Change in Iran's Foreign Policy', in Telhami and Barnett (eds), *Identity and Foreign Policy*.

279 For comments on the similarities to the Shah period see Mohsen Milani, 'Iran's Gulf Policy: From Idealism and Confrontation to Pragmatism and Moderation', in Al-Suwaidi (ed.), *Iran and the Gulf*, p. 94 and Afrasiabi, *After Khomeini*, pp. 101–102.

280 'Statement issued by the Foreign Ministry of the Islamic Republic of Iran', in *Foreign Broadcast International Service*, FBIS-NES, 22 April 1987.

281 *The Texts of Letters Exchanged between the Presidents of the Islamic Republic of Iran and the Republic of Iraq 1369 (1990)*, p. 60.

282 For the changed parameters of the Iranian foreign policy after the death of Khomeini see Ehteshami, *After Khomeini*; Afrasiabi, *After Khomeini*; Adam Tarock, *Iran's Foreign Policy Since 1990. Pragmatism Supersedes Islamic Ideology*, Commack: Nova Science, 1999 or Renate Kreile, 'Islamischer Internationalismus oder realpolitischer Pragmatismus. Zwei Jahrzehnte Aussenpolitik der Islamischen Republik Iran', *Aus Politik und Zeitgeschichte*,

B19, 7 May 1999, Bundeszentrale für politische Bildung, pp. 3–13. For a perspective from the GCC states see Hassan Hamdan al-Alkim, *The GCC States in an Unstable World. Foreign Policy Dilemmas of Small States*, London: Saqi Books, 1994, p. 104 ff.

283 For a similar assessment of the Iranian role in Iraq see Afrasiabi, *After Khomeini*, p. 72; Gargash, 'Iran, the GCC States, and the UAE: Prospects and Challenges in the Coming Decade', in Al-Suwaidi, *Iran and the Gulf*, Abu Dhabi: The Emirates Center for Strategic Studies and Research, 1996, p. 143; Milani, 'Iran's Gulf Policy: From Idealism and Confrontation to Pragmatism and Moderation', in Al-Suwaidi (ed.), *Iran and the Gulf*, Abu Dhabi: The Emirates Center for Strategic Studies and Research, 1996, pp. 92–93 and Shireen T. Hunter, 'Iran and Syria: From Hostility to Limited Alliance', in Hooshang Amirahmadi and Nader Entessar (eds), *Iran and the Arab World*, London: Macmillan, 1993, p. 199. For an analysis of the Bahraini case see Munira A. Fakhro, 'The Uprising in Bahrain. An Assessment', in Potter and Sick (eds), *The Persian Gulf*, pp. 183–184.

284 Gargash, 'Iran, the GCC states, and the UAE: Prospects and Challenges in the Coming Decade', in Al-Suwaidi (ed.), *Iran and the Gulf*, p. 145.

285 Adam Tarock, 'Iran's foreign policy since the Gulf War', *The Australian Journal of International Affairs*, Vol. 48, No.2, 1994, p. 269.

286 See *Al-Sharq al'-Awsat*, 6 February 1991, p. 6.

287 *Al-Hayat*, 29 September 1991, pp. I, 4.

288 Afrasiabi, *After Khomeini*, p. 86.

289 Charles Krauthammer, 'The Unipolar Moment', *Foreign Affairs*, Vol. 70, No. 1, 1991, p. 33.

290 Quoted in Michael T. Klare, 'The Pentagon's New Paradigm', in Sifry and Cerf (eds), *The Gulf War Reader*, p. 468.

291 See also Marc Darnovsky, L.A. Kauffman , Billy Robinson, 'What will this war mean?', in Sifry and Cerf (eds), *The Gulf War Reader*, pp. 480–486.

292 Raymond Hinnebusch, *The International Politics of the Middle East*, Manchester: Manchester UP, 2003, p. 215.

293 Noam Chomsky, 'The Use (and Abuse) of the United Nations', in Sifry and Cerf (eds), *The Gulf War Reader*, p. 308.

294 David Campbell, *Politics Without Principle: Sovereignty, Ethics, and the Narratives of the Gulf War*, London: Lynne Rienner, 1993, p. 22.

295 The US media played a key role in reproducing and by that disseminating both the 'Hitler–Hussein' and 'US-New World Order' analogies. In a study about the number of stories citing Saddam Hussein and Adolf Hitler, and the New World Order, in the *The Washington Post* before, during and after the Second Gulf War, Shaw and Martin found out a direct correlation between the intensity of conflict and the employment of the phrases by the *Post*'s reporters. In the pre-war period between 30 June 1990 until 1 August 1990, Hussein and Hitler were mentioned two times (an average of 0.06 news stories per day) and the New World Order phrase not at all (obviously because the phrase had not yet entered the jargon of US policy-makers and Iraq had not yet invaded Kuwait). In the build-up to the US offensive during 2 August 1990 and 15 January 1991, the Hussein–Hitler analogy was used 118 times (an average of 0.71 news stories per day) and the New World Order phrase 50 times (an average of 0.30 stories per day). During the air war from 16 January 1991 to 22 February 1991, the Hussein–Hitler comparison was referred to 39 times (an average of 1.03 times per day) and the New World Order phrase was mentioned 45 times (an average of 1.18 numbers of stories per day). During the US offensive on the ground, that is in a period of 4 days between 23 February 1991 and 27 February 1991, the Hussein–Hitler analogy was mentioned 7 times (an average of 1.40 number of stories per day) and the New World Order norm 5 times, (an average of one story per day). The employment of both phrases decreased in the postwar period between 28 February 1991 and 30 March 1991. The Hitler–Hussein comparison was made 7 times (an average of 0.23 stories per day) and the New World Order phrase was used 21 times (an average of 0.68 news stories per day). See Donald L. Shaw and Shannon

E. Martin, 'The Natural, and Inevitable, Phases of War Reporting: Historical Shadows, New Communication in the Persian Gulf', in Robert E. Denton Jr (ed.), *The Media and the Persian Gulf War*, Westport, CT: Praeger, 1993, p. 53.

296 The necessarily imperfect term 'neo-conservative' refers to mostly Republican (but not only) functionaries, bureaucrats, decision-makers and academics who advocate an offensive and ideologised foreign policy posture for the United States. The most prominent proponents are Paul Wolfowitz, Richard Perle, Elliott Abrams, Douglas Feith, Michael Ledeen, Charles Krauthammer, Jeane J. Kirkpatrick and William Kristol. See Julie Kosterlitz, 'The Neoconservative Moment', *National Journal*, Vol. 35, No. 20, 17 May 2003, pp. 1540–1546. In the 7 April 2002 issue of the *New Statesmen*, Michael Lind described the emergence of US neo-conservatism as follows:

> How did they get the name? Many of them started off as anti-Stalinist leftists or liberals. They are products of the largely Jewish-American Trotskyist movement of the 1930s and 1940s, which morphed into anti-communist liberalism between the 1950s and 1970s and finally into a kind of militaristic and imperial right with no precedents in American culture or political history. They call their revolutionary ideology 'Wilsonianism' (after President Woodrow Wilson), but it is really Trotsky's theory of the permanent revolution mingled with the far-right Likud strain of Zionism.

297 Hinnebush, *The International Politics of the Middle East*, pp. 218–219.
298 See Ibid., pp. 231–233 and Halliday, *Islam and the Myth of Confrontation*, p. 82.
299 PBS Frontline, 'Oral History of Gulf War II, Interview with Margaret Thatcher, Prime Minister of England'. Available at http://www.pbs.org/wgbh/pages/frontline/gulf/oral/thatcher/2.html (accessed 18 June 2002).

4 Whither the leviathan: sources of co-operation and conflict in the 'post-romantic' Persian Gulf

300 Thomas U. Berger, 'Norms, Identity and National Security in Germany and Japan', in Peter J. Katzenstein (ed.), *The Culture of National Security: Norms and Identity in World Politics*, New York: Columbia UP, 1996, p. 326.
301 See among others Ray Takeyh, 'God's Will: Iranian Democracy and the Islamic Context', *Middle East Policy*, Vol. VII, No. 4, 2000, pp. 41–49. Available at http://www.mepc.org/public_asp/journal_vol7/0010_takeyh.asp (accessed 21 January 2001) and Peter D. Schmid, 'Expect the Unexpected: A Religious Democracy in Iran', *The Brown Journal of International Affairs*, Vol. IX, No. 2, 2003, pp. 181–196.
302 For a review of the political landscape in Iran see 'Iran: The Struggle for the Revolution's Soul', *International Crisis Group*, Amman/Brussels: Middle East Report No. 5, 5 August 2002.
303 Ayatollah Montazeri was designated as the successor of Imam Khomeini after his death, but fell out of favour due to his liberal views on domestic issues.
304 Mehrzad Boroujerdi, 'The Paradoxes of Politics in Post-Revolutionary Iran', in John L. Esposito and R. K. Ramazani (eds), *Iran at the Crossroads*, Houndmills: Palgrave, 2001, p. 27.
305 Revealingly, even the centre of power associated with 'conservatism' in the Iranian context, the Supreme Leader Ayatollah Ali Khamenei, has recently employed the phrase 'religious democracy' to encourage public participation in the political process. See 'Supreme Leader: Iran is Standard Bearer of Religious Democracy'. *IRNA*, 6 August 2003.
306 Robin Wright, *The Last Great Revolution*, New York: Vintage Books, 2001, p. 9.
307 'The National Reform Document'. Available at http://www.saudiinstitute.org (accessed 21 September 2003).
308 The phrase is due to Rouhollah K. Ramazani, see his 'The Shifting Premise of Iran's Foreign Policy: Towards a Democratic Peace?', *Middle East Journal*, Vol. 52, No. 2, 1998, pp. 177–187.

309 Ibid., p. 181 ff. For the Iranian foreign policy re-formation after the election of Khatami see Hooman Peimani, *Iran and the United States. The Rise of the West Asian Regional Grouping*, London: Praeger, 1999 or Christin Marschall, *Iran's Persian Gulf Policy: From Khomeini to Khatami*, London: RoutledgeCurzon, 2003.

310 See 'Statement by H.E. Seyyed Mohammad Khatami, President of the Islamic Republic of Iran and Chairman of the Eighth Session of the Islamic Summit Conference, Tehran, 9 December 1997', in Mohammad Khatami (ed.), *Islam, Dialogue and Civil Society*, Canberra: Centre for Arab and Islamic Studies, The Australian National University, 2000, pp. 17–18.

311 See Ramazani, 'The Shifting Premise of Iran's Foreign Policy: Towards a Democratic Peace?', p. 182.

312 Khatami, *Islam, Dialogue*, p. 21.

313 See resolution 15/8-P (IS) of the Tehran Summit in 1997, *Resolutions and Declarations of the Eighth Islamic Summit*, Jeddah: OIC General Secretariat, no date.

314 'Kuwait, Iran sign agreement to fight drugs, terrorism', *AFP*, 3 October 2000.

315 *Reuters*, 28 February 1998.

316 *Reuters*, 26 May 1998.

317 *Reuters*, 27 May 1998.

318 *Reuters*, 14 May 2000.

319 'Statement by Dr Kamal Kharrazi, Foreign Minister of the Islamic Republic of Iran at the 8th Persian Gulf Seminar on Regional Approaches in the Persian Gulf, Tehran 24 February 1998', *The Iranian Journal of International Affairs*, Vol. X, Nos 1 & 2, 1998, pp. 145–146.

320 'Iran-Saudi Arabia ink landmark security deal amid warming relations', *AFP*, 18 April 2001.

321 'Gulf News says: A welcome agreement', *Gulf News*, 21 April 2001.

322 'Iran and Oman agree on joint development of offshore gas field', *AFP*, 19 June 2000.

323 For an analysis of these elections and their impact on the reform movement in Iran see Geneive Abdo, 'Electoral Politics in Iran', *Middle East Policy*, Vol. VI, No. 4, 1999, pp. 128–136. Available at http://www.mepc.org/public_asp/journal_vol6/9906_abdo.asp (accessed 12 July 2000) and Suzanne Maloney, 'A New Majlis and a Mandate for Reform', *Middle East Policy*, Vol. VII, No. 3, 2000, pp. 59–66. Available at http://www.mepc.org/public_asp/journal_vol7/0006_maloney.asp (accessed 21 July 2000).

324 'Gulf Arabs hope Iran vote aids rapprochement', *Reuters*, 21 February 2000.

325 Quoted in J.E. Peterson, 'The Historical Pattern of Gulf Security', in Lawrence G. Potter and Gary G. Sick (eds), *Security in the Persian Gulf. Origins, Obstacles, and the Search for Consensus*, Houndmills: Palgrave, 2002, p. 24.

326 Robert O. Keohane and Joseph S. Nye, *Power and Interdependence*, third edition, London: Longman, 2001, p. 10.

327 Ibid., p. 11.

328 Peter Berger, *The Sacred Canopy*, Garden City: Doubleday, 1967, p. 4.

329 John Fousek, *To Lead the Free World. American Nationalism and the Cultural Roots of the Cold War*, Chapel Hill, NC: University of North Carolina Press, 2000, p. 187.

330 Julie Kosterlitz, 'The Neoconservative Moment', *National Journal*, Vol. 35, No. 20, 17 May 2003, p. 1542.

331 See Samuel P. Huntington, *The Clash of Civilisations and the Remaking of World Order*, London: Touchstone, 1996; Francis Fukuyama, *The End of History and the Last Man*, New York: Free Press, 1992. For an examination of both paradigms after the events of 11 September 2003 see Arshin Adib-Moghaddam, 'Global Intifadah? September 11th and the Struggle within Islam', *Cambridge Review of International Affairs*, Vol. 15, No. 2, 2002, pp. 203–216.

332 David Campbell, *Politics Without Principle: Sovereignty, Ethics, and the Narratives of the Gulf War*, London: Lynne Rienner, 1993, pp. 94–95.

333　William Pfaff, 'More Likely a New World Disorder', in Micah L. Sifry and Christopher Cerf (eds), *The Gulf War Reader. History, Documents, Opinions*, New York: Times Books, 1991, p. 487.

334　Marc Darnovsky, L.A. Kauffman and Billy Robinson, 'What Will This War Mean?', in Micah L. Sifry and Christopher Cerf (eds), *The Gulf War Reader. History, Documents, Opinions*, New York: Times Books, 1991, p. 484.

335　See also David Campbell, *Writing Security: United States Foreign Policy and the Politics of Identity*, Manchester: Manchester UP, 1992.

336　See also Stephen Zunes, 'The Function of Rogue States in U.S. Middle East Policy', *Middle East Policy*, Vol. 5, No. 2, 1997, pp. 150–167.

337　For examples of this disposition see Charles Krauthammer, 'Bless our Pax Americana', *The Washington Post*, 22 March 1991 or Joshua Muravchik, 'At Last, Pax Americana', *New York Times*, 24 January 1991.

338　James Blackwell, 'US Military Response to the Iraqi invasion of Kuwait', in Robert F. Helms II and Robert H. Dorff (eds), *The Persian Gulf Crisis. Power in the Post-Cold War World*, London: Praeger, 1993, p. 127.

339　Edward W. Said, *The Politics of Dispossession. The Struggle for Palestinian Self-Determination 1969–1994*, London: Vintage, 1995, p. 298.

340　Anthony Lake, 'Confronting Backlash States', *Foreign Affairs*, Vol. 73, No. 2, 1994, p. 48.

341　Zbigniew Brzezinsky, Brent Scowcroft and Richard Murphy, 'Differentiated Containment', *Foreign Affairs*, Vol. 76, No. 3, 1997, p. 23.

342　For the impact of Jewish lobbying groups on US policy *vis-à-vis* Iran see Arshin Adib-Moghaddam, 'The Neo-conservative Factor', *bitterlemons-international*, Ed., 44, Vol. 2, 16 December 2004. Available at http://www.bitterlemons-international.org/inside.php?id=265 (accessed 12 February 2005); Bernard Burrows, John Moberly and Gerd Nonneman, 'Towards a Security Community in the Gulf', in Gerd Nonneman (ed.), *The Middle East and Europe. The Search for Stability and Integration*, London: Federal Trust for Education and Research, 1993, p. 66; Adam Tarock, 'Iran's Foreign Policy Since the Gulf War', *The Australian Journal of International Affairs*, Vol. 48, No. 2, 1994, pp. 272–273 and Bulent Aras, 'Turkish, Israeli, Iranian Relations in the Nineties: Impact on the Middle East', *Middle East Policy*, Volume VII, No. 3, 2000, pp. 151–164.

343　Michael Ledeen, 'Rediscovering American Character', *National Review Online*, 10 October 2001. Available at http://www.aei.org/news/filter.,newsID.13236/news_detail.asp (accessed 14 April 2003).

344　Quoted in Alexander L. George, 'The Gulf War's Possible Impact on the International System', in Stanley A. Renshon (ed.), *The Political Psychology of the Gulf War. Leaders, Publics, and the Process of Conflict*, Pittsburgh, PA: University of Pittsburgh Press, 1993, p. 297.

345　David C. Hendrickson, 'The Recovery of Internationalism', *Foreign Affairs*, Vol. 73, No. 5, 1994, p. 41.

346　See Herman Franssen and Elaine Morton, 'A Review of US Unilateral Sanctions Against Iran', *Middle East Economic Survey*, Vol. XLV, No. 34, 26 August 2002. According to the authors, an AIPAC spokesman was quoted as saying that 'These guys (Congress) wrote their thing (ILSA) with us sentence by sentence'. Available at http://www.mafhoum.com/press3/108E16.htm (accessed 12 January 2003).

347　See 'Country Profile Iran', *Economist Intelligence Unit (EIU)*, 1 May 2002. Available at http://www.angelfire.com/super/eiu/EIU_Country_Profile_Iran__1_May_2002.htm (accessed 23 September 2002).

348　For the official declaration by President Clinton see 'Statement by the President', The White House, 16 December 1998, Office of the Press Secretary. Available at the Internet site of the White House. http://www.whitehouse.gov

349　'Iraq Liberation Act of 1998', United States Senate, Document S.2525, 29 September 1998. Available at http://www.senate.gov/legislative/index.html (accessed 21 January 2001).

350 See Jules Lobel and Michael Ratner, 'Bypassing the Security Council: Ambiguous Authorisations to Use Force, Cease-Fires and the Iraqi Inspection Regime', *American Journal of International Law*, Vol. 93, No. 1, 1999, pp. 124–154. Available at http://www.asil.org/ajil/lobel.htm (accessed 23 August 2003).

351 Marc Lynch, 'The Politics of Consensus in the Gulf', *Middle East Report*, No. 215, Vol. 30, No. 2, 2000, p. 22.

352 See Franssen and Morton, 'A Review of US Unilateral Sanctions Against Iran', *Middle East Economic Survey*, Vol. XLV, No. 34, 26 August 2002. http://www.mafhoum.com/press3/108E16.htm

353 Rolf Ekeus interviewed in *Arms Control Today*, Vol. 30, No. 2, 2000. Available at http://www.armscontrol.org/act/2000_03/remr00.asp (accessed 22 July 2003).

354 *Middle East International*, 12 February 1999, p. 23. See also Raymond Hinnebusch, *The International Politics of the Middle East*, Manchester: Manchester UP, 2003, p. 233. Both Haliday and his successor Hans von Sponeck resigned in protest against the UN sanctions regime.

355 Charles Krauthammer, 'The Unipolar Moment Revisited: America, the Benevolent Empire', in Micah L. Sifry and Christopher Cerf (eds), *The Iraq War Reader. History, Documents, Opinions*, London: Simon & Schuster, 2003, p. 607. The article originally appeared in *The National Interest*, No. 70, 2002/2003.

356 Ibid.

357 Susan Sontag, 'Reflections on September 11th', in Sifry and Cerf (eds), *The Iraq War Reader*, p. 215. The article originally appeared in *The New Yorker*, 24 September 2001.

358 Charles Krauthammer, 'Voices of Moral Obtuseness', in Sifry and Cerf (eds), *The Iraq War Reader*, p. 218. The article originally appeared in *The Washington Post*, 21 September 2001.

359 Ann Coulter, 'Why We Hate Them', in Sifry and Cerf (eds), *The Iraq War Reader*, p. 333. The article originally appeared at *FrontPageMagazine.com*, 26 September 2003. Coulter is a political analyst and attorney. In another commentary published in the *National Review Online*, written two days after 11 September, she wrote of 'the ones cheering and dancing right now', that 'we should invade their countries, kill their leaders and convert them to Christianity', leading to her dismissal from *The National Review*. Her commentaries continue to be published at *FrontPageMagazine.com*.

360 Fred Ikle, 'Stopping the Next Sept. 11. Intelligence is one element. Offence and defence are the others', *Wall Street Journal*, 2 June 2002.

361 Later, Falwell apologised for the remarks see 'Jerry Falwell Apologises for Mohammad Criticism', *Reuters*, 12 October 2002.

362 All material quoted in relation to the Project is taken from the homepage of the organisation at http://www.newamericancentury.org/ (accessed 12 June 2001).

363 The family and friendship ties are indeed extensive. Richard Perle's close friend at the AEI is David Wurmser, who heads the Middle East Studies department at the organisation. Together with the former Israeli military intelligence official, Yigal Carmon, the wife of Mr Wurmser, Meyrav, have established the *Middle East Media Research Institute (Memri)* which selectively translates the most radical pamphlets and articles published in the Muslim world. Ms Wurmser also runs the Hudson Institute, where Richard Perle recently joined the Board of Trustees. In addition, she is a member of the Middle East Forum, where other activists with neo-conservative leanings such as Michael Rubin and Laurie Mylroie are organisers. See Brian Whitaker, 'US think tanks give lessons in foreign policy', *The Guardian*, 19 August 2002. See also his 'Selective Memri', *The Guardian*, 12 August 2002.

364 See Thomas P.M. Barnett, 'The Pentagon's New Map. It explains why we're going to war and why we'll keep going to war', *Esquire*, March 2003. The online version of this article that follows quotes referred to is available at http://www.nwc.navy.mil/newrulesets/ThePentagonsNewMap.htm (accessed 12 May 2003).

365 Unfortunately, Barnett does not provide any numbers to qualify this assertion.

366 Unfortunately, Barnett does not provide any numbers to qualify this assertion.

367 Donald Kagan, Gary Schmitt and Thomas Donnelly, 'Rebuilding America's Defences: Strategy, Forces and Resources For a New Century', A Report of *The Project for the New American Century*, September 2000.

368 'The National Security Strategy of the United States of America', September 2002. Available at http://www.whitehouse.gov/nsc/nss.pdf (accessed 12 October 2002).

369 Kagan *et al.*, 'Rebuilding America's Defences: Strategy, Forces and Resources For a New Century', p. 6.

370 'The National Security Strategy of the United States of America', p. v.

371 Kagan *et al.*, 'Rebuilding America's Defences: Strategy, Forces and Resources For a New Century', p. 75.

372 Excerpts and the quote are available at http://www.globalsecurity.org/wmd/library/policy/dod/npr.htm (accessed 1 September 2003).

373 The classified version is identified jointly as National Security Presidential Directive (NSPD) 17 and Homeland Security Presidential Directive 4. See Mike Allen and Barton Gellman, 'Preemptive Strikes Part Of U.S. Strategic Doctrine. "All Options" Open for Countering Unconventional Arms', *The Washington Post*, 11 December 2002, p. A01. Available at http://www.washingtonpost.com/ac2/wp-dyn/A36819-2002Dec10?language=printer (accessed 12 December 2002).

374 Another letter dated 25 November 2002, focused on China, another country that positions prominently on the list of potential adversaries. The signers suggest that the 'U.S. should forthrightly oppose the introduction of new national security laws and make clear that the adoption of restrictive laws would trigger a review of Hong Kong's special status under the U.S. Hong Kong Policy Act.' That letter and the following correspondences are available at the Project's homepage, note 362.

375 During a meeting in the wake of 11 September, US National Security Advisor Condoleezza Rice used the term asking her staff 'How do you capitalise on these opportunities?' A comparable reaction by Defence Secretary Donald Rumsfeld was reported by David Martin in his *CBS News* report on 4 September 2002. Martin cited notes taken by aides with Rumsfeld in the National Military Command Centre. Both citations are quoted in Sifry and Cerf, *The Iraq War Reader*, p. 241 and p. 213 respectively.

376 Estimated by Anthony Lewis, ' "First They Came for the Muslims . . ." ', in Sifry and Cerf (eds), *The Iraq War Reader*, p. 233.

377 Daniel Pipes, 'The Enemy Within', in Sifry and Cerf (eds), *The Iraq War Reader*, p. 232.

378 See Emily Eakin, 'An organisation on the lookout for patriotic incorrectness', *The New York Times*, 21 November 2001. Online available at http://www.globalpolicy.org/wtc/liberties/1124incorrect.htm (accessed 1 December 2001) and Arlene Levinson, 'Debating Terrorism Can Be Costly', *Associated Press*, 12 October 2001. Available at http://www.commondreams.org/headlines01/1013-02.htm (accessed 21 November 2002). See also Juan Cole, 'Why Are Arch Conservatives Ganging Up on the Middle East Studies Association', *History News Network*, 20 January 2003. Available at http://hnn.us/articles/1218.html (accessed 24 January 2003).

379 Graham E. Fuller, 'Repairing U.S.–Iranian Relations', *Middle East Policy*, Vol. VI, No. 2, 1998, p. 142. The online version is available at http://www.mepc.org/public_asp/journal_vol6/9810_fuller.asp (accessed 12 June 2000).

380 Stanley Hoffmann, 'The High and the Mighty: Bush's National Security Strategy and the New American Hubris', *The American Prospect*, Vol. 13, No. 24, 13 January 2003. The quote is taken from the online version available at http://www.prospect.org/print/V13/24/hoffmann-s.html (accessed 22 January 2003).

381 Available at the homepage of the Project for the new American century, note 362. Published originally in the *Frankfurter Allgemeine Zeitung*, 2 May 2002, as 'Eine Welt der Gerechtigkeit und des Friedens sieht anders aus' (A world of justice and peace looks differently).

382 The list of signatories to the letter 'What We're Fighting For: A Letter from America' is another indicator for this. The letter is available at http://www.americanvalues.org/html/wwff.html (accessed 10 August 2003).

383 'Letter from United States Citizens to Friends from Europe'. Available at http://www. americanvalues.org/html/us_letter_to_europeans.html (accessed 1 July 2003).

384 Ali Behdad, 'Nationalism and Immigration to the United States', *Diaspora* Vol. 6, No. 2, 1997, p. 161.

385 James Woolsey, 'At war for freedom', *The Observer*, 20 July 2003. Available at http://observer.guardian.co.uk/comment/story/0,6903,1001642,00.html (accessed 22 July 2003).

386 See George Monbiot, 'America is a religion', *The Guardian*, 29 July 2003, p. 19.

387 See Adib-Moghaddam, 'Global Intifadah? September 11th and the Struggle within Islam', p. 213.

388 Speech of Osama bin Laden broadcasted on *al-Jazira* television on 7 October 2001, and published on 8 October 2001 in the *International Herald Tribune*.

389 Hinnebusch, *The International Politics of the Middle East*, p. 236.

390 See Basssam Tibi, *Arab Nationalism. Between Islam and the Nation-State*, third edition, London: Macmillan 1997; Paul Salem, *Bitter Legacy. Ideology and Politics in the Arab World*, Syracuse, NY: Syracuse UP, 1994; Nazih N. Ayubi, *Over-stating the Arab State. Politics and Society in the Middle East*, London: I.B. Tauris, 1995.

391 For the influence of leftist ideas on the semantics of the Islamic revolution see Ervand Abrahamian, *Khomeinism. Essays on the Islamic Republic*, London: I.B. Tauris, 1993.

392 Jalal Al-e-Ahmad, *Plagued by the West (Gharbzadegi)*, translated from the Persian by Paul Sprachman, New York: Caravan, 1982, p. 10.

393 Ibid., p. 19.

394 Ali Rahnema, *An Islamic Utopian. A Political Biography of Ali Shariati*, London: I.B. Tauris, 2000, pp. 119–128.

395 Ibid., p. 345. In an interesting insight into the identity politics of Pahlavi Iran, Rahnema notes that Shariati's articles were printed next to another serialised article entitled 'Reza Shah the Great; Saviour and Reconstructor of Iran'.

396 For English translations see John J. Donohue and John L. Esposito (eds), *Islam in Transition. Muslim Perspectives*, Oxford: Oxford UP, 1982. For overviews see amongst others Albert Hourani, *Arabic Thought in the Liberal Age 1798–1939*, Cambridge: Cambridge UP, 1983; Nazih N. Ayubi, *Political Islam: Religion and Politics in the Arab World*, London: Routledge, 1991 and Salem, *Bitter Legacy*.

397 Al-Afghani's life and political thought are convincingly chronicled and interpreted in Nikki R. Keddie, *An Islamic Response to Imperialism: The Political and Religious Writings of Sayyid Jamal ad-Din al-Afghani*, Berkeley, CA: University of California Press, 1983. See also Elie Kedourie, *Afghani and 'Abduh: An Essay on Religious Unbelief and Political Activism in Modern Islam*, London: Frank Cass, 1966 and Hourani, *Arabic thought*, pp. 103–129.

398 Tibi, *Arab Nationalism*, p. 90.

399 Afghani's reply to Renan is translated in Keddie, *An Islamic Response*, pp. 181–187.

400 Salem, *Bitter Legacy*, p. 92.

401 Tibi, *Arab Nationalism*, p. 93.

402 Rashid Rida, *Tarikh al-ustadh al-imam al-shaykh Muhammad 'Abduh*, Vol. 1, Cairo: 1931, p. II. Quoted in Albert Hourani, *A History of the Arab Peoples*, London: Faber and Faber, 2002, p. 308.

403 See Hamid Enayat, *Modern Islamic Political Thought*, Austin, TX: Texas UP, 1982; Muhammad Iqbal, *The Reconstruction of Religious Thought in Islam*, Lahore: Iqbal Academy Pakistan, 1968; Mohammed Arkoun, *Rethinking Islam: Common Questions, Uncommon Answers*, translated and edited by Robert D. Lee, Oxford: Westview, 1994; Ali Shariati, *Man and Islam/lectures by Ali Shariati*, translated from Persian by Ghulam M. Fayez, Mashhad: University of Mashhad Press, 1982.

404 'Answer of Jamal ad-Din to Renan', *Journal des Débats*, 18 May 1883, in Keddie, *An Islamic Response*, p. 183.

405 Of course it would be a gross oversimplification to conflate the three topical areas, Ibn-Sina, al-Ghazali and Sufism. The point is that most contemporary critical Muslim thinkers find enough evidence in classical Islamic writings and practice to anchor (and legitimate) their

deconstruction of Islamic tenets. The debates between the *Asharites* and the *Mutazilites*; Avicenna and al-Ghazali; and the *Akhbaris* and the *Usulis* support their case.

406 Hourani, *Arabic Thought*, p. 18.

407 See Muhammad Rashid Rida, *al Wahabiyyun wa'l Hijaz*, Cairo 1344 (1925–1926).

408 Quoted in Richard P. Mitchel, *The Society of the Muslim Brothers*, London: Oxford UP, 1969, p. 30.

409 Ayubi, *Political Islam*, pp. 133–134.

410 Ibid., p. 128 and Salem, *Bitter Legacy*, p. 126.

411 Abu-l-Ala Mawdudi,, 'Political Theory of Islam', in John J. Donohue and John L. Esposito (eds), *Islam in Transition. Muslim Perspectives*, Oxford: Oxford UP, 1982, p. 254.

412 Sayyid Qutb, *Ma'alim fi al-tariq*, new edition, Quom: Dar al-Nashr Quom, (n.d.), pp. 21–22. Quoted in Ayubi, *Political Islam*, p. 139.

413 Quoted in Hourani, *A History of the Arab Peoples*, pp. 445–446.

414 The *Jama'at al Takfir wa al Hijra* ('The Society of Excommunication and Holy Fight') founded in Egypt after a split with the Muslim Brotherhood in 1967 by Sheikh Shukri Ahmad Mustafa, for instance, advocated armed struggle against both state and society (the same as the Egyptian *Al-Jihad*), whilst the Islamic Liberation Organisation (ILO) established in the early 1970s and led by Salih Siriyya focused its activities exclusively on combating the state. It was another neo-fundamentalist grouping, the *Munazzamat al-Jihad* ('The Holy War Organisation'), however, that was responsible for the assassination of President Anwar Sadat of Egypt on 6 October 1981. Prior to the assassination (in the late 1970s), the founders of the *Takfir* and ILO were both executed in a nation-wide crackdown of political Islamic movements.

415 Paul Eedle, 'Al-Qaeda takes fight for 'hearts and minds' to the web', *Jane's Intelligence Review*, 1 August 2002. Available at http://www.janes.com/security/international_security/news/jir/jir020715_1_n.shtml (accessed 12 August 2002).

416 Abd al-Salam Yassin, *Sur l'économie, préalables dogmatiques et régles chariques*, Rabat: Imprimerie Horizons, 1996, p. 20. Quoted in Mohammad Tozy, 'Islamism and some of its perceptions of the West', in Gema Martín Muñoz (ed.), *Islam, Modernism and the West. Cultural and Political Relations at the End of the Millennium*, London: I.B. Tauris, 1999, p. 170.

417 Notwithstanding the fact that sympathising individuals and groups are converts to Islam who have been socialised in Western European cities or in the United States.

418 These organisations are analysed in Mamoun Fandy, *Saudi Arabia and the Politics of Dissent*, London: Macmillan, 1999.

419 Quoted in ibid., p. 181.

420 Quoted in ibid., pp. 189–190.

421 Available from the members section of the Gulf/2000 Project at Columbia University, http://gulf2000.columbia.edu/ (accessed 21 September 2003).

422 See Adib-Moghaddam, 'Global Intifadah? September 11th and the Struggle Within Islam', p. 211.

423 Translation of Osama bin-Laden's tape aired on the al-Jazeera television station on 11 February 2003. Available at http://www.terrorisme.net/pdf/newcrusaderwar.pdf (accessed 11 September 2003).

424 See Fred Halliday, *Islam and the Myth of Confrontation. Religion and Politics in the Middle East*, London: I.B. Tauris, 1996, p. 81.

425 James Piscatori, 'Religion and Realpolitik: Islamic Responses to the Gulf War', in James Piscatori (ed.), *Islamic Fundamentalism and the Gulf Crisis*, Chicago, IL: The Fundamentalism Project, American Academy of Arts and Sciences, 1991, p. 3.

426 After the war in April 1991, an amalgam of Arab groups, including the Muslim Brothers and Yassir Arafat, invited to Khartoum by Hassan al-Turabi, reiterated their opposition against the US attack on Iraq.

427 *MSANews*, 14 September 2001. Available at http://msanews.mynet.net/MSANEWS/200109/20010917.15.html (accessed 13 September 2003).

428 See for instance Malise Ruthven in the afterword to Hourani, *A History of the Arab Peoples*, p. 470.

429 Sayyid Qutb, 'Social Justice in Islam', in Donohue and Esposito (eds), *Islam in Transition*, p. 126.

430 Bernard Lewis, The Roots of Muslim Rag', *The Atlantic Monthly*, Vol. 266, September 1990, p. 60.

431 Statement by the 'World Islamic Front for Jihad Against Jews and Crusaders' (Nass Bayan al-Jabhah al-Islamiyah al-Alamiyah li-Jihad al-Yahud wa-al-Salibiyin). Originally published in the Arabic newspaper *Al-Quds al-Arabi*, London, 23 February 1998, p. 3. This document is the official founding statement of al-Qaeda al-Jihad and was signed by Osama bin-Laden, Ayman al-Zawahiri, leader of the Jihad Group in Egypt, Abu-Yasir Rifa'i Ahmad Taha, from the Egyptian Islamic Group, Shaykh Mir Hamzah, Secretary of the Jamiat-ul-Ulema-e-Pakistan and Fazlur Rahman, leader of the Jihad Movement in Bangladesh. An English translation is available at http://www.fas.org/irp/world/para/docs/980223-fatwa.htm (accessed 12 September 2003).

432 See Sifry and Cerf, *The Gulf War Reader*, p. 505.

433 'Statement by the President in His Address to the Nation', 11 September 2001. Available at http://www.whitehouse.gov/news/releases/2001/09/20010911-16.html (accessed 26 September 2001).

434 'Address to a Joint Session of Congress and the American People'. 20 September 2001. Available at http://www.whitehouse.gov/news/releases/2001/09/20010920-8.html (accessed 12 February 2002).

435 'Letter dated 7 October 2001 from the Permanent Representative of the United States of America to the United Nations addressed to the President of the Security Council', UN SCOR, 56th Session, UN Document S/2001; 'Letter dated 7 October 2001 from the Chargé d'affaires a.i. of the Permanent Mission of the United Kingdom and Northern Ireland to the United Nations addressed to the President of the Security Council', UN Document S/2001/947.

436 Mary Ellen O'Connel, 'The Myth of Preemptive Self-Defense', *The American Society of International Law Task Force on Terrorism*, August 2002, p. 2.

437 Ibid., p. 21.

438 See also Arshin Adib-Moghaddam, 'American Neo-conservatives Pushed War', *bitterlemons-international*, Ed., 27, Vol. 2, 15 July 2004. Available at http://www.bitterlemons-international.org/inside.php?id=196 (accessed 25 March 2005).

439 'President Delivers State of the Union Address', 29 January 2002. Available at http://www.whitehouse.gov/news/releases/2002/01/20020129–11.html (accessed 2 February 2002).

440 Ibid.

441 Brent Scowcroft, 'Don't Attack Saddam', in Sifry and Cerf (eds), *The Iraq War Reader*, p. 297. The article originally appeared in *The Wall Street Journal*, 15 August 2002.

442 'Vice-President Speaks at VFW 103rd National Convention', 26 August 2002. Available at http://www.whitehouse.gov/news/releases/2002/08/20020826.html (accessed 18 November 2002).

443 The letter is available at http://msnbc.com/news/834690.asp?cp1=1 (accessed 18 September 2003).

444 'President Says Saddam Hussein Must Leave Iraq Within 48 Hours'. Available at http://www.whitehouse.gov/news/releases/2003/03/20030317–7.html (accessed 12 August 2003).

445 Condoleezza Rice, 'Our coalition. More than 50 countries have joined forces against Saddam', *Wall Street Journal*, 27 March 2003.

446 See 'Transnational terrorism after the Iraq war: Net Effect', International Institute for Strategic Studies (IISS), *Strategic Comments*, Vol. 9 No. 4, 2003. Available at http://www.mafhoum.com/press5/155P3.pdf (accessed 22 August 2003).

447 Sifry and Cerf, *The Iraq War Reader*, p. 502 (postscript).

448 Hinnebusch, *The International Politics of the Middle East*, p. 239.

449 William A. Rugh, 'Time to Modify Our Gulf Policy', *Middle East Policy*, Vol. V, No. 1, 1997, p. 50. The online version is available at http://www.mepc.org/public_asp/journal_vol5/9701_rugh.asp (accessed 21 November 2002).

450 See among others Henry Tajfel (ed.), *Social Identity and Intergroup Relations*, Cambridge: Cambridge UP, 1982 and Dominic Abrams and Michael Hogg (eds), *Social Identity Theory*, New York: Harvester Wheatsheaf, 1990.

451 Said, *The Politics of Dispossession*, p. 356, emphasis in original.

452 See among others Bruce Russet, 'A Neo-Kantian perspective: Democracy, Interdependence, and International Organisations in Building Security Communities', in Emanuel Adler and Michael Barnett (eds), *Security Communities*, Cambridge: Cambridge UP, 1998, pp. 368–394 and Alexander Wendt, *Social Theory of International Politics*, Cambridge: Cambridge UP, 1999, pp. 297–307.

5 Towards a cultural genealogy of anarchy in the Persian Gulf: concluding reflections and ideas for future research

453 For a comparative analysis of intervention and international order see James Mayall (ed.), *The New Interventionism 1991–1994. United Nations Experience in Cambodia, former Yugoslavia and Somalia*, Cambridge: Cambridge UP, 1996.

454 John W. Meyer, John Boli, George M. Thomas and Francisco O. Ramirez, 'World Society and the Nation-State', *American Journal of Sociology*, Vol. 103, No. 1, 1997, p. 173.

455 Karl Deutsch *et al.*, *Political Community and the North Atlantic Area*, Princeton, NJ: Princeton UP, 1957, p. 5.

456 Ibid., p. 6.

457 Ibid., p. 36.

458 David Campbell, *Politics Without Principle: Sovereignty, Ethics, and the Narratives of the Gulf War*, London: Lynne Rienner, 1993, p. 96.

459 Alexander Wendt, *Social Theory of International Politics*, Cambridge: Cambridge UP, 1999, p. 360.

460 There have been several examples of such a dialogue: In 1997, Iran's ambassador to Saudi Arabia, revealed that he had met with the Kingdom's top cleric and arbiter of Wahhabism, General Mufti Shaykh 'Abdallah Bin Baz, and other members of the Saudi Council of Senior 'Ulama (*Al-Sharq al-Awsat*, 4 July 1997); A year later protests expressed by the head of Iran's hajj delegation, Ayatollah Reyshari, led to the dismissal of the popular but anti-Shia Imam of the Medinite sanctuary, Shaykh Ali Abdal-Rahman al-Hudhayfi (See *Summary of World Broadcasts*: ME/3183 Med/17, 24 March 1998 and ME/3186 MED/15, 27 March 1998). In a remarkable step in July 2003, both countries signed a judiciary co-operation deal during the visit of Iran's Minister of the Judiciary Ayatollah Mahmoud Hashemi-Shahroudi to Riyadh ('Saudi Arabia, Iran sign judicial cooperation deal', *AFP*, 11 July 2003). The exchanges extend to the societal level as well, exemplified by increasing numbers of Saudi tourists spending their vacation in Iran. See 'Letter from Saudi Arabia: Iran current hot tourist spot for Saudis', *Gulf News*, 4 August 2003.

461 *Al-Riyadh*, 17 March 1997. Quoted in Joshua Teitelbaum, 'The Gulf States and the End of Dual Containment', *Middle East Review of International Affairs*, Vol. 2, No. 3, 1997. Available at http://www.biu.ac.il/SOC/besa/meria/journal/1998/issue3/teitelbaum.pdf (accessed 23 October 2001).

462 For the term see Emanuel Adler, 'Imagined (security) communities: Cognitive regions in international relations', *Millennium*, Vol. 26, No.2, 1997, pp. 249–277.

463 For a recent move in that direction see Richard Wyn Jones (ed.), *Critical Theory and World Politics*, London: Lynne Rienner, 2001.

Bibliography

Abdo, Geneive, 'Electoral Politics in Iran', *Middle East Policy*, Vol. VI, No. 4, 1999, pp. 128–136. http://www.mepc.org/public_asp/journal_vol6/9906_abdo.asp

Abrahamian, Ervand, *Khomeinism. Essays on the Islamic Republic*, London: I.B. Tauris, 1993.

Abrams, Dominic and Michael Hogg (eds), *Social Identity Theory*, New York: Harvester Wheatsheaf, 1990.

Adib-Moghaddam, Arshin, 'Global Intifadah? September 11th and the Struggle Within Islam', *Cambridge Review of International Affairs*, Vol. 15, No. 2, 2002, pp. 203–216.

Adib-Moghaddam, Arshin, 'American Neo-conservatives Pushed War', *bitterlemons-international*, Ed., 27, Vol. 2, 15 July 2004. http://www.bitterlemons-international.org/inside.php? id=196

Adib-Moghaddam, Arshin, 'The Neo-conservative Factor', *bitterlemons-international*, Ed., 44, Vol. 2, 16 December 2004. http://www.bitterlemons-international.org/inside.php? id=265

Adib-Moghaddam, Arshin, 'Islamic Utopian Romanticism and the Foreign policy Culture of Iran', *Critique: Critical Middle Eastern Studies*, Vol. 14, No. 3, Fall 2005, pp. 265–292.

Adler, Emanuel, 'Seizing the Middle Ground: Constructivism in World Politics', *European Journal of International Relations*, Vol. 3, No. 3, 1997, pp. 319–363.

Adler, Emanuel, 'Imagined (Security) Communities: Cognitive Regions in International Relations', *Millennium*, Vol. 26, No. 2, 1997, pp. 249–277.

Adler, Emanuel and Michael Barnett (eds), *Security Communities*, Cambridge: Cambridge UP, 1998.

Aflaq, Michel, *Fi Sabil al Ba'th*, Beirut: Dar al-Tali'ah, 1959.

Afrasiabi, Kaveh L., *After Khomeini. New Directions in Iran's Foreign Policy*, Boulder, CO: Westview, 1994.

Ahmad, Ahmad Yousef, 'The Dialectics of Domestic Environment and Role performance: The Foreign Policy of Iraq', in Bahgat Korany and Ali E. Hillal Dessouki (eds), *The Foreign Policies of Arab States*, Boulder, CO: Westview, 1984, pp. 147–174.

Ahmed, Akbar, *Discovering Islam. Making Sense of Muslim History and Society*, revised edition, London: Routledge, 2002.

Ajami, Fouad, *The Arab Predicament. Arab Political Thought and Practice Since 1967*, updated edition, Cambridge: Cambridge UP, 1992.

Alaolmolki, Nozar, *Struggle for Dominance in the Persian Gulf. Past, Present, and Future Prospects*, New York: Peter Lang, 1991.

Alaolmolki, Nozar, *The Persian Gulf Region in the Twenty First Century, Stability and Change*, London: UP of America, 1996.

Al-e-Ahmad, Jalal, *Plagued by the West (Gharbzadegi)*, translated from the Persian by Paul Sprachman, New York: Caravan, 1982.

al-Alkim, Hassan Hamdan, *The GCC States in an Unstable World. Foreign Policy Dilemmas of Small States*, London: Saqi Books, 1994.

Allport, Gordon W., 'The Role of Expectancy', in Leon Bramson and George W. Goethals (eds), *War. Studies from Psychology, Sociology, Anthropology*, London: basic books, 1964, pp. 177–194.

Alnasrawi, Abbas, *Arab Nationalism, Oil and the Political Economy of Dependency*, London: Greenwood, 1991.

Alshayji, Abdullah K., 'Mutual Realities, Perceptions, and Impediments Between the GCC States and Iran', in Lawrence G. Potter and Gary G. Sick (eds), *Security in the Persian Gulf. Origins, Obstacles, and the Search for Consensus*, Houndmills: Palgrave, 2002, pp. 217–237.

Amin, Samir, *The Arab Nation: Nationalism and Class Struggles*, London: Zed, 1978.

Amirahmadi, Hooshang and Nader Entessar (eds), *Iran and the Arab World*, London: Macmillan, 1993.

Amirsadeghi, Hossein (ed.), *The Security of the Persian Gulf*, London: Croom Helm, 1981.

Anthony, John Duke, 'The Persian Gulf in Regional and International Politics: the Arab Side of the Gulf', in Hossein Amirsadeghi (ed.), *The Security of the Persian Gulf*, London, Croom Helm, 1981, pp. 170–196.

Aras, Bulent, 'Turkish, Israeli, Iranian Relations in the Nineties: Impact on the Middle East', *Middle East Policy*, Vol. VII, No. 3, 2000, pp. 151–164.

Archer, Margaret S., *Culture and Agency: The Place of Culture in Social Theory*, revised edition, Cambridge: Cambridge UP, 1996.

Arkoun, Mohammed, *Rethinking Islam: Common Questions, Uncommon Answers*, translated and edited by Robert D. Lee, Oxford: Westview, 1994.

Ashley, Richard K., 'The Poverty of Neorealism', *International Organization*, Vol. 38, No. 2, 1984, pp. 225–286.

Ashley, Richard K., 'The Geopolitics of Geopolitical Space: Toward a Critical Social Theory of International Politics', *Alternatives*, Vol. 12, No. 4, 1987, pp. 403–434.

Ashley, Richard, 'Untying the Sovereign State: A Double Reading of the Anarchy Problematique', *Millennium*, Vol. 17, No. 2, 1988, pp. 227–262.

Atrissi, Talal, 'The Image of the Iranians in Arab Schoolbooks', in Khair el-Din Haseeb (ed.), *Arab-Iranian Relations*, Beirut: Centre for Arab Unity Studies, 1998, pp. 152–198.

Ayubi, Nazih N., *Political Islam: Religion and Politics in the Arab World*, London: Routledge, 1991.

Ayubi, Nazih N., *Over-stating the Arab State. Politics and Society in the Middle East*, London: I.B. Tauris, 1995.

Baktiari, Bahman, 'Revolutionary Iran's Persian Gulf Policy: the Quest for Regional Supremacy', in Hooshang Amirahmadi and Nader Entessar (eds), *Iran and the Arab World*, London: Macmillan, 1993, pp. 69–93.

Barnett, Michael, 'Regional Security After the Gulf War', *Political Science Quarterly*, Vol. 111, No. 4, 1996/1997, pp. 597–618.

Barnett, Michael, *Dialogues in Arab Politics: Negotiations in Regional Order*, New York: Columbia UP, 1998.

Barnett, Michael and F. Gregory Gause III, 'Caravans in Opposite Directions: Society, State and the Development of a Community in the Gulf Cooperation Council', in Emanuel Adler and Michael Barnett (eds), *Security Communities*, Cambridge: Cambridge UP, 1998, pp. 161–197.

Barnett, Michael and Jack S. Levy, 'Domestic Sources of alliances and alignments: the case of Egypt, 1962–73', *International Organization*, Vol. 45, No. 3, 1991, pp. 369–395.

Behdad, Ali, 'Nationalism and Immigration to the United States', *Diaspora*, Vol. 6, No. 2, 1997, pp. 155–178.

Bengio, Ofra, *Saddam's Word. Political Discourse in Iraq*, Oxford: Oxford UP, 1998.

Berger, Peter, *The Sacred Canopy*, Garden City: Doubleday, 1967.

Berger, Peter and Thomas Luckmann, *The Social Construction of Reality*, New York: Anchor Books, 1966.

Berger, Thomas U., 'Norms, Identity and National Security in Germany and Japan', in Peter J. Katzenstein (ed.), *The Culture of National Security: Norms and Identity in World Politics*, New York: Columbia UP, 1996, pp. 317–356.

Bilgin, Pinar, 'Inventing Middle Easts: The Making of Regions Through Security Discourses', in Bjørn Olav Utvik and Knut S. Vikør (eds), *The Middle East in a Globalised World. Papers from the Fourth Nordic Conference on Middle Eastern Studies, Oslo 1998*, London: C. Hurst & Co., 2000, pp. 10–37.

Blackwell, James, 'US Military Response to the Iraqi invasion of Kuwait', in Robert F. Helms II and Robert H. Dorff (eds), *The Persian Gulf Crisis. Power in the Post-Cold War World*, London: Praeger, 1993, pp. 121–134.

Boroujerdi, Mehrzad, *Iranian Intellectuals and the West. The Tormented Triumph of Nativism*, Syracuse, NY: Syracuse UP, 1996.

Boroujerdi, Mehrzad, 'Iranian Islam and the Faustian Bargain of Western Modernity', *Journal of Peace Research*, Vol. 34, No. 1, 1997, pp. 1–5.

Boroujerdi, Mehrzad, 'The Paradoxes of Politics in Post-Revolutionary Iran', in John L. Esposito and R.K. Ramazani (eds), *Iran at the Crossroads*, Houndmills: Palgrave, 2001, pp. 13–27.

Bramson, Leon and George W. Goethals (eds), *War. Studies from Psychology, Sociology, Anthropology*, London: Basic books, 1964.

Brinkley, Joel (ed.), *Report of the Congressional Committee Investigating the Iran-Contra Affair*. New York: Times Book, 1988.

Bromley, Simon, *American Hegemony and World Oil: The Industry, the State System and the World Economy*, Cambridge: Polity Press, 1990.

Bromley, Simon, *Rethinking Middle East Politics. State Formation and Development*, Cambridge: Polity Press, 1994.

Brown, L. Carl (ed.), *Diplomacy in the Middle East. The International Relations of Regional and Outside Powers*, London: I.B. Tauris, 2001.

Brzezinsky, Zbigniew, Brent Scowcroft and Richard Murphy, 'Differentiated Containment', *Foreign Affairs*, Vol. 76, No. 3, 1997, pp. 20–30.

Buchta, Wilfried, 'The Failed Pan-Islamic Program of the Islamic Republic: Views of the Liberal Reformers of the Religious "Semi-Opposition"', in Nikki R. Keddie and Rudi Matthee (eds), *Iran and the Surrounding World. Interactions in Culture and Cultural Politics*, Seattle, WA: University of Washington Press, 2002, pp. 281–304.

Bukovansky, Mlada, *Legitimacy and Power Politics. The American and French Revolutions in International Political Culture*, Princeton, NJ: Princeton UP, 2002.

Bull, Hedley, *The Anarchical Society. A Study of Order in World Politics*, second edition, London: Macmillan, 1995.

Burrows, Bernard, John Moberly and Gerd Nonneman, 'Towards a Security Community in the Gulf', in Gerd Nonneman (ed.), *The Middle East and Europe. The Search for Stability and Integration*, London: Federal Trust for Education and Research, 1993, pp. 63–70.

Buzan, Barry and Ole Waever, *Regions and Powers: The Structure of International Security*, Cambridge: Cambridge UP, 2003.

Campbell, David, *Writing Security: United States Foreign Policy and the Politics of Identity*, Manchester: Manchester UP, 1992.

Campbell, David, *Politics Without Principle: Sovereignty, Ethics, and the Narratives of the Gulf War*, London: Lynne Rienner, 1993.

Carr, Edward Hallett, *The Twenty Years' Crisis, 1919–1939. An Introduction to the Study of International Relations*, London: Macmillan, 1961.

Chomsky, Noam, 'The Use (and Abuse) of the United Nations', in Micah L. Sifry and Christopher Cerf (eds), *The Gulf War Reader. History, Documents, Opinions*, New York: Times Books, 1991, pp. 307–310.

Chubin, Shahram and Charles Tripp, *Iran and Iraq at War*, London: I.B. Tauris, 1988.

Cole, Juan R.I. and Nikki R. Keddie (eds), *Shi'ism and Social Protest*, New Haven: Yale UP, 1986.

Constitution of the Islamic Republic of Iran, translated from the Persian by Hamid Algar, Berkeley: Mizan, 1980.

Cooper, Scott and Brock Taylor, 'Power and Regionalism: Explaining Economic Cooperation in the Persian Gulf'. Paper prepared for the *Proceedings of the 97th Annual Meeting of the American Political Science Association*, San Francisco, 30 August–2 September 2001.

Coulter, Ann, 'Why We Hate Them', in Micah L. Sifry and Christopher Cerf (eds), *The Iraq War Reader. History, Documents, Opinions*, London: Simon & Schuster, 2003, pp. 333–335.

Cox, Robert W., 'Social Forces, States and World Orders: Beyond International Relations Theory', in Robert O. Keohane (ed.), *Neorealism and its Critics*, New York: Columbia UP, 1986.

Darnovsky, Marc, L.A. Kauffman and Billy Robinson, 'What Will this War Mean?', in Micah L. Sifry and Christopher Cerf (eds), *The Gulf War Reader. History, Documents, Opinions*, New York: Times Books, 1991, pp. 480–486.

Davison, Roderic H., 'Where is the Middle East?', in Richard Nolte (ed.), *The Modern Middle East*, New York: Columbia UP, 1963, pp. 13–29.

Dawisha, Adeed, 'Iraq: The West's Opportunity', *Foreign Policy*, Vol. 41, 1980–1981, pp. 134–148.

Dawisha, Adeed, ' "Identity" and Political Survival in Saddam's Iraq', *The Middle East Journal*, Vol. 53, No. 4, 1999, pp. 553–567.

Dawisha, Adeed, 'Footprints in the Sand. The Definition and Redefinition of Identity in Iraq's Foreign Policy', in Shibley Telhami and Michael Barnett (eds), *Identity and Foreign Policy in the Middle East*, London: Cornell UP, 2002, pp. 117–136.

Der Derian, James, *Antidiplomacy. Spies, Terror, Speed, and War*, Oxford: Blackwell, 1992.

Der Derian, James and Michael J. Shapiro (eds), *International/Intertextual Relations. Post-modern Readings in World Politics*, Lexington: Lexington Books, 1989.

Donohue, John, J. and John L. Esposito (eds), *Islam in Transition. Muslim Perspectives*, Oxford: Oxford UP, 1982.

Doyle, Michael W. and G. John Ikenberry (eds), *New Thinking in International Relations Theory*, Oxford: Westview, 1997.

Drew, Elizabeth, 'Washington Prepares for War', in Micah L. Sifry and Christopher Cerf (eds), *The Gulf War Reader. History, Documents, Opinions*, New York: Times Books, 1991, pp. 180–193.

Ebtekar, Massoumeh, *Takeover in Tehran. The Inside Story of the 1979 U.S. Embassy Capture*, as told to Fred A. Reed, Vancouver: Talonbooks, 2000.

Eedle, Paul, 'Al-Qaeda takes fight for 'hearts and minds' to the web', *Jane's Intelligence Review*, 1 August 2002. http://www.janes.com/security/international_security/news/jir/jir020715_1_n.shtml

Ehteshami, Anoushiravan, *After Khomeini. The Iranian Second Republic*, London: Routledge, 1995.

Ehteshami, Anoushiravan and Gerd Nonneman, *War and Peace in the Gulf. Domestic Politics and Regional Relations into the 1990s*, Reading, PA: Ithaca, 1991.

Enayat, Hamid, *Modern Islamic Political Thought*, Austin, TX: Texas UP, 1982.

Eribon, Didier, *Michel Foucault*, translated by Betsy Wing, London: Faber and Faber, 1991.

Esposito, John L. (ed.), *The Iranian Revolution. Its Global Impact*, Miami, FL: Florida International UP, 1990.

Fakhro, Munira A., 'The Uprising in Bahrain. An Assessment', in Lawrence G. Potter and Gary G. Sick (eds), *The Persian Gulf at the Millennium. Essays in Politics, Economy, Security, and Religion*, London: St. Martin's, 1997, pp. 167–188.

Fandy, Mamoun, *Saudi Arabia and the Politics of Dissent*, London: Macmillan, 1999.

Faour, Muhammad, *The Arab World After Desert Storm*, Washington, DC: United States Institute of Peace Process, 1993.

Finnemore, Martha and Kathryn Sikkink, International Norm Dynamics and Political Change', *International Organization*, Vol. 52, No. 4, 1998, pp. 887–917.

'First Communiqué of the Muslim Students Following the Line of Imam', in Massoumeh Ebtekar, *Takeover in Tehran. The Inside Story of the 1979 U.S. Embassy Capture*, as told to Fred A. Reed, Vancouver, WA: Talonbooks, 2000, pp. 69–70.

Foucault, Michel, 'Nietzsche, Genealogy, History', in Paul Rabinow (ed.), *The Foucault Reader*, London: Penguin Books, 1984, pp. 76–100.

Foucault, Michel, *Power: Essential Works of Foucault, 1954–1984 Vol. 3*, translated by Robert Hurley and others, London: Penguin, 1997.

Fousek, John, *To Lead the Free World. American Nationalism and the Cultural Roots of the Cold War*, Chapel Hill, NC: University of North Carolina Press, 2000.

Franssen, Herman and Elaine Morton, 'A Review of US Unilateral Sanctions Against Iran', *Middle East Economic Survey*, Vol. XLV, No. 34, 26 August 2002. http://www.mafhoum.com/press3/108E16.htm

Freedman, Lawrence and Efraim Karsh, *The Gulf Conflict 1990–1991. Diplomacy and War in the New World Order*, London: Faber and Faber, 1993.

Fukuyama, Francis, *The End of History and the Last Man*, New York: Free Press, 1992.

Fuller, Graham E., '"Repairing U.S.-Iranian Relations"', *Middle East Policy*, Vol. VI, No. 2, 1998, pp. 140–144. http://www.mepc.org/public_asp/journal_vol6/9810_fuller.asp

Gargash, Anwar, 'Iran, the GCC states, and the UAE: Prospects and Challenges in the Coming Decade', in Jamal S. Al-Suwaidi (ed.), *Iran and the Gulf. A Search for Stability*, Abu Dhabi: The Emirates Center for Strategic Studies and Research, 1996, pp. 136–157.

Gause, III, F. Gregory, 'Saudi Arabia: Desert Storm and After', in Robert O. Freedman (ed.), *The Middle East after Iraq's invasion of Kuwait*, Gainesville, FL: University Press of Florida, 1993, pp. 207–234.

Geertz, Clifford, *The Interpretation of Cultures*, New York: basic books, 1973.

George, Alexander L., 'The Gulf War's Possible Impact on the International System', in Stanley A. Renshon (ed.), *The Political Psychology of the Gulf War. Leaders, Publics, and the Process of Conflict*, Pittsburgh, PA: University of Pittsburgh Press, 1993, pp. 293–315.

George, David, 'Pax Islamica: An Alternative New World Order', in Abdel Salam Sidahmed and Anoushiravan Ehteshami (eds), *Islamic Fundamentalism*, Boulder, CO: Westview, 1996, pp. 71–90.

Goldberg, Jacob, 'The Shi'i Minority in Saudi Arabia', in Juan R. I. Cole and Nikki R. Keddie (eds), *Shi'ism and Social Protest*, New Haven, CT: Yale UP, 1986, pp. 230–246.

Grant, Rebecca and Kathleen Newland (eds), *Gender and International Relations*, Bloomington, IN: Indiana UP, 1991.

Grieco, Joseph M., 'Realist International Theory and the Study of World Politics', in Michael W. Doyle and G. John Ikenberry (eds), *New Thinking in International Relations Theory*, Oxford: Westview, 1997, pp. 163–201.

Haass, Richard, 'Saudi Arabia and Iran: The Twin Pillars in Revolutionary Times', in Hossein Amirsadeghi (ed.), *The Security of the Persian Gulf*, London: Croom Helm, 1981, pp. 151–169.

Halliday, Fred, 'Iranian Foreign Policy since 1979: Internationalism and Nationalism in the Islamic Revolution', in Juan R. I. Cole and Nikki R. Keddie (eds), *Shi'ism and Social Protest*, New Haven, CT: Yale UP, 1986, pp. 88–107.

Halliday, Fred, 'The Crisis of the Arab World', in Micah L. Sifry and Christopher Cerf (eds), *The Gulf War Reader. History, Documents, Opinions*, New York: Times Books, 1991, pp. 395–401.

Halliday, Fred, *Islam and the Myth of Confrontation. Religion and Politics in the Middle East*, London: I.B. Tauris, 1996.

Halliday, Fred, *Revolution and World Politics. The Rise and Fall of the Sixth Great Power*, Durham, NC: Duke UP, 1999.

Hansen, Birthe, *Unipolarity and the Middle East*, Richmond, Surrey: Curzon, 2000.

Haseeb, Khair el-Din (ed.), *Arab-Iranian Relations*, Beirut: Centre for Arab Unity Studies, 1998.

Hendrickson, David C., 'The Recovery of Internationalism', *Foreign Affairs*, Vol. 73, No. 5, 1994, pp. 26–43.

Hilterman, Joost, 'Elusive Justice. Trying to Try Saddam', *Middle East Report*, No. 215, Vol. 30, No. 2, 2000, pp. 32–35.

Hinnebusch, Raymond, *The International Politics of the Middle East*, Manchester: Manchester UP, 2003.

Hinnebusch, Raymond and Anoushiravan Ehteshami (eds), *The Foreign Policies of Middle East States*, London: Lynne Rienner, 2002.

Hiro, Dilip, *The Longest War: The Iran–Iraq Military Conflict*, London: Grafton, 1990.

Hiro, Dilip, 'The Iran–Iraq War', in Hooshang Amirahmadi and Nader Entessar (eds), *Iran and the Arab World*, London: Macmillan, 1993, pp. 42–68.

Hirschfeld, Lawrence A. and Susan A. Gelman (eds), *Mapping the Mind: Domain Specificity in Cognition and Culture*, Cambridge: Cambridge UP, 1994.

Hobsbawm, Eric, *Nations and Nationalism since 1780. Programme, Myth, Reality*, second edition, Cambridge: Cambridge UP, 2004.

Hoffmann, Stanley, 'The High and the Mighty: Bush's national security strategy and the new American hubris', *The American Prospect*, Vol. 13, No. 24, 13 January 2003. http://www.prospect.org/print/V13/24/hoffmann-s.html

Hourani, Albert, *Arabic Thought in the Liberal Age 1798–1939*, Cambridge: Cambridge UP, 1983.

Hourani, Albert, *A History of the Arab Peoples*, London: Faber and Faber, 2002.

Hunter, Shireen T., 'Iran and Syria: From Hostility to Limited Alliance', in Hooshang Amirahmadi and Nader Entessar (eds), *Iran and the Arab World*, London: Macmillan, 1993, pp. 198–216.

Huntington, Samuel P., *The Clash of Civilisations and the Remaking of World Order*, London: Touchstone, 1996.

al-Husri, Sati, *Ara'wa ahadith fil-qawmiyya al-'arabiyya* (Speeches and Reflections on Arab Nationalism), Egypt: Al-I'timad, 1951.

Iqbal, Muhammad, *The Reconstruction of Religious Thought in Islam*, Lahore: Iqbal Academy Pakistan, 1968.

'Iran: The Struggle for the Revolution's Soul', *International Crisis Group*, Amman/Brussels: Middle East Report No. 5, 5 August 2002.

Iraqi Revolutionary Command Council, 'Iraq is Ready to Deal (Radio Address of 15 February 1991)', in Micah L. Sifry and Christopher Cerf (eds), *The Gulf War Reader. History, Documents, Opinions*, New York: Times Books, 1991, pp. 337–342.

Ismael, Jaqueline, *Kuwait: Dependency and Class in a Rentier State*, Gainesville, FL: University Press of Florida, 1993.

Ismael, Tareq, *The Arab Left*, Syracuse, NY: Syracuse UP, 1976.

Jarvis, D.S.L., *International Relations and the Challenge of Postmodernism: Defending the Discipline*, Columbia, MO: University of South-Carolina Press, 1999.

Jepperson, Ronald L., Alexander Wendt and Peter J. Katzenstein, 'Norms, Identity, and Culture in National Security', in Peter J. Katzenstein (ed.), *The Culture of National Security. Norms and Identity in World Politics*, New York: Columbia UP, 1996, pp. 33–75.

Jochnick, C. and R. Normand, 'The Legitimation of Violence: A Critical History of the Laws of War', *Harvard International Law Journal*, Vol. 35, No. 2, 1994, pp. 49–95.

Jones, R.J. Barry, 'The English School and the Political Construction of International Society', in B.A. Roberson (ed.), *International Society and the Development of International Relations Theory*, London: Pinter, 1998.

Jones, Richard Wyn (ed.), *Critical Theory and World Politics*, London: Lynne Rienner, 2001.

Jones, Roy, 'The English School of International Relations: a case for closure', *Review of International Studies*, Vol. 7, No. 1, 1981, pp. 1–13.

Kagan, Donald Gary Schmitt and Thomas Donnelly, 'Rebuilding America's Defences: Strategy, Forces and Resources For a New Century', A Report of *The Project for the New American Century*, September 2000.

Karawan, Ibrahim, 'Arab Dilemmas in the 1990s: Breaking Taboos and Searching for Signposts', *The Middle East Journal*, Vol. 48, No. 3, 1994, pp. 433–454.

Karl W. Deutsch, Sidney A. Burrell, Robert A. Kann, Maurice Lee, J., Martin Lichtermann, Raymond E. Lindgren, Francis L. Loewenheim and Richard W. Van Wagenen. *Political Community and the North Atlantic Area*, Princeton, NJ: Princeton UP, 1957.

Kashani-Sabet, Firoozeh, 'Cultures of Iranianness: The Evolving Polemic of Iranian Nationalism', in Nikki R. Keddie and Rudi Matthee (eds), *Iran and the Surrounding World. Interactions in Culture and Cultural Politics*, Seattle, WA: University of Washington Press, 2002, pp. 162–181.

Katzenstein, Peter J. (ed.), *The Culture of National Security. Norms and Identity in World Politics*, New York: Columbia UP, 1996.

Katzman, Kenneth, 'The Gulf Co-operation Council: Prospects for Collective Security', in M.E. Ahrari and James H. Noyes (eds), *The Persian Gulf After the Cold War*, London: Praeger, 1993, pp. 197–220.

Kawtharani, Wajih, 'Mutual Awareness between Arabs and Iranians', in Khair el-Din Haseeb (ed.), *Arab-Iranian Relations*, Beirut: Centre for Arab Unity Studies, 1998, pp. 73–102.

Kechichian, Joseph A., 'The Role of the Ulama in the Politics of an Islamic State: The Case of Saudi Arabia', *International Journal of Middle East Studies*, Vol. 18, No. 1, 1986, pp. 53–71.

Keddie, Nikki R., *An Islamic Response to Imperialism: The Political and Religious Writings of Sayyid Jamal ad-Din al-Afghani*, Berkeley, CA: University of California Press, 1983.

Keddie, Nikki R. and Rudi Matthee (eds), *Iran and the Surrounding World. Interactions in Culture and Cultural Politics*, Seattle, WA: University of Washington Press, 2002.

Kedourie, Elie, *Afghani and 'Abduh: An Essay on Religious Unbelief and Political Activism in Modern Islam*, London: Frank Cass, 1966.

Keohane, Robert O. (ed.), *Neorealism and its Critics*, New York: Columbia UP, 1986.

Keohane, Robert O. and Joseph S. Nye, *Power and Interdependence*, third edition, London: Longman, 2001.

Khadduri, Majid, *The Gulf War. The Origins and Implications of the Iraq-Iran Conflict*, Oxford: Oxford UP, 1988.

Khajehpour-Khoei, Bijan, 'Mutual Perceptions in the Persian Gulf Region', in Lawrence G. Potter and Gary G. Sick (eds), *Security in the Persian Gulf. Origins, Obstacles, and the Search for Consensus*, Houndmills: Palgrave, 2002, pp. 239–251.

Khalidi, Walid, 'Iraq vs. Kuwait: Claims and Counterclaims', in Micah L. Sifry and Christopher Cerf (eds), *The Gulf War Reader. History, Documents, Opinions*, New York: Times Books, 1991, pp. 57–65.

Khatami, Mohammad, *Islam, Dialogue and Civil Society*, Canberra: Centre for Arab and Islamic Studies, The Australian National University, 2000.

Khomeini, Rouhollah, *Sahifey-e Nur*, Vol. 18, Tehran: Vezarat-e Ershad, 1364/1985.

Khomeini, Rouhollah, *Islam and Revolution. Writings and Declarations of Imam Khomeini*, translated and annotated by Hamid Algar, Berkeley, CA: Mizan, 1981.

Kissinger, Henry, *Years of Upheaval*, London: Weidenfeld and Nicolson, 1982.

Kissinger, Henry, *Years of Renewal*, London: Weidenfeld and Nicolson, 1999.

Klare, Michael T., 'The Pentagon's New Paradigm', in Micah L. Sifry and Christopher Cerf (eds), *The Gulf War Reader. History, Documents, Opinions*, New York: Times Books, 1991, pp. 466–476.

Korany, Bahgat, 'Defending the Faith: The Foreign Policy of Saudi Arabia', in Bahgat Korany and Ali E. Hillal Dessouki (eds), *The Foreign Policies of Arab States*, Boulder, CO: Westview, 1984, pp. 241–282.

Korany, Bahgat, Paul Noble and Rex Brynen (eds), *The Many Faces of National Security in the Middle East*, London: Macmillan, 1993.

Kosterlitz, Julie, 'The Neoconservative Moment', *National Journal*, Vol. 35, No. 20, 17 May 2003, pp. 1540–1546.

Krauthammer, Charles, 'The Unipolar Moment', *Foreign Affairs*, Vol. 70, No. 1, 1991, pp. 23–33.

Krauthammer, Charles, 'The Unipolar Moment Revisited: America, the Benevolent Empire', in Micah L. Sifry and Christopher Cerf (eds), *The Iraq War Reader. History, Documents, Opinions*, London: Simon & Schuster, 2003, pp. 593–607.

Krauthammer, Charles, 'Voices of Moral Obtuseness', in Micah L. Sifry and Christopher Cerf (eds), *The Iraq War Reader. History, Documents, Opinions*, London: Simon & Schuster, 2003, pp. 217–218.

Kreile, Renate, 'Islamischer Internationalismus oder realpolitischer Pragmatismus. Zwei Jahrzehnte Aussenpolitik der Islamischen Republik Iran', *Aus Politik und Zeitgeschichte*, B19, 7 May 1999, Bundeszentrale für politische Bildung, pp. 3–13.

Kukla, André, *Social Constructivism and the Philosophy of Science*, London: Routledge, 2000.

Lake, Anthony, 'Confronting Backlash States', *Foreign Affairs*, Vol. 73, No. 2, 1994, 45–55.

Lapid, Yosef and Friedrich Kratochwil (eds), *The Return of Culture and Identity in IR Theory*, London: Lynne Rienner, 1996.

Ledeen, Michael, 'Rediscovering American Character', *National Review Online*, 10 October 2001. http://www.aei.org/news/filter., newsID.13236/news_detail.asp

Lewis, Anthony, ' "First they came for the Muslims…" ', in Micah L. Sifry and Christopher Cerf (eds), *The Gulf War Reader. History, Documents, Opinions*, New York: Times Books, 1991, pp. 233–237.

Lewis, Bernard, 'The Decline of Pan-Arabism', in Micah L. Sifry and Christopher Cerf (eds), *The Gulf War Reader. History, Documents, Opinions*, New York: Times Books, 1991, pp. 405–407.

Linklater, Andrew, *Beyond Realism and Marxism: Critical Theory and International Relations*, London: Macmillan, 1990.

Linklater, Andrew (ed.), *International Relations: Critical Concepts in Political Science*, London: Routledge, 2000.

Lobel, Jules and Michael Ratner, 'Bypassing the Security Council: Ambiguous Authorisations to Use Force, Cease-Fires and the Iraqi Inspection Regime', *American Journal of International Law*, Vol. 93, No. 1, 1999, pp. 124–154. http://www.asil.org/ajil/lobel.htm

Lotfian, Saideh, 'Taking Sides: Regional Powers and the War', in Farhang Rajaee (ed.), *Iranian Perspectives on the Iran–Iraq War*, Gainesville, FL: University Press of Florida, 1997, pp. 13–28.

Lynch, Marc, 'The Politics of Consensus in the Gulf', *Middle East Report*, No. 215, Vol. 30, No. 2, 2000, pp. 20–23.

Makiya, Kanan, *Cruelty and Silence. War, Tyranny, Uprising, and the Arab World*, London: Jonathan Cape, 1993.

Makiya, Kanan, *Republic of Fear. The Politics of Modern Iraq*, updated edition with a new introduction, Berkeley, CA: University of California Press, 1998.

Maloney, Suzanne, 'A New Majlis and a Mandate for Reform', *Middle East Policy*, Vol. VII, No. 3, 2000, pp. 59–66. http://www.mepc.org/public_asp/journal_vol7/0006_maloney.asp

Maloney, Suzanne, 'Identity and Change in Iran's Foreign Policy', in Shibley Telhami and Michael Barnett (eds), *Identity and Foreign Policy in the Middle East*, London: Cornell UP, 2002, pp. 88–116.

al-Marashi, Ibrahimm, *The Mindset of Iraq's Security Apparatus*, unpublished paper presented at a workshop by the Cambridge Security Program in International Society (C-SIS), Cambridge, UK, 13 March 2003.

Marcuse, Herbert, *One-dimensional Man: Studies in the Ideology of Advanced Industrial Society*, second edition, London: Routledge, 1991.

Marschall, Christin, *Iran's Persian Gulf Policy: From Khomeini to Khatami*, London: RoutledgeCurzon, 2003.

Marx, Karl, *Survey from Exile*, edited by David Fernbach, Harmondsworth: Penguin, 1973.

Marx, Karl, 'The Eighteenth Brumaire of Louis Bonaparte', in Karl Marx, *Survey from Exile*, edited by David Fernbach, Harmondsworth: Penguin, 1973, pp. 146–249.

Mawdudi, Abu-l-Ala, 'Political Theory of Islam', in John J. Donohue and John L. Esposito (eds), *Islam in Transition. Muslim Perspectives*, Oxford: Oxford UP, 1982, pp. 94–97.

Mayall, James (ed.), *The New Interventionism 1991–1994. United Nations Experience in Cambodia, Former Yugoslavia and Somalia*, Cambridge: Cambridge UP, 1996.

Mead, George Herbert, *Mind, Self, and Society*, Chicago, IL: Chicago UP, 1934.

Mead, Margaret, 'Warfare is Only an Invention – Not a Biological Necessity', in Leon Bramson and George W. Goethals (eds), *War. Studies from Psychology, Sociology, Anthropology*, London: basic books, 1964, pp. 269–274.

Mehran, Golnar, 'The Presentation of the "Self" and the "Other" in Postrevolutionary Iranian School Textbooks', in Nikki R. Keddie and Rudi Matthee (eds), *Iran and the Surrounding World. Interactions in Culture and Cultural Politics*, Seattle, WA: University of Washington Press, 2002, pp. 232–253.

Meskoob, Shahrokh, *Iranian Nationality and the Persian Language 900–1900. The Roles of Court, Religion, and Sufism in Persian Prose Writing*, translated by Michael C. Hillmann, edited by John R. Perry, Washington, DC: Mage Publishers, 1992.

Meyer, John W., 'The World Polity and the Authority of the Nation-State', in Albert Bergesen (ed.), *Studies of the Modern World System*, New York: Academic Press, 1980, pp. 109–137.

Meyer, John W. and Ronald L. Jepperson, 'The "Actors" of Modern Society: The Cultural Construction of Social Agency', *Sociological Theory*, Vol. 18, No. 1, 2000, pp. 100–120.

Meyer, John W., John Boli, George M. Thomas and Francisco O. Ramirez, 'World Society and the Nation-State', *American Journal of Sociology*, Vol. 103, No. 1, 1997, pp. 144–181.

Milani, Mohsen, 'Iran's Gulf Policy: From Idealism and Confrontation to Pragmatism and Moderation', in Jamal S. al-Suwaidi (ed.), *Iran and the Gulf: A Search for Stability*, Abu Dhabi: The Emirates Center for Strategic Studies and Research, 1996, pp. 83–98.

Miller, James, *The Passion of Michel Foucault*, London: Harper Collins, 1993.

Mitchel, Richard P., *The Society of the Muslim Brothers*, London: Oxford UP, 1969.

Mofid, Kamran, *The Economic Consequences of the Gulf War*, London: Routledge, 1990.

Mojtahed-Zadeh, Pirouz, 'Regional Alliances in the Persian Gulf: Past Trends and Future Prospects', *The Iranian Journal of International Affairs*, Vol. X, Nos 1&2, 1998, pp. 1–20.

Mottahedeh, Roy P., 'Shi'ite Political Thought and the Destiny of the Iranian Revolution', in Jamal S. al-Suwaidi, *Iran and the Gulf: A Search for Stability*, Abu Dhabi: The Emirates Center for Strategic Studies and Research, 1996, pp. 70–80.

Muñoz, Gema Martín (ed.), *Islam, Modernism and the West. Cultural and Political Relations at the End of the Millennium*, London: I.B. Tauris, 1999.

Muttahari, Morteza, *Islam and Iran*, Beirut: Dar al-Ta'aruf, n.d.

Nelson, Alan, 'How "Could" Scientific Facts be Socially Constructed?', *Studies in History and Philosophy of Science*, Vol. 25, No. 4, 1994, pp. 535–547.

Neuman, Stephanie G. (ed.), *International Relations Theory and the Third World*, London: Macmillan, 1998.

Nietzsche, Friedrich, *The Birth of Tragedy; and The Genealogy of Morals*, translated by Francis Golffing, Garden City: Anchor Books, 1956.

Nonneman, Gerd, *Iraq, the Gulf States & the War: A changing Relationship, 1980–1986 and beyond*, London: Ithaca, 1986.

Owen, Roger, *State, Power and Politics in the Making of the Modern Middle East*, second edition, London: Routledge, 2000.

Pahlavi, Mohammad Reza, *Answer to History*, New York: Stein and Day, 1980.

Parsons, Anthony, 'Iran and the United Nations, with Particular Reference to the Iran–Iraq War', in Anoushiravan Ehteshami and Manshour Varasteh (eds), *Iran and the International Community*, London: Routledge, 1991, pp. 7–30.

Peimani, Hooman, *Iran and the United States. The Rise of the West Asian Regional Grouping*, London: Praeger, 1999.

Peterson, J.E., 'The Historical Pattern of Gulf Security', in Lawrence G. Potter and Gary G. Sick (eds), *Security in the Persian Gulf. Origins, Obstacles, and the Search for Consensus*, Houndmills: Palgrave, 2002, pp. 7–31.

Pfaff, William, 'More Likely a New World Disorder', in Micah L. Sifry and Christopher Cerf (eds), *The Gulf War Reader. History, Documents, Opinions*, New York: Times Books, 1991, pp. 487–491.

Pipes, Daniel, 'The Enemy Within', in Micah L. Sifry and Christopher Cerf (eds), *The Iraq War Reader. History, Documents, Opinions*, London: Simon & Schuster, 2003, pp. 231–232.

Piscatori, James, 'Religion and Realpolitik: Islamic Responses to the Gulf War', in James Piscatori (ed.), *Islamic Fundamentalism and the Gulf Crisis*, Chicago, IL: The Fundamentalism Project, American Academy of Arts and Sciences, 1991, pp. 1–27.

Potter, Lawrence G. and Gary G. Sick (eds), *The Persian Gulf at the Millennium. Essays in Politics, Economy, Security, and Religion*, London: St Martin's, 1997.

Potter, Lawrence G. and Gary G. Sick (eds), *Security in the Persian Gulf. Origins, Obstacles, and the Search for Consensus*, Houndmills: Palgrave, 2002.

Qutb, Sayyid, 'Social Justice in Islam', in John J. Donohue and John L. Esposito (eds), *Islam in Transition. Muslim Perspectives*, Oxford: Oxford UP, 1982, pp. 123–128.

Rahnema, Ali, *An Islamic Utopian. A Political Biography of Ali Shariati*, London: I.B. Tauris, 2000.

Rajaee, Farhang, *Islamic Values and World View: Khomeyni on Man, the State and International Politics, Volume XIII*, Lanham, MD: University Press of America, 1983.

Rajaee, Farhang, 'Iranian Ideology and Worldview: The Cultural Export of Revolution', in John L. Esposito (ed.), *The Iranian Revolution. Its Global Impact*, Miami, FL: Florida International UP, 1990, pp. 63–80.

Rajaee, Farhang (ed.), *Iranian Perspectives on the Iran–Iraq War*, Gainesville, FL: University Press of Florida, 1997.

Ramazani, Rouhollah K., *The Persian Gulf: Iran's Role*, Charlottesville, VA: University of Virginia Press, 1972.

Ramazani, Rouhollah K., *Revolutionary Iran. Challenge and Response in the Middle-East*, Baltimore, MD: Johns Hopkins UP, 1986.

Ramazani, Rouhollah K., 'Shi'ism in the Persian Gulf', in Juan R.I. Cole and Nikki R. Keddie (eds), *Shi'ism and Social Protest*, New Haven, CT: Yale UP, 1986, pp. 30–54.

Ramazani, Rouhollah K., 'The Shifting Premise of Iran's Foreign Policy: Towards a Democratic Peace?', *Middle East Journal*, Vol. 52, No. 2, 1998, pp. 177–187.

Renshon, Stanley A. (ed.), *The Political Psychology of the Gulf War. Leaders, Publics, and the Process of Conflict*, Pittsburgh, PA: University of Pittsburgh Press, 1993.

Rida, Rashid, *Tarikh al-ustadh al-imam al-shaykh Muhammad 'Abduh*, Vol. 1, Cairo: 1931.

Robinson, Julian Perry and Jozef Goldblat, 'Chemical Warfare in the Iraq-Iran War', Stockholm International Peace Research Institute, *SIPRI Fact Sheet*, Chemical Weapons I, May 1984.

Rosenau, Pauline Marie, *Postmodernism and the Social Sciences: Insights, Inroads and Intrusions*, Princeton, NJ: Princeton UP, 1992.

Roy, Olivier, *The Failure of Political Islam*, translated by Carol Volk, London: I.B. Tauris, 1999.

Ruggie, John, 'Continuity and Transformation in the World Polity: Toward a Neorealist Synthesis', *World Politics*, Vol. 35, No. 2, 1983, pp. 261–285.

Ruggie, John Gerard, 'Territoriality and Beyond: Problematising Modernity in International Relations', *International Organization*, Vol. 47, No. 1, 1993, pp. 139–174.

Ruggie, John Gerard, 'What Makes the World Hang Together? Neo-utilitarianism and the Social Constructivist Challenge', *International Organization*, Vol. 52, No. 4, 1998, pp. 855–885.

Rugh, William A., 'Time to Modify Our Gulf Policy', *Middle East Policy*, Vol. V, No. 1, 1997, pp. 46–57. http://www.mepc.org/public_asp/journal_vol5/9701_rugh.asp

Russet, Bruce, 'A Neo-Kantian Perspective: Democracy, Interdependence, and International Organisations in Building Security Communities', in Emanuel Adler and Michael Barnett (eds), *Security Communities*, Cambridge: Cambridge UP, 1998, pp. 368–394.

Saad, Joya Blondel, *The Image of Arabs in Modern Persian Literature*, Lanham: University Press of America, 1996.

Said, Edward W., *Orientalism*, London: Penguin, 1995.

Said, Edward W., *The Politics of Dispossession. The Struggle for Palestinian Self-Determination 1969–1994*, London: Vintage, 1995.

Salamé, Ghassan, 'The Middle East: Elusive Security, Indefinable Region', *Security Dialogue*, Vol. 25, No. 1, 1994, pp. 17–35.

Salem, Paul, *Bitter Legacy. Ideology and Politics in the Arab World*, Syracuse, NY: Syracuse UP, 1994.

Sariolghalam, Mahmood, 'Conceptual Sources of Post-Revolutionary Iranian Behaviour toward the Arab World', in Hooshang Amirahmadi and Nader Entessar (eds), *Iran and the Arab World*, London: Macmillan, 1993, pp. 19–27.

Schmid, Peter D., 'Expect the Unexpected: A Religious Democracy in Iran', *The Brown Journal of International Affairs*, Vol. IX, No. 2, 2003, pp. 181–196.

Schofield, Richard N., 'Border Disputes in the Gulf: Past, Present and Future', in Lawrence G. Potter and Gary G. Sick (eds), *The Persian Gulf at the Millennium. Essays in Politics, Economy, Security, and Religion*, London: St Martin's, 1997, pp. 127–165.

Sciolino, Elaine, *The Outlaw State*, New York: John Wiley & Sons, 1991.

Scowcroft, Brent, 'Don't attack Saddam', in Micah L. Sifry and Christopher Cerf (eds), *The Iraq War Reader. History, Documents, Opinions*, London: Simon & Schuster, 2003, pp. 295–297.

Shariati, Ali, *Man and Islam/Lectures by Ali Shariati*, translated from Persian by Ghulam M. Fayez, Mashhad: University of Mashhad Press, 1982.

Shaw, Donald L. and Shannon E. Martin, 'The Natural, and Inevitable, Phases of War Reporting: Historical Shadows, New Communication in the Persian Gulf', in Robert E. Denton Jr (ed.), *The Media and the Persian Gulf War*, Westport, CT: Praeger, 1993, pp. 43–70.

Sifry, Micah L. and Christopher Cerf (eds), *The Gulf War Reader. History, Documents, Opinions*, New York: Times Books, 1991.

Sifry, Micah L. and Christopher Cerf (eds), *The Iraq War Reader. History, Documents, Opinions*, London: Simon & Schuster, 2003.

Sindi, A.M., 'King Faisal and Pan-Islamism', in Willard A. Beling (ed.), *King Faisal and the Modernisation of Saudi Arabia*, London: Croom Helm, 1986, pp. 184–201.

Sontag, Susan, 'Reflections on September 11th', in Micah L. Sifry and Christopher Cerf (eds), *The Iraq War Reader. History, Documents, Opinions*, London: Simon & Schuster, 2003, pp. 215–216.

Springborg, Robert, 'Selling War in the Gulf', in St. John Kettle and Stephanie Dowrick (eds), *After the Gulf War*, Sydney: Pluto, 1991, pp. 26–43.

'Statement by Dr. Kamal Kharrazi, Foreign Minister of the Islamic Republic of Iran at the 8th Persian Gulf Seminar on Regional Approaches in the Persian Gulf, Tehran 24 February 1998', *The Iranian Journal of International Affairs*, Vol. X, Nos 1&2, 1998, pp. 144–147.

Tajfel, Henry (ed.), *Social Identity and Intergroup Relations*, Cambridge: Cambridge UP, 1982.

Takeyh, Ray, 'Gods Will: Iranian Democracy and the Islamic Context', *Middle East Policy*, Vol. VII, No. 4, 2000, pp. 41–49. http://www.mepc.org/public_asp/journal_vol7/0010_takeyh.asp

Tarock, Adam, 'Iran's Foreign Policy Since the Gulf War', *The Australian Journal of International Affairs*, Vol. 48, No. 2, 1994, pp. 267–280.

Tarock, Adam, *The Superpowers Involvement in the Iran–Iraq War*, Commack: Nova Science, 1998.

Tarock, Adam, *Iran's Foreign Policy since 1990. Pragmatism Supersedes Islamic Ideology*, Commack: Nova Science, 1999.

Telhami, Shibley, *Power and Leadership in International Bargaining: the Path to the Camp David Accords*, New York: Columbia UP, 1990.

Telhami, Shibley and Michael Barnett (eds), *Identity and Foreign Policy in the Middle East*, London: Cornell UP, 2002.

The Final Report of the Assessment of the Economic Damages of the War Imposed by Iraq on the I.R. of Iran (1980–1988), Tehran: Plan and Budget Minsitry, 1991.

'The Glaspie Transcript: Saddam Meets the US Ambassador (25 July 1990)', in Micah L. Sifry and Christopher Cerf (eds), *The Gulf War Reader. History, Documents, Opinions*, New York: Times Books, 1991, pp. 122–133.

The Military Balance Between 1987–1988, London: International Institute for Strategic Studies (IISS), 1987.

The Modern and Contemporary History of the Arab Homeland, for Third Year Intermediate, Ministry of Education, Baghdad 1994.

The Texts of Letters Exchanged Between the Presidents of the Islamic Republic of Iran and the Republic of Iraq 1369 (1990), translated by Maryam Daftari, Tehran: Publishing House of the Ministry of Foreign Affairs, The Institute for Political and International Studies, 1374/1995.

Tibi, Basssam, *Arab Nationalism. Between Islam and the Nation-State*, third edition, Macmillan: London 1997.

Tibi, Bassam, *Conflict and War in the Middle East. From Interstate War to New Security*, second edition, London: Macmillan, 1998.

Tickner, Arlene, 'Seeing IR Differently: Notes From the Third World', *Millennium: Journal of International Studies*, Vol. 32, No. 2, 2003, pp. 295–324.

Tickner, J. Ann, *Gender in International Relations: Feminist Perspectives on Achieving Global Security*, New York: Columbia UP, 1992.

Tripp, Charles, 'The Future of Iraq and of Regional Security', in Geoffrey Kemp and Janice Gross Stein (eds), *Powder Keg in the Middle East: The Struggle for Gulf Security*, London: Rowman & Littlefield, 1995, pp. 133–159.

Tripp, Charles, *A History of Iraq*, second edition, Cambridge: Cambridge UP, 2000.

Walt, Stephen, *The Origins of Alliances*, Ithaca, NY: Cornell UP, 1987.

Waltz, Kenneth N., *Theory of International Politics*, New York: McGraw-Hill, 1979.

Wendt, Alexander, *Social Theory of International Politics*, Cambridge: Cambridge UP, 1999.

Wendt, Alexander, 'Anarchy is What States Make of It: the Social Construction of Power Politics', *International Organization*, Vol. 46, No. 2, 1992, pp. 391–425.

Wilson, Peter, 'The English School of International Relations: A Reply to Sheila Grader', *Review of International Studies*, Vol. 15, No. 1, 1989, pp. 49–58.

Wright, Robin, *The Last Great Revolution*, New York: Vintage Books, 2001.

Wuthnow, Robert, James Davison Hunter, Albert Bergesen and Edith Kurzweil, *Cultural Analysis. The Work of Peter L. Berger, Mary Douglas, Michel Foucault, and Jürgen Habermas*, London: Routledge & Kegan Paul, 1984.

Yassin, Abd al-Salam, *Sur l'économie, préalables dogmatiques et régles charïques*, Rabat: Imprimerie Horizons, 1996.

Yavari, Neguin, 'National, Ethnic and Sectarian Issues in the Iran–Iraq War', in Farhang Rajaee (ed.), *Iranian Perspectives on the Iran–Iraq War*, Gainesville, FL: University Press of Florida, 1997, pp. 75–89.

Zahlan, Rosemary Said, *The Making of the Modern Gulf States: Kuwait, Bahrain, Qatar, the United Arab Emirates and Oman*, Reading, PA: Ithaca Press, 1998.

Zunes, Stephen, 'The Function of Rogue States in U.S. Middle East Policy', *Middle East Policy*, Vol. 5, No. 2, 1997, pp. 150–167.

Newspapers, News Agencies and Periodicals

Agence France Press (AFP)

American Journal of International Law

Associated Press (AP)

BBC Summary of World Broadcasts

bitterlemons-international

Al-Ahram

Arms Control Today

Aus Politik und Zeitgeschichte

BBC Survey of World Broadcasts

Cambridge Review of International Affairs

Critique: Critical Middle Eastern Studies
Diaspora
European Journal of International Relations
Foreign Broadcast Information Service (FBIS)
Frankfurter Allgemeine Zeitung (FAZ)
Harvard International Law Journal
History and Theory
International Organization
International Studies Quarterly
Iran Times
Islamic Republic News Agency (IRNA)
Journal of Peace Research
Middle East International
Middle East Policy
National Journal
Reuters News Agency
Security Dialogue
Al-Sharq al'-Awsat
Tehran Times
The Australian Journal of International Affairs

The Daily Star (Beirut)
The Independent
The International Journal of Middle East Studies

The Middle East Economic Survey
The National Interest
The New Statesmen
The New York Times
The Wall Street Journal

Counterpunch
Economist Intelligence Unit (EIU)
Foreign Affairs
Foreign Policy
Gulf News
Al-Hayat
History News Network
International Security
International Studies Review
Al-'Iraq
Jane's Intelligence Review
Kayhan
Middle East Journal
Millennium
Political Science Quarterly
Al-Riyadh
Shargh Newspaper
Strategic Comment
The American Prospect
The Brown Journal of International Affairs
The Guardian
The International Herald Tribune
The Iranian Journal of International Affairs
The Middle East Journal
The National Review
The New Yorker
The Observer
The Washington Post

Internet sources

Gulf/2000 Project at Columbia University, New York. http://gulf2000.columbia.edu/
Human Right's Watch Report. 'Genocide in Iraq. The Anfal Campaign Against the Kurds'. http//:www.hrw.org/reports/1993/iraqanfal/
Iraq Research and Documentation Program. Centre for Middle East Studies, Harvard University. http://www.fas.harvard.edu/~irdp/
National Security Archive (NSA), George Washington University. National Security Archive Electronic Briefing Book No. 82, 25 February 2003, edited by Joyce Battle: 'Shaking Hands with Saddam Hussein. The U.S. Tilts toward Iraq, 1980–1984'. http://www.gwu.edu/~nsarchiv/NSAEBB/NSAEBB82/index.htm
PBS Frontline, 'Oral History of Gulf War II, Interview with Brent Scowcroft, US National Security Advisor'. http://www.pbs.org/wgbh/pages/frontline/gulf/oral/scowcroft/1.html
PBS Frontline, 'Oral History of Gulf War II, Interview with Margaret Thatcher, Prime Minister of England'. http://www.pbs.org/wgbh/pages/frontline/gulf/oral/thatcher/2.html

The Project for the New American Century. http://www.newamericancentury.org/

United States Senate, 103rd Congress, Second Session, 25 May 1994. A Report of Chairman Donald W. Riegle, Jr and Ranking Member Alfonse M. D'Amato of the Committee on Banking, Housing and Urban Affairs with Respect to Export Administration: 'The Riegle Report. US Chemical and Biological Warfare-Related Dual Use Exports to Iraq and their Possible Impact on the Health Consequences of the Gulf War'. http://www.gulfweb.org/bigdoc/report/riegle1.html

US House of Representatives, 27 July 1992. Speech by Henry B. Gonzalez: 'Bush Administration Had Acute Knowledge of Iraq's Military Industrialisation Plans'. http://www.fas.org/spp/starwars/congress/1992/h920727g.htm

US Senate Committee on Banking, Housing, and Urban Affairs, 7 October 1994: Committee Staff Report No. 3: Chemical Warfare Agent Identification, Chemical Injuries, and Other Findings. Principal Investigator James J. Tuite III: 'U.S. Chemical and Biological Exports to Iraq and their Possible Impact on the Health Consequences of the Persian Gulf War'. http://www.chronicillnet.org/PGWS/tuite/chembio.html

Index

eBooks – at www.eBookstore.tandf.co.uk

A library at your fingertips!

eBooks are electronic versions of printed books. You can store them on your PC/laptop or browse them online.

They have advantages for anyone needing rapid access to a wide variety of published, copyright information.

eBooks can help your research by enabling you to bookmark chapters, annotate text and use instant searches to find specific words or phrases. Several eBook files would fit on even a small laptop or PDA.

NEW: Save money by eSubscribing: cheap, online access to any eBook for as long as you need it.

Annual subscription packages

We now offer special low-cost bulk subscriptions to packages of eBooks in certain subject areas. These are available to libraries or to individuals.

For more information please contact
webmaster.ebooks@tandf.co.uk

We're continually developing the eBook concept, so keep up to date by visiting the website.

www.eBookstore.tandf.co.uk